Mental health policy and practice

Mental health policy and practice

Helen Lester and Jon Glasby

Consultant Editor: Jo Campling

First published 2006 by
PALGRAVE MACMILLAN
Houndmills, Basingstoke, Hampshire RG21 6XS and
175 Fifth Avenue, New York, N. Y. 10010
Companies and representatives throughout the world

PALGRAVE MACMILLAN is the global academic imprint of the Palgrave Macmillan division of St. Martin's Press, LLC and of Palgrave Macmillan Ltd. Macmillan® is a registered trademark in the United States, United Kingdom and other countries. Palgrave is a registered trademark in the European Union and other countries.

ISBN-13: 978–1–4039–3543–4 paperback
ISBN-10: 1–4039–3543–2   paperback

This book is printed on paper suitable for recycling and made from fully managed and sustained forest sources. Logging, pulping and manufacturing processes are expected to conform to the environmental regulations of the country of origin

A catalogue record for this book is available from the British Library.

A catalog record for this book is available from the Library of Congress.

Library of Congress Catalogue Card mumber- 2005056-732

10   9   8   7   6   5   4   3   2
15   14   13   12   11   10   09   08   07

Printed in China

To Huw   — for being there in all weathers
For Mary — may the world always be as exciting as you think it is

Contents

List of Figures

Abbreviations

Mental health services use a large number of acronyms and abbreviations. To aid readers new to this language, we have set out the main terms below:

ACT	Assertive Community Treatment
A&E	Accident and Emergency
AO(T)	Assertive Outreach (Team)
BMA	British Medical Association
BPS	Biopsychosocial
CAIPE	Centre for the Advancement of Interprofessional Education
CBT	Cognitive Behavioural Therapy
CEHR	Commission for Equality and Human Rights
CHI	Commission for Health Improvement
CMHT	Community Mental Health Team
CPA	Care Programme Approach
CPN	Community Psychiatric Nurse
CR	Crisis Resolution
CTO	Community Treatment Order
DDA	Disability Discrimination Act
DoH/DHSS	Department of Health/of Health and Social Security
DRC	Disability Rights Commission
DSM	Diagnostic and Statistical Manual of Mental Disorders
DSPD	Dangerous Severe Personality Disorder
DUP	Duration of Untreated Psychosis
ECR	Extra-contractual referral
ECT	Electro-Convulsive Therapy
EI(S)	Early Intervention (Service)
EU	European Union
FLEAT	Forensic, Liaison, Emergency and Assessment Team
GDP	Gross Domestic Produce
(n)GMS	(new) General Medical Services
GP	General Practitioner
GPwSI	GP with a special interest
HIV	Human Immuno deficiency Virus
HMSO/TSO	Her Majesty's Stationery Office/The Stationery Office
HT	Home Treatment
ICD	International Classification of Disease

IRTC	In-Reach and Through-Care Service
IT	Information Technology
MH–PIG	Mental Health Policy Implementation Guide
NDDP	New Deal for Disabled People
NHS	National Health Service
NICE	National Institute for Clinical Excellence
NIMBY	Not in my back yard
NIMHE	National Institute of Mental Health in England
NSF	National Service Framework
ODPM	Office of the Deputy Prime Minister
OECD	Organisation for Economic Co-operation and Development
ONS	Office for National Statistics
PACT	Programme for Assertive Community Treatment
PALS	Patient Advisory and Liaison Services
PCG/T	Primary Care Group/Trust
PCGMHW	Primary Care Graduate Mental Health Worker
PCO	Primary Care Organisation
PET	Psychiatric Emergency Team
PMS	Personal Medical Services
PRiSM	Psychiatric Research in Service Measurement
RCGP	Royal College of General Practitioners
RCT	Randomised Controlled Trial
SDO	Supervised Discharge Order
SCIE	Social Care Institute for Excellence
SSI	Social Services Inspectorate
STR	Support Time and Recovery
SURGE	Service User-Led Research Hub
SWOT	Strengths, Weaknesses, Opportunities and Threats
TAPS	Team for the Assessment of Psychiatric Services
UKAN	UK Advocacy Network
UPIAS	Union of the Physically Impaired Against Segregation
WHO	World Health Organisation

Acknowledgements

The authors are grateful to all the friends and colleagues who reviewed chapters of this book and commented on our early drafts. There are too many people to name individually, but each person acted as a critical friend and had a key role to play in producing this book. We would also like to acknowledge the many people with mental health problems who have helped us, through their lived experience, think through what mental health care could and should look like.

We are also very grateful to Palgrave and to Jo Campling for all their advice and assistance.

Chapter 7 of the book draws on material published in the *Journal of Interprofessional Care* 18(1), 7–16.

1 Introduction

In this chapter we discuss:

- What we mean by mental health and illness
- The strategic importance of mental health and illness
- The changing constructions of mental illness
- The incidence and prevalence of mental illness

This book is designed as an introduction to mental health policy and practice for students as well as for qualified practitioners, their managers and policy makers. Each chapter follows the same basic style, with key points highlighted at the beginning, and a series of reflection exercises and suggestions for further reading at the end. You might find the exercises useful in helping to consider how the issues raised in the chapter relate to your own geographical area or personal context.

Each chapter has been written to 'stand alone', that is, to make sense and be of use if read in isolation from the rest of the book. Occasionally, this may mean that some chapters briefly summarise material presented in more detail elsewhere, but the book signposts readers to the relevant section so that they can follow this up in greater depth. However, as with most aspects of life (and indeed, as we argue below with regard to mental health services), the whole is always greater than the sum of its parts, and you will achieve a better understanding of the mental health system if you read each chapter sequentially.

We have not taken a particular political or theoretical stance since this might lead us to offer a less 'balanced' overview of the mental health system. This does not, however, equate to a non-critical approach. As health and social care practitioners as well as researchers and teachers, we have day to day experience of the frustrations and the very real rewards of working with people with mental health problems within the National Health Service (NHS) and social care and have, as you will see, highlighted not only the successes and exemplars of positive working practices but also policy non-sequiturs and disempowering aspects of the system. Above all, this book is an introductory text, written to help you begin to explore this interesting and complex aspect of health and social care. We hope you enjoy the journey and are encouraged to translate some of the ideas from paper to practice.

Throughout the book, we attempt to present what we describe as 'a whole systems approach' (that is, trying to see the mental health system from the perspective of somebody using services and viewing individual components as part of a wider spectrum of interdependent services). However, within this 'whole system', we place particular emphasis on those health and social care services that specialise in working with people with mental health problems. While we recognise that people with mental health problems are often much more affected by and concerned with the everyday services and supports that are so essential to all of us (for example, housing, employment, income, education, family, neighbourhoods, transport, leisure and community safety), there is nevertheless a range of health and social care services that devote themselves to working with people with mental health problems. Although we acknowledge the importance of wider services whenever possible, it is these specialist mental health services that form the focus of this book.

What do we mean by mental health and illness?

Mental health is more than simply an absence of symptoms of mental illness or distress. Mental health refers to a positive sense of well-being and a belief in our own worth and the worth of others (Health Education Authority, 1997). Everyone has mental health needs, whether or not they have a diagnosis of mental illness. Positive mental health includes the ability to understand and make sense of our surroundings, to be able to cope with change and to communicate effectively with other people. When mentally well, we are aware of and have control over different strands of our life; we have the will to live life to its full potential; things make sense to us. In other people's eyes, a mentally healthy person talks and behaves in a culturally appropriate way; there is an apparent ability to maintain their health and develop a role in society. Mental health is therefore an essential component of our general health.

It is, however, even more difficult to define what is meant by 'mental illness'. This is largely because the meaning has changed across time, and is influenced by geography, discipline and personal perspective. A lawyer will have one definition, a psychiatrist another, a service user another still.

The legal definition, at least under the 1983 *Mental Health Act*, includes four types of mental disorder:

1. Mental illness – although this is not defined
2. Mental impairment – this refers to people with learning difficulties
3. Severe mental impairment – this refers to people with severe learning difficulties
4. Psychopathic disorder – this refers to antisocial individuals who manifest seriously irresponsible conduct.

The second revision of the 2002 *Draft Mental Health Bill* gives a single definition of mental disorder as 'an impairment of or a disturbance in the functioning of the mind or brain resulting from any disability or disorder of the mind or brain. Examples of mental disorder include schizophrenia, depression or a learning disability'.

The writings of people who have experienced mental illness first hand are invaluable in providing an insight that neither romanticises nor underestimates the meaning, effects and consequences of mental illness. William Styron (2001, pp. 46–7) describes his depression as: 'a storm of murk ... near paralysis, psychic energies throttle back close to zero. Ultimately the body is affected and feels sapped, drained...I began to conceive that my mind itself was like one of those outmoded small town telephone exchanges, being gradually inundated by flood waters: one by one, the normal circuits began to drown, causing some of the functions of the body and nearly all those of instincts and intellect to slowly disconnect'.

Users' experience and writings can, however, also demonstrate the ways in which people find value even in the most difficult circumstances. David Karp (1996, p. 104) records how one of his interviewees, a female freelance writer, aged 41, described her depression as a gift: 'that if we can befriend it, if we can travel with it, that it is showing us things. Somewhere along the line we have got to integrate it into our lives. All of us are depressed someway, somewhere at sometime. If we don't allow it in, it can be disruptive. If we allow it in, it is a teacher'.

As we discuss in Chapter 2, it is largely through the writings of mental health service users that the notion of recovery from mental illness has become an increasing part of the discourse of mental illness.

The strategic importance of mental health and illness

Mental illness now touches many peoples' lives. At a global level, depression will be the second most common cause of 'disability', after ischaemic heart disease, by 2020, and currently accounts for 10.5 per cent of the 'total global burden of disease' calculated by combining years of life as a disabled person, years of life lost and mortality rates (World Health Organisation, 1999). The burden of psychosis is exceeded only by quadriplegia and dementia at a global level, when assessed by people's perception of disease burden (Ustun *et al.*, 1999).

At a national level, antidepressant medication accounts for seven per cent of the United Kingdom (UK) primary care drug budget. In 2002, over 32 million prescription items were dispensed for mental health problems, costing over £540 million. The Sainsbury Centre for Mental Health (2003a) has estimated that the annual costs of mental health problems in England are £77.4 billion (see Figure 1.1), leading to reduced quality of life, missed employment and significant social security costs. Overall, the total cost to the economy of people with serious mental illness and common mental health problems is greater than ischaemic heart disease, breast cancer and diabetes combined (Dawson and Tylee, 2001).

The Sainsbury Centre for Mental Health (2003b) has also calculated the breakdown of direct NHS and local authority costs by type of service (see Figure 1.2) and found that inpatient care still accounts for the largest percentage spent on mental health.

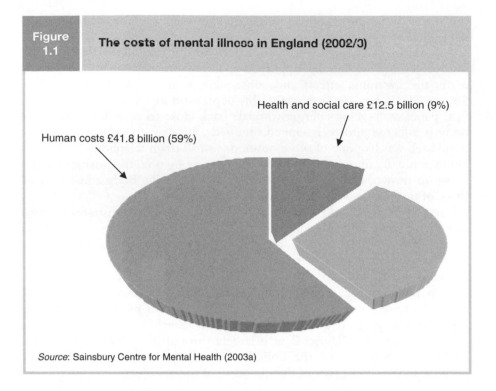

Figure 1.1

The costs of mental illness in England (2002/3)

Health and social care £12.5 billion (9%)

Human costs £41.8 billion (59%)

Source: Sainsbury Centre for Mental Health (2003a)

Figure 1.2

Mental health expenditure (2002/3)

	Per cent
Clinical services including inpatient care	24.6
Community mental health teams	17.2
Secure/high dependency provision	12.3
Continuing care	12.3
Accommodation	10.3
Access and crisis services	6.6
Day services	5.3
Psychological therapy services	4.6
Home support services	2.1
Other community/hospital teams	1.6
Support services	1.5
Services for mentally disordered offenders	1.1
Services for carers	0.3
Mental health promotion	0.1
Direct payments	0.1

Source: Sainsbury Centre for Mental Health (2003b)

On an individual level, there are about 200,000 hospital admissions relating to mental health problems each year in England and Wales alone, and over 4000 people take their own lives each year (Healthcare Commission, 2004; Mind, n.d.). Mental illness also contributes to individual as well as national poverty through lost production from people being unable to work, reduced productivity from people who are ill at work, lost production from absenteeism, and loss of the bread winner of a dependant family. This cycle can sometimes be perpetuated to future generations through untreated illness in a parent leading to childhood educational failure, future unemployment and perhaps illness in adult life.

The prevalence of mental illness also impacts on the emotional well-being of a nation and, it has been argued, through the medium of social exclusion and poverty, on the social capital of society (Wilkinson, 1996; see also Figure 1.3).

Figure 1.3	The effects of common mental health problems

It is no longer tenable to argue that the burden of common mental disorders can be ignored – the costs of doing so are immense in terms of repeated GP consultations, sickness absence, labour turnover, reduced productivity, impact on families and children. In addition, there is the more difficult to quantify but nonetheless important concept of the emotional well being of the country and nation which undoubtedly influences its future.

(Jenkins *et al.*, 1998, p. 138)

The changing constructions of mental illness

As Coppock and Hopton (2000) have suggested, there is a tendency for mental health professionals to opt for one particular approach to understanding mental illness, often allied to their training and professional background (see Figure 1.4). We firmly believe, however, that no one approach has all the answers and that the origin of mental illness must inevitably represent a confluence of different factors. This implies that we need to be reflexive in our thinking rather than holding fast to one particular conceptual model. As Tyrer and Steinberg suggest 'those who imprison themselves within the confines of one model only have the perspective of the keyhole' (2003, p. 138).

We have therefore deliberately chosen to discuss a range of perspectives on the nature and cause of mental illness, some of which are frankly contradictory, and hope this will allow you to understand something of the age old debates in this area and why your own views will not always be readily accepted by the people you are talking to. Our discussion, however, aims to give you a flavour rather than a detailed exploration of the area and we make suggestions for further reading to enable you to follow up these and other models in greater depth at the end of the chapter.

Figure 1.4	Difficulties in conceptualising mental illness

Despite over a hundred years of scientific research into the causation and treatment of mental distress, we are still unable to provide any incontrovertible evidence of either what causes mental distress or how it can be treated effectively. There is though a considerable body of circumstantial evidence, which suggests that mental distress is the product of the interplay between various psychological, social, political, environmental and biological factors. Regrettably few mental health professionals are willing to take account of all of these factors. Instead many adopt one theoretical perspective and therapeutic approach as their own and disregard any new research findings, which might challenge their belief. While such identity politics and celebration of difference are in keeping with the post modernist zeitgeist of the time, it will not necessary lead to us furthering our understanding of what causes mental distress, how to prevent it and how to respond to it.

(Coppock and Hopton, 2000, p. 10)

Whatever your belief about the origins of mental illness, the notion of 'madness' is indisputably ancient and ubiquitous. There is probably no society past or present that has failed to acknowledge its existence. Madness became associated with health and sickness through the writings of the early Greeks, particularly Hippocrates (470–10 BC). Hippocratic medicine explained health and illness in terms of the rhythms and shifting balances of humours (juices or fluids). Within this belief system, 'humoral balance' of vital fluids was essential for good health, and illness was the result of an increase or decrease in the humours. In terms of mental illness, excess blood and yellow bile were thought to lead to mania and surplus black bile to melancholy or depression.

Perhaps the next great leap in thinking, at least in terms of rationalising madness, came from the work of René Descartes (1594–1650), who moved away from the more mystical elements of the Hippocratic tradition, towards a theory of particles of matter obeying mathematical laws. Descartes proposed that there are two types of material in the world: the mental or mind, and the physical or body. He equated the mind with the soul and stated that the mind docked with the body at the pineal gland. He also proposed that the mind and body were therefore separate entities (sometimes talked about as 'Cartesian dualism'). This had significant consequences for thinking about madness since, in effect, it implied that mental and physical health are separate entities.

That madness was the result of a disease process and a bodily malfunction became the dominant paradigm of the Enlightenment. In the UK, Thomas Willis (1621–75) coined the term 'neurology', and, as an avid dissector, tried to localise mental functions to particular regions of the brain. In Philadelphia, Benjamin Rush (1745–1813), the physician officially acknowledged by the American Psychiatric Association as 'the father of American psychiatry', believed that 'madness' was an arterial disease for which the logical remedy was, therefore, blood letting.

By the late nineteenth century, the main priority for the growing number of psychiatrists was to legitimise their discipline as a hard biomedical science alongside neurology and pathology. Creating a credible knowledge base for psychiatry helped to underpin psychiatrists' claims for their medical authority over 'madness'. Scull (1979) cites an editorial from the Journal of Mental Science (the former title of the British Journal of Psychiatry) in 1858 that captures this early biomedical professional justification: 'Insanity is purely a disease of the brain. The physician is now the responsible guardian of the lunatic and must remain so.'

A key figure in this movement was Emil Kraepelin (1856–1926), a German psychiatrist who assumed that there were a discrete and discoverable number of psychiatric disorders and argued that each disorder had a typical symptom picture. He also believed that each disorder was associated with a different brain pathology and different aetiology (that is, cause and origin). As Bentall (2003, p. 13) suggests 'on Kraepelin's analysis, therefore the correct classification of mental illness according to symptoms would provide a kind of Rosetta stone, which would point directly to the biological origins of madness'. Kraepelin also highlighted the importance of long-term outcomes and of illness trajectories by suggesting that the natural history of psychiatric illness was a better clue to its nature than the symptoms a patient showed at one particular point in time. Kraepelin was therefore responsible for a significant innovation in the conceptualisation and classification of illness, encouraging psychiatrists to describe and taxonomise mental disorders and informing and shaping the dominant disease model in twenty-first century psychiatry (see Figure 1.5).

The persistence of Kraepelinian ideology is also demonstrated by the influence of the ever expanding World Health Organisation (WHO) produced International Classification of Disease (ICD) and the Diagnostic and Statistical Manual of Mental Disorders (DSM) published by the American Psychiatric Association (see Figure 1.6).

The notion of mental illness as a biomedical entity was challenged in the 1960s by a number of disparate individuals and groups, including UK anti-psychiatrists such as Ronny (RD) Laing and the American psychiatrist,

Figure 1.5	Central tenets of the disease model

- Mental pathology is accompanied by physical pathology
- Mental illness can be classified as different disorders which each have characteristic common features
- Mental illness is biologically disadvantageous
- The causes of physical and mental pathology in psychiatric illness are all explicable in terms of physical illness

(Tyrer and Steinberg, 2003, p. 10)

Figure 1.6	The growth of the Diagnostic and Statistical Manual of Mental Disorders

- In 1917, the American Psychiatric Association recognised 59 psychiatric disorders
- With the introduction of the diagnostic and statistical manual (DSM) in 1952, this rose to 128
- The second edition, DSM 2 (1968), had 159 categories
- DSM 3 (1980) had 227 and the revised DSM 3R (1987) had 253 categories
- DSM 4 (2000), the current system, has 374 categories
- The DSM 5 is tentatively scheduled for 2010. With tongue firmly in cheek, the American psychologist Roger Blashfield (1996) has suggested that, based on the escalation of categories to date, DSM 5 will be over 1200 pages long and contain over 1800 diagnostic criteria

Thomas Szasz. Laing, in classic texts such as *The Divided Self* (1960) and *The Self and Others* (1961), claimed that psychotic symptoms are meaningful in themselves and therefore cannot be understood as medical phenomena. Szasz (who vehemently denied any association with the anti-psychiatry movement), claimed that the concept of mental illness is incoherent and that mental illness is not a disease, but a myth fabricated by psychiatrists for reasons of professional advancement and endorsed by a society looking for easy solutions for problem people (1960). Szasz (1970, p. 23) stated that:

> the expression mental illness is a metaphor which we have come to mistake for a fact. We call people physically ill when their body functioning violates certain anatomical and physiological norms; similarly we call people mentally ill when their personal conduct violates certain ethical, political and social norms. This explains why many historical figures from Jesus to Castro and from Job to Hitler, have been diagnosed as suffering from this or that psychiatric malady.

Although intellectually influential, Szasz's views have not been widely accepted. However, as we shall see in Chapter 2, they resonate with proposed notions in the UK for treatment orders in the community and the preventive detention of people with Dangerous Severe Personality Disorder (DSPD).

Michael Foucault, a French historian, argued that mental illness is a cultural construct, sustained by a grid of administrative and medico-psychiatric practices (1961). The history of madness is therefore less an account of disease and treatment but of freedom and control, of knowledge and power. The American sociologist, Irving Zola, similarly argued that:

> medicine is becoming a major institution of social control, nudging aside, if not incorporating, the more traditional institutions of religion

and law... this is not occurring through the political power physicians hold or can influence, but is largely an insidious and often un-dramatic phenomenon accomplished by 'medicalising' much of daily living, by making medicine and the labels healthy and ill relevant to an ever increasing part of human existence (Kosa and Zola, 1975, p. 170).

This social construction of mental illness sees the primary function of mental health policy as the regulation of behaviour, with the process of categorising and labelling people a way of pathologising rule-breaking behaviour that is unacceptable to wider society.

The social causation model of mental illness has also become an increasingly important model, and argues that social forces are the most important influence in the aetiology of mental illness (see Figure 1.7). Key figures in this movement include Emil Durkheim (1897) who, in his classic work on suicide, argued that social factors, especially isolation and loss of social bonds, were important in predicting and even causing suicide. More recently, Brown and Harris (1978) found that depressed women living in a London borough were more likely to have more young children at home, less part time or full time employment, and fewer confidantes with whom they could discuss their worries than non-depressed women. This increasing evidence base has led many people working in mental health to recognise the influence of social factors and the environment on developing mental illness and to focus treatment on helping individuals find an acceptable social role and addressing underlying social issues rather than on treating presumed biochemical imbalances.

Closely allied to the social causation model is the biopsychosocial (BPS) model of illness. The BPS model refers to a position spelt out perhaps most clearly by George Engel (1980) where he argued that, for psychiatry to generate a fully scientific and inclusive account of mental disorder, biomedical accounts needed to be superceded by ones that incorporated ideas from general systems theory. In contrast to the biomedical model, this approach recognises that psychological and social factors influence patients' perceptions and actions and therefore the experience of what it feels like to be ill. Pilgrim (2002)

Figure 1.7	Central tenets of the social causation model

- Mental disorder is often triggered by life events that appear to be independent
- Social forces linked to class, occupational status and social role are the precipitants of mental disorder
- People with mental disorder often become and remain disordered because of societal influences

(Tyrer and Steinberg, 2003, p. 87)

suggests that the BPS model does not object to diagnosis in principle, but that it privileges the patient and their longitudinal context over the medical categories applied to them and that the model's inclusive approach creates the possibility of thinking about mental health problems on both scientific and humanistic terms. Certainly the BPS model appears to have achieved recognition and popularity in many branches of medicine, but Pilgrim also warns that in mental health, its popularity may reflect service level pragmatism and a form of mutual tolerance within increasingly multi-disciplinary teams rather than its acceptance as a stable theoretical orthodoxy.

Writing from a somewhat provocative psychological perspective, Bentall (2003) has recently challenged the entire Kraepelinian foundation of psychiatric practice, suggesting that psychosis in particular should be seen as just part and parcel of human variation, rather than as an illness. He cites studies showing that up to 11–13 per cent of people have experienced hallucinations at some point in their lives (Tien, 1991) and the work of Marius Romme and Sandra Escher (1989) in the Netherlands who have suggested that many people hear voices, but have little difficulty coping with them and indeed have never sought psychiatric treatment for them. Bentall argues that the boundaries of madness are fluid and that many experiences that might be attributed, on DSM criteria, to a psychotic illness, are not necessarily pathological. His 'Post Kraepelinian' position is that:

> ...we should abandon psychiatric diagnoses altogether and instead try to explain and understand the actual experiences and behaviours of psychotic people...Once these complaints have been explained, there is no ghostly disease remaining that also requires an explanation. Complaints are all there is...an advantage of this approach is that it does not require us to draw a clear dividing line between madness and sanity (2003, pp. 141–2).

At the beginning of the twenty-first century, it could be argued that the biomedical disease model of mental illness is enjoying a resurgence, driven by the development of new physical treatments, of brain scans assessing differences in brain size and composition between people with and without mental illness and the success and publicity accorded to the human genome project. Of course the fact that medically trained psychiatrists (described by Pilgrim as 'chemotherapists with a prescription pad' (2002, p. 591)) and General Practitioners (GPs) remain influential professionals within the diagnostic and treatment process also affects the emphasis accorded to different viewpoints of the causation and construction of mental illness. This biomedical approach, with its strong links to 'mind-body dualism' where the body and mind are seen as separate and unconnected entities, is also, as we shall see throughout this book, reflected in the separate services for people with physical and mental health problems. As Wade and Halligan suggest:

> Health commissioners, budgetary systems, health care professionals and the public all act if there is some clear, inescapable separation between

physical and mental health problems, ignoring evidence that a person's emotional state always affects their function and presentation of physical symptoms (2004, pp. 1398–99).

The incidence and prevalence of mental illness

From a pragmatic point of view, this book talks about mental illness as being either a 'serious mental illness' or a 'common mental health problem'. We are mindful, however, that people can have both a serious and a common mental health problem sequentially or at the same time, and some common mental health problems such as obsessive compulsive disorder can be just as disabling in terms of activities of daily living as the more 'serious' problems such as schizophrenia and bipolar affective disorder.

It is difficult to quote gold standard statistics for the incidence and prevalence of mental illness (prevalence refers to the number of people with a particular illness at a point in time in the population, whereas incidence refers to new cases). A definition based on service contact only captures people who become patients and not the real number of people within society who have mental illness. Previous community surveys (Goldberg and Huxley, 1992; Hannay, 1979) suggest that many more people experience symptoms than are diagnosed with a specific illness. Results of prevalence studies also vary greatly both between and within countries due to differences in diagnostic practices and to social and environmental factors (Warner, 1985).

The latest Office National Statistics (ONS) statistics suggest that an estimated one in two hundred people have experienced a psychotic disorder in the past year (Singleton *et al.*, 2001; see Figure 1.8), although this survey is

Figure 1.8	Prevalence of mental disorders (rates per 1000)		
	Men	*Women*	*Total*
All neurosis	135	194	164
Mixed anxiety and depression	68	108	88
Generalised anxiety	43	46	44
Depression	23	28	26
Phobias	13	22	18
Obsessive-compulsive disorder	9	13	11
Panic	7	7	7
Personality disorder	54	34	44
Probable psychosis	6	5	5

Source: Singleton *et al.* (2001)

likely to underestimate the true prevalence as it only reflects people living in private households, not those living in institutions or who are homeless. People with serious mental illness are also less likely to respond to surveys than the general public, once again leading to an underestimate of the real figure. Using available data, however, it appears that up to 16 per cent of people have common mental health problems at any one time, a figure that has been stable for approximately the last ten years (Fryers *et al.*, 2002; Singleton *et al.*, 2001).

The prevalence of mental illness is also affected by a number of different factors including ethnicity, age, gender, occupation, education and family responsibilities (see Figure 1.9).

Figure 1.9	Factors affecting prevalence rates of mental illness

Ethnicity and gender: See Chapter 9 for further detail on the over-representation of some minority ethnic communities and of women in some sections of the mental health system.

Age: The highest rates of suicide are in young men aged 25 to 34; 1300 young men died by suicide in 2001, and suicide accounts for one in five deaths of young people (Department of Health, 1998a, 2001a). Common mental health problems peak for men aged 45–49 years and for women from 50–54 years (Singleton *et al.*, 2001).

Occupation: People working in certain jobs can be at particular risk of mental health problems, with those working in the medical and farming professions being at the greatest risk of suicide.

Education: Having less education, and being unemployed or economically inactive are the most consistent risk factors associated with common mental health problems (Fryers *et al.*, 2002).

Family responsibilities: An estimated 28 per cent of lone parents have common mental health problems (Melzer *et al.*, 2002). Approximately 1.26 million people in the UK care for someone with a mental health problem (National Schizophrenia Fellowship, n.d.), including between 6000 and 17,000 young carers (Aldridge and Becker, 2003). Carers are twice as likely to have mental health problems themselves if they provide substantial care (Singleton *et al.*, 2002) (see also Chapters 9 and 10 for further detail on anti-discriminatory practice and carers' perspectives).

Key themes in each chapter

Mental health policy and practice has eleven chapters in total, spanning the mental health system from professional, user and carer perspectives. An initial policy overview is followed by chapters on four specific service areas: primary care, community mental health, hospital services and forensic mental health services. Chapters 7 to 10 address broader issues of partnership working, user involvement, anti-discriminatory practice and carers' perspectives. The final chapter draws together key themes and suggests underlying reasons for the rhetoric/reality gap between policy and practice. In particular, the book builds on a previous literature review published in 2003 by the National Institute for Mental Health in England (NIMHE) (Glasby et al., 2003). Summarising 'what works' in adult mental health, this study was based on a review of the research from 1997–2002 and was designed to provide an accessible guide to the key issues for service users, practitioners, managers and policy makers. This book updates this initial search and, crucially, places many of the issues raised in their historical and policy context. Traditionally, mental health services have tended to see themselves as different from the rest of health and social care because of the unique challenges they face. However, as we demonstrate throughout this book, mental health is also influenced by broader policy changes in health and social care and in social policy more generally. As a result, it is important for mental health students, workers and managers to understand how the issues and pressures they face fit into wider debates about welfare and service provision.

As you read through this book, you may notice recurring themes of a lack of real voice and choice for services users and carers, the rhetoric/reality gaps between policy prose and implementation in practice and the constant call by health and social care professionals and users and carers for a 'whole systems approach' to mental health. There are also a series of critical but uncomfortable issues that individuals and teams face around the culture of their organisation and the underlying attitudes and values of the staff, managers and policy makers towards people with mental health problems. This book will, we hope, enable you to explore these issues, understand historical and current strengths and weaknesses of services and, above all, discover what we might be able to do to work towards more inclusive, integrated, user-focused services that make sense both to those providing and receiving them.

In Chapter 2, we provide an overview of mental health policy, which is key to understanding many aspects of the subsequent chapters. The chapter begins with a discussion of the meaning of the term 'policy' and influences on how policy is made, and concludes with some of the reasons why policies are not always implemented in practice. It also presents a detailed chronological history of mental health policy, contextualised, from the 1970s onwards, through discussions of wider policy issues in generic health and social care. While the detail relates to English law, the underlying principles and wider service implications are applicable throughout the UK. We suggest that although there is growing evidence that mental health has moved up the political agenda during the last decade, chronic long-term underfunding means that many aspects of the mental health system are starting from a low baseline relative to services within the wider NHS. There are also a series of unresolved tensions particularly between the wider modernisation agenda of partnership working and patient choice, and mental health policy that appears increasingly coercive and controlling. In addition to summarising influential policy initiatives, this chapter also presents some key theoretical frameworks for explaining current policy tensions and dilemmas.

Chapter 3 describes the complex and often messy world of primary care, which, with the emergence of Primary Care Trusts (PCTs), is the most rapidly changing part of the NHS. Primary care is a key partner in providing good quality mental health services since most people with mental heath issues, including serious mental illness, are seen and treated within this setting. After describing the history and current state of primary care in the UK, we focus on users' views of services and on the potential benefits offered by workforce developments such as the extended role of practice nurses, primary care graduate mental health workers (PCGMHW) and GPs with a special clinical interest (GPwSI). The chapter concludes with a discussion of new integrated models of working in primary care mental health. We also suggest that although new roles and responsibilities may create opportunities for greater choice for patients and more seamless services, they could also lead to poorer continuity and fragmented provision of care.

Community mental health services are a complex and controversial area of practice that have received increasing attention in the last decade, within the context of wider deinstitutionalisation debates. Against this background, Chapter 4 discusses the uncertain origins of community mental health care, the development and roles of generic community mental health teams (CMHTs), the advent and impact of more specialised functionalised teams and alternative ways of providing community based services. We also discuss the multiple and reinforcing ways that people with mental illness are excluded from wider society, and examples of positive practice in community inclusion. We suggest that to provide good quality care for people with mental health problems, community mental health, assertive outreach (AO), home treatment/crisis resolution (HT/CR) and early intervention (EI) teams need to work together with clear lines of communication, an understanding of each others' roles and responsibilities and with additional rather than redistributed funding streams. Health and social care workers also have a part to play in encouraging wider community acceptance of people with mental illness, so that community care becomes more than simply a geographical concept.

Hospital services still play a key role in the UK health care system and mental health inpatient care costs approximately £800 million per year, representing nearly 25 per cent of the total health and social care budget for mental health. However, largely as a result of the current emphasis on community care, acute mental health services have tended to be neglected by policy makers and researchers. In Chapter 5, we discuss trends in acute psychiatric care, highlighting key concerns about pressures on acute beds, changes in admissions thresholds, the effects of high bed occupancy on standards of care and the poor quality of some service users' experiences of hospital services. We also discuss grounds for optimism, including national guidance to improve the physical environment of acute wards, and initiatives to develop a generalisable model of care that users experience as both safe and therapeutic, and where staff strengthen their skills and experience.

Forensic mental health services are both extremely complex and high profile. They involve working with a wide range of partners and with people with potentially challenging behaviour and very different needs. There are also a large number of people with unmet mental health needs in prison and a significant number of people inappropriately placed in secure settings. In Chapter 6, we discuss these issues in more depth and suggest that placing and moving people through the system in an appropriate manner could free up capacity to help with current unmet needs in other parts of the system, including prisons. Successful forensic mental health care therefore requires a spectrum of services and more effective partnership working between key agencies. We also discuss the 'mad v bad' debate, and, in particular, stereotypes and misunderstandings about the alleged link between mental illness and crime/violence, and the difficulties inherent in assuming that risk assessment is a precise science rather than a subjective art.

Partnership working between different agencies is crucial if users are to receive co-ordinated services that meet all of their needs. Chapter 7 discusses how the UK welfare state has tended to be relatively fragmented, the consequences of failure to work together (for example the death of Victoria Climbié or the care of Christopher Clunis) and the recent impetus to partnership working including the formation of Care Trusts and the impact of the *Health Act* flexibilities (1999). Different models of partnership working are discussed, along with key barriers and success factors. We conclude that partnership working remains a complex task and that there are few quick fixes. The way forward may lie in an incremental approach, with individual partners making use of whatever avenue they think may be beneficial and locally appropriate.

Until very recently, mental health service users have been almost universally perceived as passive recipients of care. However, over the past 20 years, users' views on service provision have become more accepted as a valuable part of health and social care. Chapter 8 charts the many, varied and overlapping meanings of the term 'mental health service user' and the history of user involvement in mental health services. We discuss the importance of user involvement in developing mental health services, barriers to user involvement and examples of positive practice. Tensions between notions of partnership and coercion of mental health service users, and evidence of professional ambivalence towards greater user involvement, are also highlighted. We conclude that meaningful user involvement cannot be a one-off intervention or a discrete programme of work, but a much broader and more empowering way of working which affects every aspect of mental health provision.

Discrimination exists at many different levels, both within mental health services and wider society. Chapter 9 discusses the concept of discrimination and anti-discriminatory practice, the current policy context and relevant legislation. Discrimination in mental health services and in particular the experience of women, people from minority ethnic communities, people with physical impairments, people with learning difficulties, older people and gay men, lesbian and bisexual people are highlighted. We suggest that discrimination, like social exclusion, cannot be tackled simply by changing the way individuals behave. Instead, attempts to root out discrimination in mental health services need to be accompanied by similar efforts within wider society at a personal, cultural and structural level.

The majority of community care is provided not by statutory services, but by carers – often family, friends and neighbours supporting others on a voluntary basis. While caring can be a positive experience, it can also bring a series of negative consequences, both for the carer and for the person being cared for. Despite much greater recent recognition of the needs of carers in a range of policies, many carers continue to feel unsupported. In Chapter 10, we discuss the complex definition and importance of carers, the policy context (including the relative neglect of carers of people with mental health problems) and carers' own needs. We suggest that a way forward may lie in providing a range of support from accessible information and practical advice to specialist and crisis support. However, we also highlight the importance of the value base and interpersonal skills of individual workers, with a need for human skills such as empathy and the ability to listen, and a much greater willingness to acknowledge the expertise of carers and value them as people with a key contribution to make.

Suggestions for further reading

1. Key statistics on mental health and illness can be found in: Singleton et al. (2001) *Psychiatric morbidity among adults living in private households. 2000: summary report.* London, Office for National Statistics
2. Pilgrim, D. and Rogers, A. (1999) *A sociology of mental health and illness.* Buckingham, Open University Press

   This classic text has a useful overview of perspectives on mental health and illness from both within and beyond sociology, including sections on labelling theory, critical theory and social constructivism.
3. Rosenhan, D.L. (1973) On being sane in insane places, *Science*, 179, 250–8

   For readers interested in social construction, Rosenhan's (1973) classic paper on what happens when 'normal' people feign mental health symptoms to gain admission to a psychiatric hospital, and are then treated as an inpatient with a presumed diagnosis of schizophrenia, is essential reading.
4. Bentall, R. (2003) *Madness explained: psychosis and human nature.* London, Allen Lane

   This doorstop-sized tome is an interesting and deliberately provocative read that draws on a wide range of evidence from psychology, psychiatry, anthropology and the neurosciences, arguing that there is no discrete dividing line between mental health and illness. Bentall suggests that we can explain and understand many psychotic symptoms as part and parcel (or at least at the extreme end) of normal psychological processes.
5. Tyrer, P. and Steinberg, D. (2003) *Models for mental disorders: conceptual models in psychiatry.* Chichester, John Wiley and Sons

   This book describes a number of the main models currently used in psychiatry (biological, psychodynamic, social and behavioural), and also includes a discussion of a hybrid correlative model.

2 Mental Health Policy

In this chapter we discuss:

- The meaning of the term 'policy' and influences on how policy is made
- The theoretical frameworks that help to understand key policy dilemmas and debates
- A chronological history of mental health policy within the broader context of generic NHS and social care policy
- The influence of the modernisation agenda on mental health policy and practice
- The reasons why policies are not always implemented in practice

In trying to unravel the complexities of mental health policy and practice, the most useful organising principle is probably a chronological (historical) perspective (Porter, 1987). Comparing mental health policy over time enables us to see how successive governments have built on or responded to previous policy and to the social, political and economic climate of the time (see Appendix A for a full policy chronology). Although we concentrate on mental health, we have also sought to contextualise more recent debates in mental health policy and practice through discussions of wider policy issues in generic health and social care. This approach enables us to see the origins of current policy and to appreciate that many current key debates have been rehearsed for decades. This, of itself, raises a number of interesting questions about the barriers and facilitators to implementation and the differences between policy rhetoric and the practical realities of delivering mental health services on the ground. The end result is, unsurprisingly, less a neat sign-posted pathway of incremental, evidence based change than a messy trek with missed turns, sudden deviations from the highway and, at times, a sense of muddling through. Before setting out on the journey, however, it is worthwhile reflecting briefly on what we mean by the term 'policy' and on how policy is made. It is also important to have a grasp of some of the basic concepts that recur throughout this book to see how they help us understand why policy is formulated in certain ways and also why it sometimes fails to deliver services in ways that make sense at an individual and community level. We will therefore also discuss three useful underlying theoretical frameworks that can help to illuminate some of the tensions and dilemmas in current policy and practice.

What do we mean by 'policy'?

The concept of 'policy' is both highly contested and difficult to encapsulate. Ham (1999, pp. 98–9) suggests that the notion of policy is complex, involving a series of related decisions and a number of different people, many of whom are responsible only for the policy making rather than the implementation phase: 'Policy may involve a web of decisions rather than one decision. There are two aspects to this. First the actors who make decisions are rarely the same people as those responsible for implementation...the second aspect is that even at the policy making level, policy is not usually expressed in a single decision. It tends to be defined in terms of a series of decisions which taken together comprise a more or less common understanding of what policy is'.

In terms of mental health policy, Rogers and Pilgrim (2001, p. 226) suggest: 'The term mental health policy at the turn of the twenty-first century refers to legal arrangements, policy directives and service investments in relation to the aggregate picture which have accumulated over the past 100 years. It is partly about the control of behaviour, partly about promoting well-being, partly about ameliorating distress and partly about responding to dysfunction'. With such a broad remit, it is perhaps unsurprising that the mental health policy narrative is a complex and at times paradoxical story.

How is policy formed?

One of the consequences, Ham (1999) suggests, of the diverse interests in the policy community is that the history of the development of health and social care is characterised by long periods of incremental change and only occasional episodes of radical reform. Indeed, as we shall see, the move towards emptying asylums and providing care in the community is a story of slow, gradual change. Kingdon (1995) suggests that a 'step change' in policy is only likely to occur under two circumstances: a major event like war or an economic crisis that forces politicians to go beyond the accepted realms of possibilities (indeed the NHS itself was established under such circumstances), and as a response to events that cast doubt on the credibility of insider groups such as the British Medical Association (BMA). This happened to some extent in the late 1990s when plans to regulate the medical profession (including compulsory revalidation and appraisal procedures) were introduced in many ways as a response to scandals involving poor outcomes for children undergoing heart surgery in Bristol and the discovery that a GP, Dr Harold Shipman, had been able to murder many of his patients without detection over a period of years.

Sometimes policy has been made as a result of a bargain struck with key stakeholders. The concessions made to hospital doctors in terms of options for private practice and access to pay beds in NHS hospitals, for example, helped pave the way for the birth of the NHS in 1948. However, at other times, policy has been made and implemented despite opposition from the field. For example, the *NHS and Community Care Act* 1990, which introduced the controversial idea of the purchaser/provider split, was bitterly opposed by many in the medical profession. However, it was championed by a Conservative government sure of its majority and not afraid of taking on significant pressure groups.

Policy is also not always fully thought through at the time it becomes law. For example, a number of aspects of the *NHS and Community Care Act* 1990 were delayed in terms of implementation and modified and adapted as policy makers and practitioners realised that they needed to sort out how the new system was going to work, with the full Act not coming into force until 1993.

Is policy evidence based?

From the discussion above, it is perhaps not surprising to learn that policy is not always evidence based. White Papers do not automatically carry annexes with detailed analysis of policy evaluations; ministerial speeches are not published with a list of references.

However, since the mid-1990s, government circles and the health and social care professions have actively moved from a system based on expert knowledge to one founded more on principles of evidence based practice. At a national level, official health and social care research and development programmes are now in place and actively commissioning research to provide an underpinning evidence base for policy and practice (Parker, 2002). Recent policy documents including the *National Service Framework for Mental Health* (NSF) (Department of Health, 1999a) and the Quality and Outcomes Framework in the new GP contract (BMA/NHS Confederation, 2003) are, at least in part, evidence based.

Indeed, 6 (2002) argues that policy makers are, in fact, frequently faced with excessive rather than insufficient evidence about what works. The major difficulty for policy makers is then to reconcile the interests of multiple partners and to ensure that policy reflects government pledges and financial flows. As Marmot (2004, p. 906) suggests: 'A simple prescription would be to review the scientific evidence of what would make a difference, formulate policies and implement them – evidence based policy making. Unfortunately, this simple prescription, applied to real life, is simplistic. The relationship between science and policy is more complicated. Scientific findings do not fall on blank minds that get made up as a result. Science engages with busy minds that have strong views about how things are and ought to be'.

It could, of course, be argued that basing policy only on research evidence might also be detrimental to health and social care. Research tends to focus on selected patient populations and so cannot tell clinicians what to do with specific individuals. There is also often an unacceptably long delay in publishing research findings, with a definite publication bias for studies that have positive findings (Higgitt and Fonagy, 2002). There are also debates over what we mean by 'evidence'. Often traditional research hierarchies favour more quantitative approaches such as systematic reviews and randomised controlled trials (RCTs) (often known as 'type I' or 'type II' evidence). However, small-scale qualitative work can provide a collectively powerful evidence base. For example, the collation of individual patient views (including 65,000 telephone calls, 124,000 website hits and 1374 emails) over the antidepressant medication paroxetine in response to the television programme Panorama in 2001 helped to influence National Institute for Clinical Excellence (NICE) guidelines on depression (NICE, 2004) and was a key factor in prompting subsequent calls for an investigation into the regulation of the pharmaceutical industry (Medawar *et al.*, 2002).

Useful theoretical frameworks

There are a number of theoretical frameworks that are helpful in making sense of the way in which policy is both formulated and implemented. We highlight three frameworks that we have used throughout this book to illuminate the way in which recent mental health policy has developed and influenced practice to greater and lesser extents.

The social model of disability

In the UK in the mid-1970s, the concept of disability began to be challenged by a number of different groups including Union of the Physically Impaired Against Segregation (UPIAS, 1976) and disability was recast in a socio-political light. Oliver (1983) identified 'the social model of disability' in order to reflect the growing demand by disabled people and their allies for:

> ...nothing more fundamental than a switch away from focusing on
> the physical limitations of particular individuals to the way in which
> the physical and social environments impose limitations on certain
> groups or categories of people (Oliver 1983, p. 23).

The social model of disability is based on the principle that disability is a denial of civil rights caused by exclusionary practices in all sectors of society. It recognises that people have impairments but argues that it is society which disables them. The social model has arguably, provided the basis for a transformed approach to disability among disabled people, and informed the politics of the Disability Movement (Oliver 1990; 1996). This has led to major changes in the UK and internationally in disability legislation, policy, practice and thinking including the passage of the Disability Discrimination Act (DDA) (1995), direct payments legislation (1996) and the establishment of the Disability Rights Commission (DRC) (2000).

The place of impairment within the social model of disability has been hotly disputed. At times, particularly within what is known as the purist 'strong' model, it has been excluded from analysis with Oliver (1996) and Barnes (1998), key thinkers in the disability movement, both arguing that the personal experience of dealing with impairment is not the concern of disability studies and instead that intellectual and political energies should be concentrated on understanding and tackling the wider social causes of disability. In contrast, the importance of attention to impairment has been made on a number of different grounds. Feminist writers in particular have argued that impairment does restrict activities in important ways. French (1993), for example, argues that her visual impairment imposes some social restrictions such as an inability to recognise people and read non-verbal clues in social interactions that cannot be resolved by the application of the principles of the social model. Lee (2002) suggests it is politically dangerous to accept that adapting the environment is a sufficient response to the issues of disability since it minimises, and indeed potentially trivialises, the social care and accommodation needs that many disabled people have.

Initially, the social model of disability focused almost exclusively on physical illness (Campbell and Oliver, 1996), which may perhaps reflect the relative invisibility of conditions that primarily affect the way someone feels rather than the more 'discrediting' stigma associated with congenital or acquired physical impairments. More recently, work around 'embodied irrationality', that is, the impact of having and living with a mental illness, has helped to focus thinking on aspects of mental illness as impairment and the ways in which impairment interacts with disability (Mulvany, 2000). Beresford also argues that there are at least three key reasons why people with mental illness should recognise and indeed use the social model of disability:

> Survivors are now also among those experiencing the sticks and carrots of government welfare to work policy as disabled people. Thus *regardless of what survivors themselves may think*, they are frequently officially included as disabled. Secondly, there are significant overlaps between the two populations. Some survivors also have impairments, sometimes related to the damaging effects of the chemical and other treatments they have received, or to impoverishment…Thirdly, disabled people and psychiatric system survivors are both subject to discrimination and oppression. While the forms these take may vary and restriction of rights is an explicit commitment of policy for psychiatric system survivors, the denial of their human and civil rights is a shared experience of disabled people and survivors (2000, pp. 169–70).

Political action is therefore as important as talking or pharmaceutical treatments. This model can, however, alienate some mental health service users who do not necessarily identify themselves with the notion of being disabled (see also Chapters 8 and 9).

The recovery model

Deinstitutionalisation, the emergence of community care and psychosocial rehabilitation, the growth of the user movement and the publication of a small number of longitudinal studies of people with serious mental illness that suggested that significant numbers of patients had positive outcomes (Harding *et al.*, 1994; Harrison *et al.*, 2001) all paved the way for the emergence of the recovery model in the 1980s. The recovery model is quite different from the deficit approach that has perhaps been dominant amongst many health and social care professionals for decades.

There is no single agreed upon definition of recovery nor a single way to measure it, but perhaps the most prominent professional proponent of recovery, William Anthony, has used the following definition:

> a person with mental illness can recover even though the illness is not cured...recovery is a way of living and having a satisfying hopeful and contributing life even with the limitations caused by illness. Recovery involves the development of new meaning and purpose in one's life as one goes beyond the catastrophic effects of mental illness (1993, p. 11).

A further pioneering mental health service user, Patricia Deegan, talks about recovery as 'lived experience in gaining a new and valued sense of self and purpose' (1988, p. 15).

Recovery from mental illness, according to mental health service users' writings, involves much more than recovery from the symptoms themselves but also recovering from the stigma people experience and internalise, from the side effects of treatments and treatment settings, and from the negative effects of social exclusion such as unemployment and reduced social networks. Service users describe recovery as a process of making sense of what has happened to them, reconstructing a positive identity, accepting, living with and growing beyond the limits of their mental health problem. It incorporates notions of hope for the future, of taking the least amount of medication necessary, of being involved in treatment planning in a partnership with professionals, of taking control over your life, of tapping into multiple sources of support and of learning about the illness to have better control over it. Anthony also suggests that recovery can occur without professional intervention and even though symptoms are present. It is also not a linear process. Thus, periods of insight or growth can happen unexpectedly while at other times there may be no change for months on end.

We will argue, however, that recent policy developments suggest that the current mental health policy framework does not necessarily encourage recovery for people with mental health problems.

Communitarianism

The term 'communitarianism' was first used in 1841 by Barmby who founded the Universal Communitarian Association. In this and other nineteenth century usage, communitarian meant 'a member of a community formed to put into practice communistic or socialist theories'. The more common and contemporary usage of 'pertaining to or characteristic of a community' first appeared in Webster's dictionary in 1909. Etzioni (1995), perhaps the most well known current thinker in this field, suggests that communities are webs of social relations that encompass shared meanings and shared values. He suggests that families may qualify as mini communities as do some neighbourhoods and cities. Well-integrated national societies may also be said to have communitarian elements. Specifically Etzioni suggests that:

> a communitarian perspective recognises both individual human dignity and the social dimension of human existence. A communitarian perspective recognises that the preservation of individual liberty depends on the act of maintenance of the institutions of civil society where citizens learn respect for others as well as self respect... a communitarian perspective recognises that communities and policies too have obligations – including the duty to be responsive to their members and to foster participation and deliberation in social and political life (1995, p. 25).

Etzioni also suggests that a communitarian social movement has an important role in 'asserting moral voices that should be heeded in a society that increasingly threatens to become normless, self centred and driven by greed' (1995, p. 26) and that the best place to start in terms of building a communitarian platform is where each generation acquires its moral anchoring; in the family.

The communitarians have had a direct influence on New Labour thinking, representing a 'call to restore civic virtues ... and to shore up the moral foundations of society' (Etzioni 1995, p. 31) and in the emphasis on the responsibilities of individuals to each other as members of communities of people living in proximity to each other.

However, communitarianism has a number of associated problems. If they become too strong, communities can breed identity politics and therefore have a potential for social division or even disintegration rather than cohesion. Barnes (1997) suggests that community can mean much more than geographical locality and that notions of communities of interests and of identity are becoming increasingly important, yet are largely ignored in communitarian theory. The normative assumptions on which communitarianism is based, for example the acceptance of traditional gender subordination and the emphasis on family and geographical communities, can therefore exclude people whose identities and affiliations come from a different type of collectively. Communitarianism from the standpoint of people with mental health problems, black people or gay and lesbian people can therefore potentially be a source of oppression and social exclusion.

A 'brief history' of mental health policy

Locking up the mad: the rise of the asylum

On the whole, throughout history and across civilisations, madness has usually been seen as a domestic responsibility, something that friends and families deal with (see Chapter 10 for a discussion of the role of carers). Indeed, it was not until the end of the Middle Ages that separation from society was used as a management strategy, with, for example, the religious house of St Mary of Bethlehem, known as Bethlem (Bedlam), set up to care for 'distracted' patients in London in 1377. Treatment was rudimentary, with patients chained to the wall in leg irons and whipped or ducked in water. From the early 1600s, visitors were allowed in to view the patients for a penny. A trip to Bedlam became a great treat for Londoners, with over 100,000 people a year paying to see the patients, who were placed in cages on the hospital's galleries.

The practice of private madhouses in England began in 1670, with some degree of licensing imposed a century later through the 1774 *Madhouses Act*. Some of these early private madhouses like Ticehurst House in Sussex allowed patients to bring their own personal servants and even to follow the hounds (Porter, 2002).

By 1800, there were approximately 5000 people housed in a mixed economy of private asylums, far less salubrious state run county asylums and workhouses. However, during the nineteenth century, the number of asylums and inmates increased dramatically. The underlying reasons for the rise in asylum care are complex (see Figure 2.1).

Figure 2.1	The rise of the asylum in Victorian England

- The most popular theory at the time was that there had been a rise in the rate of mental illness, particularly schizophrenia
- It has been suggested that the sheer force of human misery in an increasingly industrialised and urbanised nation pricked a new social conscience, sparking off philanthropic gestures including developing charitable institutions in which 'insanity might be healed by a gentle system of rewards and punishments, amusements, occupation and kind but firm discipline' (Murphy (1991, p. 34) rather than leaving vulnerable mentally ill people open to exploitation in workhouses
- Scull (1993, p. 3) suggests that the increase in institutionalisation was 'embedded in far more complex ways in broader transformations of the English political and social structure' as the asylum became a convenient dumping ground for a wide range of individuals who could not cope in the community and hence could not contribute to the political economy of early Victorian England
- Pilgrim and Rogers (1999) suggest the change reflects the general move towards increased state intervention in social problems including the *Poor Law Act* of 1834, the *Factory Acts* of 1833 and 1844, the *Mines Act* of 1842 and the *Public Health Act* of 1848

The 1845 *Lunatics Act* required the building of a network of publicly owned county asylums and formally established the Lunacy Commission, which inspected, licensed and reported (indeed performance managed) the progress of the new institutions. However the new state asylums largely failed to live up to early expectations, particularly of the philanthropists and proponents of moral therapy and non-restraint, and for most people in Victorian England, as the number of inpatients increased, asylums became effectively warehouses for the unwanted.

To some extent, psychiatrists and policy makers were also victims of their own propaganda. The proclamation by Lord Ashley during debates around the 1845 *Lunatics Act* that asylum treatment would 'effect a cure in seventy cases out of every hundred' (Hansard 6.6, 1845 column 193) was, to say the least, overly ambitious. Older people with dementia, people with general paralysis of the insane and people with epilepsy were increasingly admitted to asylums yet were never realistically going to recover and leave. By 1890, Gibbons (1988, p. 161) describes a situation where 'there were 66 county and borough Asylums in England and Wales with an average 802 inmates and 86,067 officially certified cases of insanity – more than four times as many as 45 years earlier'. The 1890 *Lunacy Act* was also the first time that mental health legislation prioritised and protected the civil rights of individuals outside the asylum, rehearsing current debates around *The Draft Mental Health Bill.*

The influence of the First World War

A major change in government policy and public attitudes occurred quite swiftly during and immediately after the First World War in response to the recognition and treatment of soldiers with shell shock. Until then, asylum doctors had emphasised the inherited vulnerability of mental illness and argued that a tainted gene pool accounted for most forms of madness, criminality, alcoholism, epilepsy, physical disability, prostitution and idiocy (Marshall, 1990), a eugenic view that was common across Europe and North America at that time. However during the First World War, between four to seven per cent of volunteer soldiers were deemed to be suffering from shell-shock (now commonly known as Post Traumatic Stress Disorder), including officers and gentlemen thought of as England's 'finest blood'. In some sense, this made the eugenic view of mental illness both illogical and indeed a form of near treason (Stone, 1985).

Prior to 1914, there had also been only a handful of British doctors using psychological methods of treatment, but by the end of the First World War this had also changed dramatically. There was a relative boom in outpatient facilities in an attempt to deal with the thousands of ex-soldiers suffering from the effects of shell shock, and an accompanying emphasis on using new psychological techniques (Coppock and Hopton, 2000).

The 1930 *Mental Treatment Act* gave full legislative support to the introduction of voluntary treatment and to local authorities spending money on outpatient facilities at a time when only seven per cent of all admissions were voluntary (Leff, 1997). However there was no central money allocated to implement many of the changes in the Act, a recurring theme in the story of mental health and community care throughout the twentieth century.

The birth of the NHS

The 1911 *National Insurance Act* enabled working men to access free health care and was, in part, responsible for enabling debates on the benefits of a free NHS. However, it was William Beveridge's well-received 1942 report on the development of a cradle to grave welfare state (Beveridge, 1942), followed by the success of the wartime Emergency Medical Service, that created a political climate where a huge step change in health and welfare policy could be both conceived and implemented. The NHS was born on the 5th July 1948, after negotiations with the medical community that Aneurin Bevan, the Health Minister, rather euphemistically described as 'not... altogether trouble free' (Bevan, 1948).

A central tenet of the vision for the new NHS was that it would be free at the point of use. The first page of the explanatory leaflet distributed to all homes at the outset of the new service proudly declared: 'It will provide you with all medical, dental and nursing care. Everyone – rich or poor, man, woman or child – can use it or any part of it. There are no charges except for a few special items. There are no insurance qualifications. But it is not a charity. You are all paying for it, mainly as tax payers, and it will relieve your money worries in time of illness' (cited in Webster, 2002, p. 24).

The NHS assumed responsibility for mental health which, up to that point, had been under the jurisdiction of the county councils and boroughs, a move that could potentially have led to equality of care between mental health and non-mental health services. However by the 1950s, Mental Health Hospitals (the terminology introduced in the 1930 *Mental Treatment Act*) and Mental Deficiency Hospitals (for people with learning disabilities) were still overcrowded and under-funded. They contained 40 per cent of NHS inpatient beds but received only 20 per cent of the hospital budget (Goodwin, 1997). The average cost of treating a mental health inpatient was 3 pound 15 shillings and 11 pence in 1951 compared with 4 pound 13 shillings and 11 pence in 1959/60 (at 1950/1951 prices). However during the same period, the cost of inpatient maternity care rose from 6 pound 9 shillings and 5 pence to 16 pound 11 shillings and 3 pence. Goodwin suggests 'these figures clearly underline why the mental health services have earned the tag of a Cinderella service' (1990, p. 67).

Community care policy imperatives

By the late 1950s, there had certainly been some progress towards community care as the number of outpatient clinic attendances increased from virtually none in 1930 to 144,000 in 1959. However, mental health was still dominated by a hospital based approach. The need to move towards a more community based system of care and treatment was again highlighted by the

Royal Commission on Mental Illness and Mental Deficiency (1954–57) (the Percy Commission). The report suggested 'in relation to almost all forms of mental disorder, there is increasing medical emphasis on forms of treatment and training and social services which can be given without bringing patients into hospitals as inpatients or which make it possible to discharge them from hospital sooner than in the past' (1957, p. 207). It endorsed the development of a complex infrastructure of local authority community services such as hostels, day care, social work support and sheltered employment schemes that would support a policy of deinstitutionalisation and encourage greater use of treatments in a community setting. However, in a pattern repeated across the decades, the aspirations of the Percy Commission were never fully supported in legislation since the *Mental Health Act* of 1959 simply invited local authorities rather than required them to produce community care plans and no additional money was made available (Goodwin, 1990).

In 1961, Enoch Powell's now infamous 'water tower speech' once again heralded government policy intentions to shift the focus of mental health practice from the institution to the community (see Figure 2.2).

A Hospital Plan for England and Wales (1962) proposed the development of small-scale psychiatric units in District General Hospitals and envisaged that local authorities would provide a full range of domiciliary services to support patients in their own homes. However despite the recognition of what needed to be done, financial pressures continued to undermine community care policy.

It is also interesting to note that even at that stage, a time long before community care was a significant reality, concerns were beginning to be

Figure 2.2	The water tower speech

I have intimated to the hospital authorities who will be producing the constituent elements of the national Hospital Plan that in 15 years time there may well be needed not more than half as many places in hospitals for mental illness as there are today. Expressed in numerical terms, this would represent a redundancy of no fewer than 75,000 hospital beds... Now look and see what are the implications of these bold words. They imply nothing less than the elimination of by far the greater part of this country's mental hospitals as they exist today. This is a colossal undertaking, not so much in the new physical provision which it involves, as in the sheer inertia of mind and matter which it requires to overcome. There they stand, isolated, majestic, imperious, brooded over by the gigantic water tower and chimney combined, rising unmistakable and daunting out of the countryside – the asylums which our forefathers built with such immense solidity to express the notions of their day. Do not for a moment underestimate their powers of resistance to our assault.

(Powell, 1961)

expressed about both the real meaning of the word and, allied to this, the rhetoric/reality gap of an underfunded and understaffed community service. As Richard Titmuss, Professor of Social Administration at the London School of Economics suggested:

> We pontificate about the philosophy of community care; we may feel righteous because we have a civilised mental health act on the statute books; but unless we are prepared to examine it…at the level of concrete reality, what we mean by community care is simply indulging in wishful thinking…at present we are drifting into a situation in which, by shifting the emphasis from the institution to the community – a trend which, in principle and with qualifications, we all applaud – we are transferring the care of the mentally ill from trained staff to untrained or ill equipped staff or no staff at all (1968, pp. 106–7).

By 1974, there were 100,000 people in UK mental hospitals (60,000 fewer residents than there had been in 1954), but very few extra services to support the people who had been discharged into the community, prompting notions of a 'careless community' (Harrison, 1973). Indeed, it is more than a little ironic that the push for deinstitutionalisation was in part a result of concerns about conditions experienced by long-term residents in the old mental hospitals yet, as Grove (1994, p. 433), claims 'it is clear that this group who were supposed to benefit most from the closure of the institutions have in many cases fared worse'. While subsequent research has highlighted the usually positive outcomes of discharging people from hospitals into the community, this was not the case for everyone (Leff, 1997; see Chapters 4 and 5 for further discussion).

Causes of deinstitutionalisation

There are a number of competing theories on the causes of deinstitutionalisation. Goodwin (1997) proposes the following ideas (see Figure 2.3).

Figure 2.3	Deinstitutionalisation

1. *The development of new treatments*
   The development of anti-psychotic medication in the late 1950s is the most frequently cited factor for the shift from institutional to community based services. However there is little evidence to suggest a strong causal link since the coincidence of the introduction of psychotropic drugs and peaks of mental health inpatient populations are largely confined to the UK and the United States (US), not to other western countries.
2. *The development of social psychiatry*
   The association between the move towards community care and progressive social psychiatrists (that is, people interested in the effects of social conditions on behaviour and the relationship between psychiatric disorders and the social

Figure 2.3	Deinstitutionalisation *(continued)*

environment) are also inadequate since some professionals' livelihoods depended on the continued existence of the asylums.

3. *The emergence of anti psychiatry and the civil rights movement*

   The views of the anti psychiatrists (that is, a group of psychiatrists who by and large felt that mental illness was a myth and a societal construct) and civil rights activists in the 1960s provided an academic impetus for arguing for greater equality and better provision of community health care for people with mental illness. However the influence of these groups was relatively limited in policy circles.

4. *The poor conditions in the old asylums*

   By the late 1950s, many of the old asylums were overcrowded and increasingly dilapidated. However this of itself was insufficient to provide a direct impetus for deinstitutionalisation.

5. *Increased community tolerance*

   In the 1950s, a number of policy statements suggested a substantial change in the general climate of public opinion so that people were more ready to tolerate mental illness in the community. However the supporting evidence base for this is slim.

6. *Constitutional structures*

   Differences in constitutional structures between countries with similar onsets of deinstitutionalisation suggests that structures per se do not have a clear relationship with the development of community care.

7. *Funding systems*

   There is some evidence that insurance based funding systems tended to hinder policy change in the direction of community care. However this is still only a relatively marginal influence concerned with the rate of policy change rather than its instigation or implementation.

8. *Fiscal pressure*

   Scull (1977) argues that after the Second World War, the government increasingly struggled to contain the fiscal pressures of the welfare state and community care was seen as a cheaper option. However, analysis of the relative costs and effectiveness suggests that adequate community care is no cheaper than inadequate hospital care.

9. *The changing nature of mental illness*

   Goodwin (1997, p. 111) suggests that 'the shift in the second half of the twentieth century from an institutional to a community based system of mental health service provision represents little more than the administrative façade for the more substantial aspects of this process: an increase in accessibility of treatment facilities in order to address the newly defined and expanded range of mental health problems'. This is supported by the rapid increase in the number of conditions, particularly more common mental health problems, classified as a mental illness throughout the twentieth century. Community care may therefore represent a policy response to the changing nature and expansion of mental health problems in the twentieth century.

   In summary, the causes of deinstitutionalisation are multiple and often interlinked and it is overly simplistic to suggest that a single theory is sufficient to explain this complex transition within mental health policy and practice.

Better services for the mentally ill?

In 1975, the White Paper *Better Services for the Mentally Ill*, as the 1930 *Mental Treatment Act*, the *Mental Health Act* of 1959 and the *Hospital Plan* in 1962 had before it, explicitly stated that developing community care would be encouraged and would need significant financial investment (see Figure 2.4). It also stated that 'joint planning of health and local authority services is essential' (p. 86) given that it is 'not easy to draw an exact line between the functions of day centres... (managed by local authority Social Services Departments) and those of day hospitals...(managed by the NHS)' (p. 34) (see Chapter 7 for further discussion of partnership working between health and social care).

However, by the mid-1970s, the Labour government, struggling with debt problems amplified by the oil crisis in 1973, approached the International Monetary Fund for a loan. A condition of the loan was that public spending had to be brought under control, precipitating a series of welfare cuts. As Webster points out (2002, p. 74):

> the oil crisis precipitated an economic collapse throughout the western world. The economic growth rate which had been maintained since 1960 at an average of about 5 per cent in the OECD (Organisation for Economic Co-operation and Development) area slumped to nothing. From 1975 onwards the entire OECD area shared the UK's experience of low growth, high inflation, high unemployment and an adverse balance of trade...gloomy voices declared that 1975 represented the death knell of the welfare state.

Lack of funds to fully implement community care policies in the face of hospital closures has been, as we have seen, a recurring theme throughout

Figure 2.4	Better services for the mentally ill

Mental illness is... perhaps the major health problem of our time. It is also a major social problem... What we have to do is get to grips with shifting the emphasis to community care. The problems are many. Social services facilities have to be built up... Staff to run them have to be recruited and trained...Psychiatric services have to be developed locally, in general and community hospitals and in health centres. We have to recognise, moreover, that the pace at which community based care can be introduced depends not only on resources but on the pace of response of the community itself... Local services mean more day hospital treatment, more day care, more treatment and support in the home itself and less in-patient treatment... The policy can only be achieved if there is substantial capital investment in new facilities and if there is a significant shift in the balance of services between health and the local authority.

(Department of Health and Social Security (DHSS), 1975, pp. 2–3)

the history of mental health services but, set within this particular economic context, it is perhaps less surprising that few of the proposals and principles enshrined in *Better Services for the Mentally Ill* were implemented in practice.

The NHS: under new management?

When the Conservative government came to power under Margaret Thatcher in 1979, the main focus of welfare policy was how to make it more business-like in the face of increasing demands from an ageing population, rising patient expectations and advances in medical technology (Bloor and Maynard, 1994). The first defining NHS policy report associated with the Thatcher era was the *NHS management inquiry report* (DHSS, 1983), produced by a team led by Roy Griffiths, who was then Managing Director of the Sainsbury supermarket chain. The report identified the absence of a clearly defined general management function as the main weakness of the NHS and recommended that consensus management should be replaced by a system of general management at all levels (see Figure 2.5)

Part of the government's overall efficiency drive also included a programme of privatisation of state-owned enterprises, reductions in some forms of taxation and tighter controls over public spending. This tight fiscal background had a direct effect on the NHS. By 1988, the cumulative shortfall in hospital and community health service funding since 1981–82 amounted to 1.8 billion. For 1987–88 alone, expenditure was almost 400 million below the government's own estimated target funding level (King's Fund Institute, 1988).

In the face of a developing NHS funding crisis, highlighted by growing medical disquiet and perennial winter bed shortage crises, the BMA called for additional resources to help meet the financial shortfall. The immediate government response included an additional £101 million funding in December 1987 and a Ministerial Review on the future of the NHS. There was little desire in the Review for a major change in how the NHS was financed since experience from other countries suggested that the funding mechanism per se was not the key to running an efficient health service.

Figure 2.5	The Griffiths Report (1983)

The absence of this general management support means that there is no driving force seeking and accepting direct and personal responsibility for developing management plans, securing their implementation, and monitoring actual achievement. It means that the process of devolution of responsibility, including discharging responsibility to the units, is far too slow…If Florence Nightingale were carrying her lamps through the corridors of the NHS today, she would almost certainly be searching for the people in charge.

(DHSS, 1983: para 5 and 12)

The Review instead focused on how resources could be used more efficiently through changes in how health services are delivered. A key proposal, based on the ideas of an American economist Alain Enthoven (1985), was that responsibility for purchasing care and providing services should be separated (the purchaser/provider split) to create the conditions for a competitive internal market within the NHS. In essence, services would be provided by hospitals and community units as self-governing Trusts, and these services would be bought by the Health Authorities and also by fund holding practices (practices with a budget to purchase a limited range of services for their patients by negotiating contracts with NHS Trusts). This meant, in effect, that providers would compete with each other to sell their services, creating a quasi market, that would, in theory, encourage more cost effective services and make the NHS more efficient.

At the same time, the pressures for reform of community care were also beginning to build up again, with growing criticism of a lack of joined-up working between health ands social care (Audit Commission, 1986). In social services in particular, this was linked to concerns about the rapidly rising cost of care home placements for older people and a desire to bring this budget back under control (see Means and Smith, 1998 for an overview). At the same time, there were also growing concerns about the essentially unpaid and significant contribution that informal, often family carers, were increasingly being expected to provide, harking back to the pre-Victorian, pre-asylum era of mental health care (see Chapter 10 for further discussion of carers).

In 1988, the government commissioned Roy Griffiths (again) to review the funding and organisation of community care. His report *Community Care: an Agenda for Action* (1988) reaffirmed criticisms of inadequate resources and the apparent abdication of responsibility by central government: 'community care, everyone's distant relative but no-body's baby' (Griffiths, 1988: iv). Griffiths recommended that in order to reduce the confusion between agencies, local authority social services departments should be given the lead role in the provision of community care and suggested an increased role for the private and voluntary sectors. Many of these proposals were later enshrined in the White Paper *Caring for People* (Department of Health, 1989a) and the *NHS and Community Care Act* (1990) (see below).

Within the NHS, ideas from the Ministerial Review and the 1988 Griffiths Report were drawn together in the White Paper *Working for Patients* (Department of Health, 1989b). These proposals were described by Margaret Thatcher as 'the most far-reaching reform of the National Health Service in its forty year history' (Foreword to *Working for Patients*, 1989). The paper, however, provoked a storm of protest and opposition from the medical profession and others, and was further complicated by the difficult negotiations taking place with the BMA at the same time over a new contract for GPs. In spite of opposition, the timetable for implementation set out in *Working for Patients* was largely achieved and *The NHS and Community Care Act* (1990) became law in 1990 with many of its recommendations effective from April 1991 and full implementation by 1993 (see Figure 2.6).

Figure 2.6	The NHS and Community Care Act 1990

The Act, which brought in some of the biggest changes in the welfare state since the Second World War, represented the first occasion on which community care per se had provided the central focus for welfare legislation and aimed to enable people to live an independent and dignified life at home or elsewhere within the community for as long as they were able and wished to do so. It also recommended that service providers made practical support to carers a high priority. Significantly it also set out the role of health services as well as local authority social services in the provision of community care.

Specific provisions included:

- Giving local authority social services departments lead responsibility for community care
- The introduction of market principles into the provision of publicly funded health and welfare services including purchasing from private and voluntary agencies. Further impetus for this policy also came when it was announced that 85 per cent of the funding for social services' new responsibilities would have to be spent in the independent sector. From the early 1990s onwards, this meant that social care practitioners gained considerable experience of working with a 'mixed economy of care' (that is, with the public, private and voluntary sectors)
- Health Authorities assuming responsibility for purchasing health care with NHS trusts taking the responsibility for providing services. GP fund holders were able to purchase care for their patients as well as provide primary health care to individuals and families
- A requirement for local authorities to produce and publish community care plans
- Recognition of the importance of carers' roles and their need for practical support

However, a number of difficulties soon became apparent in terms of implementing the provisions of the Act. Inefficient inter-agency collaboration (particularly where different parts of the system – NHS, Social Services, voluntary and private sectors – had different ideologies and priorities), inadequate mechanisms for enabling the shift of finance from hospitals to community care and professional attachment to traditional working practices meant that problems soon developed. Partnership working was, in effect, part of government rhetoric rather than a practical reality (Bean and Mounser, 1993) (see also Chapter 7).

In the specific context of mental health, the BMA (1992, p. 30) indicated that 'there is concern that most local authorities lack the skills and expertise to take on the responsibility for supporting mentally ill people in the community' (an accusation that some in local government would probably also level at the medical profession). As Coppock and Hopton suggest, moreover, 'while the rhetoric of government ministers focused on a commitment to giving people who use mental health services more of a

Figure 2.7	Role confusion over the continuity of care

A good example of this role confusion is the dual development of the health-led care programme approach (CPA) for people under the care of specialist mental health services, and the social services-led care management approach (Department of Health, 1990a).

    As Hannigan suggests 'confusingly, both care management and CPA were introduced as mechanisms through which multi-disciplinary and multi-agency continuity of care could be organised and delivered. In many areas the lack of integration between the two methods resulted in duplication of effort, excessive bureaucracy and construction of a barrier to effective joint working' (2003, p. 32).

say, the reality highlighted a system plagued by gross under funding and role confusion' (2000, p. 43) (see Figure 2.7).

Of course, not all the evidence on co-operation between sectors was as bleak, and there were examples throughout the 1990s of excellent dialogue between health and social services as a result of the community care reforms, especially where boundaries were co-terminous (Means *et al.*, 2003). However, as we shall see, high profile cases of poor joint working also led to significant shifts in community mental health policy and practice.

Increasing resistance to community care

The difficulties inherent in joint working, duplication of effort and indeed the potential for no-one taking ultimate responsibility were highlighted by the Ritchie Report (1994), which, with the benefit of hindsight, was a watershed in the history of mental health in the last decade. The Ritchie Report was the culmination of the inquiry into the killing of Jonathan Zito by Christopher Clunis at a London underground station on 2nd December 1992 (before the full implementation of the Community Care Act). Although there were other high profile cases of people with mental health problems harming themselves or others, this particular event helped to shift the emphasis from talking about greater care in the community to fear about the risk posed by a small number of people with mental health problems to the community. The Ritchie Report did not, on the whole, blame individuals or suggest that the policy of community care should be reversed (and indeed noted that Christopher Clunis was in some sense a victim of the system since he had spent over five years moving between different sectors of the health and welfare service, between hospital, hostels and prison, with no overall plan for his care). However, the Report did state that 'the serious harm that may be inflicted by severely mentally ill people to themselves and others is a cost of care in the community which no society should tolerate' (paragraph 47.0.1).

Despite this, the notion of dangerousness implied by the Report is not evidence based. This is discussed in much more detail in Chapter 6, with recent research suggesting that the proportion of homicides committed by people with a mental health problem is not only very small, but has also fallen. Nevertheless, the intensity of the media coverage of Christopher Clunis and a small number of other cases in the 1990s (including the 1996 murders of Lin and Megan Russell by Michael Stone, diagnosed as having an untreatable personality disorder) created considerable public unease and a series of government policies focused on notions of public safety (see Figure 2.8).

Figure 2.8	Care in the community?

- In April 1994, supervision registers were introduced to identify and provide information on service users 'who are and are liable to be at risk of committing serious violence or suicide or serious self neglect' (NHS Executive 1994, p. 1)
- In 1995, Supervised Discharge Orders (SDOs) allowed clinicians to specify where patients should live, to require them to attend for treatment and to require that they allow access to members of a clinical team for the purpose of assessment
- In 1995, the government produced good practice guidance (Department of Health, 1995) that stressed that the CPA and care management were based on the same principles and so should be capable of being fully integrated

It is interesting, however, to note that supervision registers were used inconsistently between Trusts (Bindman *et al.*, 2000) and that revised guidance (Department of Health, 1999b) removed the requirement to maintain a supervision register if a simplified two tier CPA is in place. Evidence also suggests that SDOs are rarely used and are of limited effectiveness (Pinfold *et al.*, 2001). Perhaps this suggests that policies based primarily on public safety are actually very difficult to enforce?

New Labour and the Modernisation Agenda

In May 1997, New Labour swept into government vowing to save and rebuild the NHS. However, within months, the political rhetoric began to change, with an announcement that there would be a continuation of Conservative spending plans (Department of Health, 1997a). This lack of immediate change was also, to some extent, a reflection that from 1991 onwards, the tone of successive Conservative Health Ministers had slowly changed, with partnership rather than competition increasingly emphasised. This position was most clearly expressed in the 1996 White Paper, *A Service with Ambitions*, which outlined a future in which priority would be given to information technology (IT), professional development and managing quality rather than to further developing the market economy in public services (Department of Health, 1996a).

New Labour's big policy ideas across all sectors of government were largely focused on the notion of modernisation (see Figure 2.9), reflected in key policy documents including *Modernising Social Services* (Department of Health, 1998d), *Modernising Local Government* (Department of the Environment Employment, Transport and the Regions, 1998) and *Modernising Government* (Cabinet Office, 1999).

The Labour government's first substantive NHS proposals were published towards the end of the first year in office in the White Paper *The New NHS: Modern, Dependable* (Department of Health, 1997a). It stressed the modernisation principles of partnership working and the importance of a 'third way' in running the NHS:

> The Government is committed to building on what has worked but discarding what has failed. There will be no return to the old centralised command and control of the 1970s...but nor will there be a continuation of the divisive internal market system of the 1990s... Instead there will be a third way of running the NHS – a system based on partnership and driven by performance (Secretary of State for Health, 1997a, p. 10).

The concept of the 'third way' (part of the language of social democracy throughout most of the twentieth century), took on particular meaning at this time as it became associated not only with the politics of the Labour party in the UK but also with the New Democrats led by Bill Clinton in the US. Tony Giddens, a Professor at the London School of Economics, who has written extensively about the meaning and implication of the third way (Giddens, 1998; Giddens, 2000), suggested the third way proposed to construct a new social contract based on the idea of:

> ... no rights without responsibilities. Those who profit from social goods should both use them responsibly and give something back to the

Figure 2.9	**Principles of modernisation**

- A focus on outcomes to enable working across organisational structures
- The promotion of partnership between different areas of government and with the voluntary and private sectors
- Greater use of evidence in research
- Consultation with service users
- The use of targets and performance monitoring to secure quality and continuous improvement in public services
- Additional investment to be conditional on improved results
- A greater valuing of public services by developing skills and rewarding results
- The development of information technology (IT) throughout government

(Cabinet Office, 1999)

Figure 2.10	Monitoring performance in health and social care

Key mechanisms included:

- The introduction of National Service Frameworks (the first of which, in 1999, addressed mental health)
- Star rating systems to assess the performance of health and of social care
- The creation of NICE (an organisation that develops and publishes cost benefit analysis for specific technologies and pharmaceuticals) and the Social Care Institute for Excellence (SCIE) (to identify and disseminate 'what works' in social care)
- The creation of the Commission for Health Care Inspection (CHI) (now known as The Healthcare Commission) and the Commission for Social Care Inspection

wider social community in return. Seen as the feature of citizenship no rights without responsibilities has to apply to politicians as well as citizens, to the rich as well as the poor, to business corporations as much as the private individual. A left of centre government should be prepared to act upon it in all these areas (1998, p. 52).

Third way politics also emphasises the need for active government intervention to respond to social exclusion with a transition from passive to active welfare policies.

The New NHS also included a clear commitment to abolish the internal market but retain the Conservatives' provider/purchaser split. The main change was that commissioning would be in the hands of new Primary Care Groups (PCGs) (now replaced by PCTs) covering an average of 100,000 patients rather than Health Authorities and GP fund holders, and that competition would be replaced by collaboration and partnership between commissioners and providers. This structural decentralisation also enabled the integration, at least in theory, of primary care and community services, and, by linking provision with commissioning powers, could theoretically address longstanding issues of fragmentation within the NHS. However, modernisation also encompassed a greater use of targets and performance monitoring to make sure that any new funding provided was spent in different ways in the future to improve services (see Figure 2.10).

Modernising mental health services

As we have suggested throughout this chapter, there has been much to modernise in mental health. *The Journey to Recovery* (Department of Health, 2001b) admitted that mental heath was a poor relation among services with 'shabby and depressing wards that would never have been tolerated in medicine or surgery' and care in the community that 'too often became a bleak and neglected environment' (p. 4). However, by the end of the 1990s, a number of seemingly separate but ultimately inter-linking factors such as the adverse publicity of a small number of high profile cases including violence and people with serious mental illness, the appointment of mental health champions such as John Mahoney and Antony Sheehan to key policy posts, and an increasingly vocal mental health service user movement (see Chapter 8) meant that mental health began to become more of a political priority.

The mental health modernisation agenda was heralded and imple-mented through two key policy documents: *Modernising Mental Health Services: Safe, Sound and Supportive* (Department of Health, 1998a) (see Figure 2.11) and *The National Service Framework for Mental Health* (Department of Health, 1999a). *Modernising Mental Health Services* was, in effect, the first comprehensive government statement about the future direction of mental health policy since *Better Services for the Mentally Ill* in 1975 and, unlike that White Paper, was underpinned by £700 million of new investment over three years.

The supportive element of the White Paper, working with patients and services users, families and carers to build healthier communities, reflected the increasingly overt communitarian approach adopted by New Labour.

However, it is also interesting to note that the major emphasis was on public safety rather than support for service users (an issue we return to later in this chapter). Frank Dobson, the Health Secretary at the time, echoed the rhetoric of the Ritchie Report in his introduction to the White Paper (Department of Health, 1998b) stating that:

> care in the community has failed because while it improved the
> treatment of many people who were mentally ill, it left far too many
> walking the streets, often at risk to themselves and a nuisance to

Figure 2.11	*Modernising Mental Health Services* (1998a)

The key recommendations in the White Paper were to:

- Strengthen comprehensive care (with particular emphasis on services for people with severe mental illness, including acute beds, 24-hour nursed care secure beds, assertive outreach teams and crisis intervention teams)
- Provide 24-hour access to services
- Develop, train and recruit staff with the skills and motivation to deliver modern services
- Improve the planning and commissioning of services
- Develop partnership
- Develop mental health promotion
- Improve the use of information technology

others…Discharging people from institutions has brought benefits to some, but it has left many vulnerable patients trying to cope on their own…A small but significant minority have become a danger to the public as well as themselves… We are going to ensure that patients who might otherwise be a danger to themselves and others are no longer able to refuse to comply with the treatment they need.

The following year, *The National Service Framework for Mental Health* (Department of Health, 1999a), set out a ten-year plan for the development and delivery of mental health services for adults of working age (see Figure 2.12).

The *National Service Framework* or NSF (Department of Health, 1999a) had a number of key strengths including the fact that it was the first document in mental health to set a common agenda for local agencies. It was comprehensive in scope and focused as much on health promotion and common mental illness within primary care as it did on serious mental illness. As *Modernising Mental Health Services* had done, the NSF also reflected a communitarian philosophy of promoting access to the mainstream for people with mental illness through social inclusion involving the wider community as well as through developing health and social care services. It was also partially evidence based, which, as we suggested at the beginning of this chapter, is relatively rare in a policy report. However, as the Sainsbury Centre for Mental Health at the time (1999) and the Wanless report since

Figure 2.12	*The National Service Framework for Mental Health* (1999a)

The framework included seven standards in five areas of care:

1. *Mental health promotion* – to ensure health and social services promote mental health and reduce discrimination and social exclusion associated with mental health problems.
2. *Primary care and access to services* – to deliver better primary mental health care, and to ensure consistent advice and help for people with mental health needs, including primary care services for individuals with severe mental illness.
3. *Effective services for people with severe mental illness* – to ensure that each person with severe mental illness receives the range of mental health services they need; that crises are anticipated or prevented where possible; to ensure prompt and effective help if a crisis does occur, and timely access to an appropriate and safe mental health place or hospital bed, as close to home as possible.
4. *Caring about carers* – to ensure health and social services assess the needs of carers who provide regular and substantial care for those with severe mental illness and provide care to meet their needs.
5. *Preventing suicide* – to ensure that health and social services play their full part in reducing the suicide rate by at least one fifth by 2010.

have recognised (Wanless, 2002), it was not a fully resourced document. There were also basic inequities in a framework devoting a standard to carers but not service users. Indeed, users are depicted largely as recipients of services and, once again, as potential sources of risk to the community.

The costs of modernisation

By 2000, despite the plethora of policy reforms, a desire to stick within the previous administration's spending limits meant that 'Ministers were deluded by their own rhetoric into thinking that Labour's programme of modernisation possessed some kind of magic that permitted miracles to be wrought without the application of resources' (Webster, 2002, p. 215). In 1998, UK total health care expenditure was 6.8 per cent of Gross Domestic Produce (GDP) compared with an income weighted average of 8.4 per cent in European Union (EU) countries. The UK's total health care spending per capita was then about 25–30 per cent lower than in Australia, France and The Netherlands, around 35 per cent lower than in Canada and Germany (OECD, 2001) and comparable to that of the Czech Republic, Poland and South Korea. The OECD statistics show that the UK spent £863 per person on health in 1999, while Norway spent £1484 on each person (Wanless, 2002).

Public disquiet over long waiting lists and variable treatment experiences, negative publicity and public criticism of the government's record on the NHS by respected experts put pressure on the government to consider changes in NHS funding. The Prime Minister announced that the government would, over a period of five years, increase the level of health spending to the European average (Tony Blair, interviewed by David Frost, BBC TV, 16 January 2000). The budget that year gave sufficient money to the NHS to allow it to grow in real terms by 6.1 per cent, nearly twice the historic average.

In July 2000, *The NHS Plan* (Department of Health, 2000a) represented, in many senses, a re-launch of Labour's now more robustly funded NHS policy. New investment in staff and IT systems and new NHS structures including Care Trusts (new integrated health and social care bodies; see Chapter 7) were announced. Three clinical priority areas were highlighted: cancer, coronary heart disease and mental health. From a mental health perspective, *The NHS Plan* promised an extra annual investment of over £300 million by 2003/4 to fast forward the NSF but was also, true to the principles of modernisation, fundamentally concerned with what had to be delivered in return for the money (see Figure 2.13).

Unfortunately, despite pledges on primary and community care, there was relatively little emphasis on acute services (see Chapter 5) or mental health promotion. Indeed, it could be argued that the overall mental health emphasis was on compulsion and perhaps even reinstitutionalisation, with funding being directed towards forensic beds, involuntary hospital admissions and places in supported housing to provide proactive care for people traditionally seen as difficult to engage in the community (Priebe *et al.*, 2005). *The NHS Plan*

Figure 2.13	Mental health policy and *The NHS Plan*

- 1000 new graduate mental health staff to work in primary care
- An extra 500 community mental health team workers
- 50 early intervention teams to provide treatment and support to young people with psychosis
- 335 crisis resolution teams
- An increase to 220 assertive outreach teams
- Provision of women only day services
- 700 extra staff to work with carers
- More suitable accommodation for up to 400 people currently in high secure hospital
- Better services for prisoners with mental illness
- Additional placements and staff for people with severe personality disorder

(Department of Health, 2000a) also relied heavily on a flourishing well-trained and motivated workforce for implementation, which in terms of mental health, as in many other areas of the NHS, has not necessarily materialised.

In addition, *The NHS Plan* also assumed that the NHS had a management structure that could embrace and lead change. Although the 1983 Griffiths report arguably laid the foundations for such significant changes by creating a group of staff receptive to management ideas and policies, *The NHS Plan* was introduced at a time in NHS history when significant change was occurring at all levels of the service (Department of Health, 2001c, 2002b) which led to a dilution of management expertise. New PCTs for example were given specific responsibility for commissioning services including mental health services, and in April 2002, Health Authorities in England were replaced by 28 larger Strategic Health Authorities with a performance management brief.

The organisation of mental health services also changed rapidly with the creation in England of specialist Mental Health Trusts and the increasing integration of health and social care provision. At the time of writing there are 85 providers of secondary mental health services in England including 18 PCT providers. Five Mental Health Care Trusts have been established, while other NHS trusts and local authorities have used the *Health Act* (1999) flexibilities to develop integrated provision (see Chapter 7). As these NHS structures and functions changed and people moved around the system with new roles and responsibilities, it is also perhaps not surprising that there has been slippage in implementing many of the mental health and wider *NHS Plan* targets.

To help resolve uncertainty about future NHS finances, the Treasury asked Derek Wanless, the former chief executive of the National Westminster Bank, to produce a report on future NHS funding. In 2002, the Wanless Report concluded that 'to deliver the high quality service envisaged, the review projects that NHS costs will rise to between 154 billion and 184 billion by 2022–23 (in 2002/03 prices). Across the 20 year period this implies total NHS spending increasing at an average rate of between 4.2 and 5.1 per cent a year in real terms' (Wanless, 2002, Introduction).

In response, the April 2002 budget announced significant new investment in the NHS from 2003–08, financed in part by an extra one per cent on national insurance. Spending on the NHS should now rise by an average of 7.4 per cent annually, reaching £105.6 billion by 2007/8, compared to £65.4 billion in 2002/3 and £40 billion in 1999–2000. This represents a rise in the share of GDP spent on health care to 9.4 per cent. If these increases are achieved, the next few years will more than double the historical rate of annual increases and should provide significant extra investment for generic and mental health services, although this is still far less than many other countries including France, Germany and the US (Robinson, 2002). However, concern has also been raised that funding for social care will not rise by the same rate, creating possible future funding difficulties when considering integrated working (Kenny, 2004). There are also on-going concerns over transparency in tracing money with Rethink (2002), for example, estimating that only £632 million of the promised £700 million in *Modernising Mental Health Services* was received by mental health services.

The continuing debate about community care

By the late 1990s, patient choice and partnership working were becoming buzz words within the wider health and social care community, and were, to a lesser extent, also beginning to impact on mental health services (see Chapters 7 and 8). Issues of social inclusion, represented perhaps most starkly by the unacceptably high unemployment rates for people with mental illness, were also beginning to be addressed by a series of policy initiatives (see Figure 2.14).

It was, paradoxically, against this emerging more inclusive policy background that service users and professionals clashed with a government that seemed determined to prioritise media spun notions of public safety over the evidence base on community care. Frank Dobson's statement in the House of Commons on 29th July 1998 that care in the community had failed heralded a series of papers and consultation documents on the revision of the 1983 *Mental Health Act*, including a report from an expert committee chaired by Genevra Richardson and a Green Paper, *Reform of the Mental Health Act 1983: proposals for consultation* (Department of Health, 1999c, 1999d). In particular, Richardson argued that issues of capacity, reciprocity (that is, safeguarding patient's rights and providing appropriate services), a statutory right to early advocacy and the inclusion of advanced statements needed to be recognised in future legislation.

The Green Paper, however, ignored these recommendations and instead emphasised questions of risk in a traditional paternalistic sense, referring to compulsory treatment orders (CTOs) for those posing a risk to self or

Figure 2.14	Mental illness and the wider social inclusion agenda

- The *Disability Discrimination Act* (1995) was the first attempt by a British government to legislate against the discrimination faced by disabled people including people with mental illness. The number of disabled people with mental health problems in Britain covered by the DDA definition is estimated to be 580,783, just over ten per cent of the total DDA disabled population of working age (ONS, 2003)
- *Welfare to Work*, the government's overall policy framework and programme for reform of the welfare state includes the New Deal for Disabled People (NDDP) which addresses the needs of mental health services users. The NDDP recognises the particular barriers to employment and education faced by this group in society, and includes new advisory services and a limited range of more intensive support aimed at enabling people claiming disability benefits to return to work. (see Chapter 4 for further discussion of social inclusion and employment issues)
- There is, however, an inherent tension within the *Welfare to Work* programme between the very low rates of employment for people with mental health problems, the resulting poverty and additional social exclusion that this can lead to, and also the recognition that, for some people, full time paid work may never be possible. There is, however, still a need for people to engage in meaningful activity that keeps them well in the community with the open-ended possibility of recovery

(Rankin, 2005)

others. The subsequent White Paper, *Reforming the Mental Health Act* (Department of Health, 2001d, 2001e) attracted a great deal of attention, largely because of its over-riding emphasis on public safety (Grounds, 2001). The first *Draft Mental Health Bill*, published on 25th July 2002, contained safeguards of rights of appeal and access to advocacy services and safeguards for certain patients treated informally who are not capable of consenting, but also included a number of issues that create considerable concerns for health and social care professionals, services users and for wider society particularly in terms of increased powers of compulsion (see Figure 2.15). An umbrella organisation, the Mental Health Alliance, consisting of over 60 mental health organisations was established in response to the Bill and was vociferous in its opposition. The second (revised) Draft Bill was published on 8th September 2004. Although there appeared to be some improvements, critics still argue that services provided to an individual will be largely determined by the risk they post to society rather than, as the Richardson report proposed, the level of their mental capacity (Mooney, 2004). The BMA has called the Draft Bill too complex, unethical and unworkable (Kmietowicz, 2005). The Bill was subjected to pre-legislative scrutiny in March 2005 and looks set to be introduced in Parliament in 2006/7.

Overall, it is difficult to see how the Draft Bill fits with the modernisation agenda of partnership working, access, and patient choice. It also fails to

Figure 2.15	Key concerns within the first and second Draft Mental Health Bill (Deparment of Health 2002a)

- The treatability clause in the 1983 Act was effectively abolished in the first draft. A compulsory order can therefore be placed 'in the case of a person who is at substantial risk of causing serious harm to other persons, that it is necessary for the protection of those persons that medical treatment be provided to him' and 'in any other case that it is necessary for the health or safety of the patient or the protection of other person that medical treatment be provided to him' (TSO 2002, part 2, 1.6). People with Dangerous Severe Personality Disorder (DSPD) can be detained if they pose 'a substantial risk of serious harm to others'. This means that in practice the notion of preventive detention has been introduced into English law for the first time outside wartime or the prevention of terrorism, despite the fact that there is no evidence base to support the idea that the behaviour of people with a diagnosis of personality disorder can be predicted with sufficient certainty to justify preventive detention. The second draft however introduced the definition of 'clinical appropriateness' which means the clinician must decide whether it is clinically appropriate for the patient
- Community treatment orders mean patients can effectively be detained in the community. Patients will be required to attend for their injection or their oral medication at a certain place at a certain time and, if they don't comply, they may be removed to a clinical setting where the drugs can then be administered. This, of course, places real tensions on the doctor/patient relationship and mental health service user groups have warned that it may also drive users away from services. The revised Bill however limits these extended powers to some extent so that only patients previously detained for inpatient care can be forcibly treated in the community
- The broad definition of mental disorder in both drafts as 'an impairment of or a disturbance in the functioning of the mind or brain resulting from any disability or disorder of the mind or brain. Examples of mental disorder include schizophrenia, depression or a learning disability' raises the possibility of compulsory treatment for a broader group of people, for example, for people who are dependent on alcohol or drugs
- The extra appeals, tribunals and hearings that the new system may generate will require an estimated 1000 additional staff (NHS Confederation, 2003a), at a time when there are workforce shortages

recognise notions of the possibility of recovery from mental illness. Instead, a more effective way of improving the safety of the public and the care of people with mental health problems is surely to devise mental health services where users have information and are truly consulted and given control over aspects of their care (see Chapter 8). As Laurance suggests (2003, p. xxi):

> The most effective way to improve the safety of the public and the care of those who are mentally ill is to devise services that genuinely engage users and meet their desire for greater control so that they are

encouraged to seek treatment and lead stable, risk-free lives. If instead, politicians pander to public prejudice and adopt a heavy handed, coercive approach, they will drive people away from services.

Implementation rhetoric and reality

Despite the policy focus and extra funding, mental health services, like many other generic aspects of the NHS, are still getting 'mixed reviews' particularly in terms of implementation. A recent review (Commission for Health Improvement, 2003a) found that while some mental health trusts were performing well, particularly in the areas of user involvement, innovative practices and links with community organisations, there were significant problems created by:

- The national shortages of psychiatrists and nurses
- Poor physical facilities for service provision
- Pressures on inpatient beds
- Poor information systems and significant lack of management capacity
- Low priority for services to older people and children

There has also been significant slippage in the time frame of many of the new mental health initiatives announced in *The NHS Plan* (Department of Health, 2000a) with, for example, only 150 of the 1000 primary mental health workers in place by April 2004 (Rushforth, personal communication, 2004). An interesting question, and one that could have been asked at almost any point in the last 150 years, is therefore why central policy imperatives are not consistently implemented on the ground. There appear to be at least four key issues that affect implementation:

1. Implementation is more likely to occur if different organisations have clear roles and responsibilities. However, in terms of mental health, there is significant overlap between different programmes and organisations. Suicide prevention, for example, is tackled not only as Standard 7 of *The NSF*, but specifically within the *National Confidential Inquiry into Suicide and Homicide*, *The NHS Plan*, *Adult Acute In-Patient Care Provision* guidance and the *National Suicide Prevention Strategy* (Department of Health, 1999a, 2000a, 2001a, 2002c, 2002d).
2. The culture of an organisation is also important in implementing change. In a study exploring the relationship between organisational culture and performance in the NHS, Mannion *et al.* (2003) identified a range of cultural characteristics that appeared to be linked to positive organisational performance including:

   - Strong leadership
   - A culture of clear and explicit performance objectives
   - Clear lines of upward accountability

■ A pro-active approach to managing the local health community
■ A considerable emphasis on developing and harnessing staff potential

Despite this, the evidence base on the nature of organisational culture in the NHS, its role in performance and quality, and the extent to which policies have succeeded in securing change is still relatively sparse (Leatherman and Sutherland, 2003) and more work is needed to understand this link in the context of the NHS.

3. It is also difficult to implement new working practices within a system that is in a constant state of change. It is interesting that the shape and size of PCTs and strategic Health Authorities are once again changing with further reorganisation and mergers in 2006 to reduce their number by half across England at precisely the point in their history when they require space to work on implementing current policy initiatives, build relations with local health care communities and secure much needed clinical engagement and improvements in service (Walshe et al., 2004). As Means et al. suggest, there is: 'the impression of a modernisation muddle in which managers and field level staff are struggling to keep pace with the demand for policy change and the ever increasing flood of directives, guidelines and indicators' (2003, p. 214). Successful implementation requires a break from new policy and time and space to understand and implement existing directives.

4. Perhaps the key barrier to implementation is the age-old tension between central policy edicts and local flexibility, with implementation deficits due either to top down or bottom up problems (Hill and Hupe, 2002). In a seminal book on implementation deficit, Pressman and Wildavsky (1973) argue that relatively small failures of co-operation between different organisations can easily multiply to create a major implementation deficit. Major policy change is especially likely to create an implementation deficit because of the complexity it both requires and engenders. As the government attempts to enforce change through a top down approach, they are likely to provoke resistance from vested interests and also generate a mass of unintended consequences. In practice, the policy directives from the Department of Health have to be filtered down through Strategic Health Authorities, PCTs and Acute Trusts before they can have an impact on services. All of these bodies are semi-autonomous organisations and can influence if and how central policy is implemented. In addition, social care is overseen by local councillors, and services are therefore accountable to locally elected representatives rather than nationally.

Structural decentralisation in the NHS, through the creation of PCTs and Strategic Health Authorities to performance manage their local health system, suggests that local control and autonomy at the coalface are becoming increasingly common. The creation and promotion of Foundation Trusts also demonstrates the government's desire to delegate autonomy to the field through the *Community Health and Standards Act* (2003) since Foundation Trusts can opt out of central government control and have greater flexibility over their financial position. However the modernisation agenda with its organisations, frameworks and widespread central quality controls has and continues to exert a powerful centralising influence within health and social care and the latest *Priorities and Planning Framework* (2002d) is explicit in its arrangements for monitoring and performance management. The clash of top down and bottom up approaches creates tensions within the system and means that policies may not necessarily be implemented in practice.

Conclusion

Aneurin Bevan said: 'we ought to take a pride in the fact that despite our financial and economic anxieties, we are still able to do the most civilised thing in the world – put the welfare of the sick in front of every other consideration' (House of Commons, 1948). However as this chapter has suggested, over the intervening five and a half decades, the NHS has slipped from being the number one government priority, and indeed has been, at times, both poorly managed and financially neglected.

The place and relative importance of the NHS, of course, needs to be viewed within the broader political context. The Chancellor of the Exchequer, Gordon Brown, recently declared that the government's task is to 'push forward with all radical long term reforms necessary to enhance productivity and to improve public services, health being in that basket along with transportation, higher education and utilities' (Brown, 2003). In other words, health needs to be seen in the context of the macro political and economic picture. There is however definite evidence of a change in the political priority accorded to the NHS since 2000, underpinned by the five-year funding infusion of £40 billion announced in April 2002. Quite where social care fits in with this agenda is harder to gauge – sometimes included in policies that focus primarily on health care, sometimes receiving additional funding (but less than the NHS) and sometimes receiving relatively little attention at all.

Is Cinderella finally going to the ball?

Mental health has also been seen as an increasing political priority since 1998, the subject of the first National Service Framework in 1999, a key area within *The NHS Plan* (Department of Health, 2000a) and prominent as one of the three highlighted clinical areas in the *Priorities and Planning Framework* for 2003–06 (Department of Health, 2002e). The NIMHE was also established in 2002 to help oversee changes in mental health services, while the now established Mental Health Research Network may, help to provide high quality evidence to inform policy and underpin service developments. However practitioners still face a series of particular challenges in practice.

Within the new Planning Framework, mental health has a joint lead agency, which means that leadership responsibilities are shared between the NHS and social services. Good partnership working will therefore be crucial in implementing change and lessons need to be heeded from previous attempts at 'power sharing', for example, in implementing provisions within the *NHS and Community Care Act* 1990 (see Chapter 7).

Sufficient financial investment is, of course, also crucial in improving mental health services. Twelve per cent of the NHS budget is currently spent on mental health, but as the Wanless report suggested 'The additional annual cost of implementing the NSF for mental health is estimated to be 3.1 billion a year by 2010/11, roughly doubling existing spending on mental health services for adults' (2002, p. 24). It remains to be seen if this funding materialises.

However, there is a still a central paradox at the heart of mental health policy and practice. While there are legal structures that encourage partnership working, policy that finally begins to address shortfalls in acute and community mental health provision and financial investment in public services, there are also moves to introduce compulsory mental health treatment in the community and to detain people on suspicion that they might harm someone, prioritising coercion rather than care in the community. In a health and social care system that increasingly values patient and user choice, mental health in a new century poses a particular paradox for policy makers and presents a series of challenges to practitioners and users to shape mental health services in a way that truly reflects what users want, what the country can afford and what the workforce is able to deliver.

Suggestions for further reading

For those wishing to explore the policy context in more detail, the following books offer critical and well-written appraisals of the history and politics of the NHS and social care:

1. Coppock, V. and Hopton, J. (2000) *Critical perspectives on mental health*. London, Routledge
    This book explores the social, political and intellectual developments that have shaped mental health practice over the last four decades, using as a guiding framework the ideas of the anti-psychiatry, anti-racism and radical feminism movements.
2. Rogers, A. and Pilgrim, D. (2001) *Mental health policy in Britain* (2nd edn.). Basingstoke, Palgrave
    This key text offers a critical analysis of mental health policy including a discussion of the mental health users' movement and the influence of users' views on policy formation.
3. Webster, C. (2002) Th*e National Health Service: a political history.* Oxford, Oxford University Press
    This book provides an overview of the key issues that have shaped the NHS during the past 50 years. Although mental health does not feature prominently within the text, the political and economic influences on generic NHS policy are helpful in contextualising the position of mental health.
4. Laurance, J. (2003) *Pure madness: how fear drives the mental health system.* London, Routledge
    Pure Madness is an impressionistic, anecdotal, but nevertheless powerful account of the state of mental health care in Britain today, written by the health editor of *The Independent*. Laurance examines issues of care or control in the community and explores alternatives to inpatient treatment.
5. For anyone interested in the history of madness, there is no better source than the unique and always fascinating Roy Porter. Try:

    ■ Porter, R. (2002) *Madness: a brief history.* Oxford, Oxford University; or
    ■ Porter R. (1999) *A social history of madness: stories of the insane.* London, Phoenix

6. Means, R., Richards, S. and Smith, R. (2003) *Community care: policy and practice* (3rd edn.). Basingstoke, Palgrave Macmillan
    For a general overview of community care services for older people, people with learning difficulties and people with mental health problems, Means *et al.* offer a detailed but accessible account that helps to place many of this issues discussed in this chapter in a wider social policy context.
7. Details of government policy documents are available on: www.official-documents.co.uk. Relevant statutes can be found on: www.hmso.gov.uk

3 Primary Care and Mental Health

In this chapter we discuss:

- The structure and workload of primary care
- The exceptional potential of primary care
- The history of primary care
- Primary care and mental health
- The value of primary care from the service user perspective
- The role of practice nurses in primary care and mental health
- The new primary care mental health workforce
- Creating a new model of primary care mental health care
- Barriers to partnership working

The structure and workload of primary care in the UK

GPs, practice nurses, dentists, pharmacists and opticians form the primary care level of the NHS and, as such, are the 'front line' of the health service. On the whole, patients cannot consult a doctor in secondary care such as a hospital consultant or member of a community mental health team unless they are referred by a GP. This filtering process has led to GPs being described as the 'gate keepers' of the NHS.

The core group of staff working in a practice is known as the 'primary health care team' (see Figure 3.1). The actual composition of any primary health care team differs between practices but the Royal College of General Practitioners (RCGP, 2002) has identified a core team as consisting of:

- GPs
- Practice nurses
- District nurses
- Health visitors
- Practice managers
- Administrative staff

In some surgeries, midwives, physiotherapists, counsellors and psychiatric nurses are also members of the team.

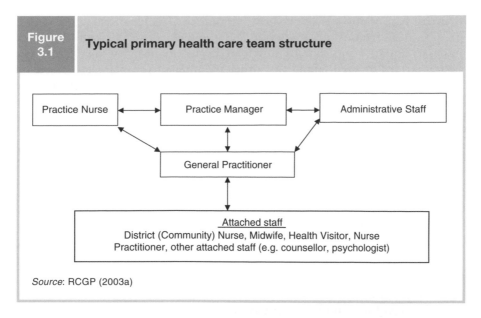

Figure 3.1   Typical primary health care team structure

Source: RCGP (2003a)

Ninety seven per cent of the population are registered with one of the approximately 36,000 GPs in the UK and see them on average four times each year (OPCS, 2000; RCGP, 2003b). GPs in the UK carry out over 269 million consultations each year, broadly equivalent to 740,000 consultations each day or 8000 consultations per GP per year (Office of Health Economics, 2000).

The exceptional potential of primary care?

Primary care in the UK has a number of unique strengths (see Figure 3.2). It offers rapid access for routine and crisis care in a low stigma setting. It occupies an important space at the interface of users, families, communities and professional worlds and is able to address mental, physical and social aspects of care. It has, until very recently, also been able to guarantee a cradle to grave doctor–patient relationship, with informational, longitudinal and interpersonal continuity of care (Saultz, 2003).

Figure 3.2   The strengths of primary care

- Offers a low stigma and accessible setting
- Enables a holistic approach to problems
- Provides informational, longitudinal and interpersonal continuity of care
- Sees individuals in the context of their past, their social networks and the wider community
- Is able to deal with both the general and the particular

Primary care is also a place of great complexity. As Heath suggests (1999, p. 565). 'Uncertainty, contradiction and complexity are the stuff of general practice and the measure of much of its fascination for us'. Each day, people arrive to see their GP or other member of the primary care team with coughs and colds and cancer and depression and have on average ten minutes to explain their problems and negotiate a solution. This compares to 20–30 minutes in a hospital setting where a referral letter has set the agenda and the doctor is an acknowledged specialist in that clinical area. Primary care is, by way of contrast, delivered by specialists in generalism (Willis, 1995), by people taking an interest in whatever is of interest to the patient. As a result, primary care has developed sophisticated ways of working with the uncertainty and complexity of its environment (Wilson and Holt, 2001). Decisions, for example, may be based more on intuition, experience and knowledge of the patient's previous history than slavish adherence to medical algorithms. General practitioners are also able, although not all are necessarily willing, to act not only as an individual's advocate within the wider system, but can combine this role with a wider social and political responsibility to speak out on behalf of the most needy and least heard within our society. As Tudor Hart suggests (1998, p. 332): 'If social factors influence the behaviour of disease on a community-wide scale, GPs and other primary care workers must concern themselves with them as a normal and central part of their work, not a fringe option to be added by some doctors and ignored by others'.

Primary care practitioners are also uniquely placed to understand both the general and the particular, an ability that Heath (1999) has termed the 'oscillating gaze'. Thus, when a practitioner focuses on the individual, they see the patient as a single human being (perhaps a tearful young woman with a new baby and sleep problems), and when they focus on the group, they see that young woman as part of a broader group within social life (that is, as a person with possible postnatal depression):

> The categorisation of people devalues individual experience and can leave individuals feeling unrecognised and the reality of their symptoms unheard…. the general practitioner while actively using the generalisation for biomedical science, has a constant responsibility to refocus on the individual, the detail of their experience and the meaning they attach to that experience. We cannot see the particular patient and the generalisation simultaneously. At a given instance we have to choose one way of seeing or the other. If we are to maximise our understanding, if we are not to become stranded and impotent at one pole of the dualism, we must learn to oscillate our gaze.
>
> (Heath, 1999, p. 652).

The history of primary care

The structure of primary care in the UK has its roots in the nineteenth century when medical care was provided by three groups of people – apothecaries, physicians and surgeons. The latter two had superior qualifications and status. During the early nineteenth century, the term GP came to be applied to a growing number of apothecaries who took the membership examination of the Royal College of Surgeons of England. However, at that stage there was still considerable freedom to move between the branches of the profession.

The practice of GPs referring patients to specialists began at the end of the nineteenth century and was well established by the time of the 1911 *National Insurance Act* which ensured free state primary care provision for a proportion of the population (working men).

The birth of the NHS as we might begin to recognise it today was in 1948. From the beginning there were complex negotiations. Ultimately, GPs agreed to register all patients and provide 24-hour care for them, establishing universal access to family doctors for the first time in the UK, but were allowed to retain their 'independent contractor status' so that they, in effect, remained their own bosses. Hospital consultants still had the option of private practice and access to pay beds in NHS hospitals and negotiated a system of financially advantageous 'merit awards' (now known as clinical excellence awards), leading Bevan to admit he had 'stuffed their mouths with gold' (Abel-Smith 1964, p. 480) to achieve agreement.

Ham (1999) has argued that an important outcome of the negotiations was to effectively divide the medical profession in two, winning the support of hospital consultants with generous financial payments and isolating and further reducing the power and status of GPs, reinforcing the notion of second–class citizenship created by the subordinate position of the apothecaries. Calnan and Gabe (1991) have argued that between 1948 and the negotiation of the next new contract in 1966, this lower status was demonstrated by GPs seeking to emulate hospital medical practice, for example by undertaking sessional clinical attachments in local hospitals.

However, from the mid–1960s onwards, GPs became swept up by a series of changes which transformed their practices and brought them into the mainstream of the health service. The Contract introduced in 1966 encouraged a move from single handed to group practices through the introduction of the 'group practice allowance' (funding specifically for multi-doctor practices). GPs were able to claim 70 per cent reimbursement of salary costs for up to two staff per full time GP partner, encouraging the employment of ancillary staff such as receptionists and practice nurses. A new terminology appeared, with uni-professional general practice being replaced with the notion of a multi-professional primary health care team working from a health centre.

These changes were underpinned by changes in vocational training. The Royal Commission on Medical Education (The Todd Report) made a series of recommendations designed to achieve parity between GPs and other specialities in terms of undergraduate education, postgraduate training, continuing education and a higher profile academic role in medical schools (Todd, 1968).

The work of GPs was also changing out of all recognition, largely due to the decline of infectious diseases, the ageing population and a recognition of

Figure 3.3	The changing workload of primary care

The old emergencies, lobar pneumonia, empyema, mastoids, have disappeared: doctors are being cast whether they like it or not in a new role as interested in and responsible for all the human frailties.

(Butterfield, 1964, Foreword)

The primary physician has an unequalled opportunity to balance long-term health needs against short-term clinical pressures. He can practise from a broad clinical base by integrating the psychosocial and biological components of each illness. He can implement applied continuity of care to defined population by learning to use the skills and aids which are required to achieve this. He can also make maximum use of the opportunities for health promotion and thereby begin to discover the need to modify the traditional clinical approach. Finally, he can permit his knowledge and skills in the modification of help-seeking behaviour to influence his clinical decisions, his practice organisation and his relationship with his patients. The larger number of patients coming to primary care, the nature of their problems, and the relationship they may have with their doctor – all reinforced these opportunities in a way not usually possible for other specialities.

(Stott and Davis, 1979, pp. 204–5)

the central importance of proactive as well as reactive care (see Figure 3.3). Reactive care (fire fighting), with a limited number of drugs, was replaced by a growing emphasis on holistic care and on health promotion and health prevention as well as addressing acute and on–going health complaints (Stott and Davis, 1979). These changes required a new workforce and a new approach to work in primary care.

Primary care since 1990

During the last 15 years, primary care has become increasingly central to the development and delivery of health services, an emphasis that is a global phenomenon (Rogers and Pilgrim, 2003). The political and fiscal context of the 1980s are described in detail in Chapter 2, but essentially, changes in terms of tighter public spending controls and the dominant political ideology focused on the importance of market forces led to a series of reviews of NHS funding mechanisms and organisation that culminated in the late 1980s, in the White Paper *Working for Patients* (Department of Health, 1989b). This included radical ideas about the delivery of health services, creating competition through the separation of purchaser and provider responsibilities and the establishment of self-governing NHS Trusts and GP fund holding (where practices were given a budget to purchase a limited range of services for their patients by negotiating contracts with NHS Trusts).

At the same time, the new 1990 GP Contract included provision for health checks for new patients, three yearly checks for patients not otherwise seen by a GP, and annual checks for patients aged 75 or over. Targets were also set for vaccinations, immunisation and cervical cancer screening and financial encouragement was given for the development of health promotion clinics. The Contract monies attached to health prevention and promotion were a significant stimulus to employing practice nurses. A survey at the time found that 51 per cent of GPs had created new practice nurse posts because of the Contract (Robinson *et al.*, 1993). Overall, the proportion of GP income that derived from capitation payments (where money was attached to each individual registered patient regardless of their health status or use of the health service) was increased from 46 per cent to 60 per cent, which could of course be seen as an incentive to increase list sizes rather than improve quality of care.

During the 1990s, the proposals in *Working for Patients* were implemented, but in a progressively modified form. For example, the rules on GP fund holding changed on a number of occasions. Initially, only practices with 11,000 or more patients could apply to become a GP fund holder, but this limit was subsequently reduced to 7000, 5000 and eventually 3000 patients. In the process, various options were offered to GPs, ranging from a limited version of the scheme known as community fund holding through standard fund holding to total purchasing. Fund holding was voluntary but by 1997 nearly half the GPs in the UK had become fund holders of some description.

The election of a Labour government in 1997 theoretically offered the prospect of quieter times for the NHS although, as we have seen in Chapter 2, in fact the Blair government developed policies for the modernisation of the NHS that were in many ways as radical as those contained in *Working for Patients*. Within months of coming into office, the publication of *The New NHS: Modern, Dependable* (Department of Health, 1997a) announced the demise of GP fund holding and the internal market. Instead it placed an emphasis on equity of access and provision and the need to ensure quality through clinical governance and accountability to local communities. However, *The New NHS* conceded that fund holding had demonstrated the value of GP commissioning of services and Labour aimed to optimise the benefits of commissioning by GP practices. Its new policy could therefore be regarded as a universalisation of fund holding rather than its abolition (Webster, 2002).

The introduction of Primary Care Groups/Trusts

The major structural change introduced to deliver these policy goals was the formation of PCGs with the expectations that they would mature to PCTs (that is, fully autonomous bodies commissioning a much broader range of services). In April 1999, 481 PCGs were established throughout England. Seventeen of these formed the first wave of PCTs a year later. When PCGs were formed, their Board was constituted to have a majority of GPs. However as PCGs developed into PCTs, the focus changed to one of stronger managerial leadership and greater accountability. The number of GPs on the PCT Board was reduced and the post of chairman of the PCT board became an independent lay appointment. The professional voice was still influential through PCT Professional Executive Committees although their overall influence was reduced.

Shifting the Balance of Power (Department of Health, 2001c) dramatically accelerated the timeframe for maturation from PCGs to PCTs and acknowledged them as the leading NHS organisation. In *Shifting the Balance of Power – the next steps* (Department of Health, 2002b), PCTs were specifically given responsibility for commissioning all mental health services. The strength of PCTs was also increased by giving them complete control over the new personal medical services (PMS) schemes, an initiative developed under the 1997 *Primary Care Act* to encourage new ways of working in primary care, particularly in deprived areas. PCTs in England in effect became substitute Health Authorities for their geographical areas, but operating from primary care rather than acute care platforms. There was also significant financial investment in primary care with an additional £1.9 billion in the three years to 2005/6, an average increase of 11 per cent per year in cash terms (Department of Health, 2002f).

Concentrating power at the PCT level exercised a domino effect on the rest of the system. Health Authorities lost their main function, replaced by a smaller number of Strategic Health Authorities, and the balance between the hospital and primary care sector tipped further in favour of primary care. However, the rate and pace of change may have been too great for some PCTs. Surveys have suggested problems with management capacity and expertise in commissioning services including mental health (Sainsbury Centre for Mental Health, 2001; Audit Commission, 2004). The experience of forerunners to PCT commissioning such as the total purchasing pilots and GP commissioning schemes also found difficulty in achieving effective involvement of grass roots GPs, and noted the demands on lead GPs and the importance of good management in enabling improvements in services (Mays *et al.*, 1998; Regen *et al.*, 1999). Some PCTs have also inherited debts from the old Health Authorities making it more difficult to plan and provide new services. There are additional pressures from a raft of performance targets and, since 2003, the introduction of star rating systems akin to secondary care Hospital and Trust rating schemes.

Primary care is currently going through another major structural reform. In July 2005, the chief executive of the NHS, Sir Nigel Crisp, announced in *Commissioning A Patient-Led NHS* (Department of Health, 2005a) that the number, size and responsibilities of PCTs would be reconfigured from the end of 2006. The number of PCTs will be almost halved to approximately 150 and greater co-ordination is expected between PCTs and local authority social service boundaries. In future, there will be greater separation of commissioning and provision and a greater emphasis on contestability in healthcare provision in primary as well as secondary care. One of the consequences of these changes is yet more instability at PCT level, with managers reapplying for their own jobs and loss of organisational memory.

The impact of the new GP Contract

Primary care underwent a further fundamental revolution with the acceptance in June 2003 of a new General Medical Services (nGMS) Contract, effective from April 2004 (BMA/NHS Confederation, 2003). Although, as in 1948, 1966 and 1990, there was something of a bitter and bloody battle between the health professionals and the government (on this occasion focused on a flawed resource allocation formula that initially suggested GPs would be paid less for doing more work), seven out of ten GPs voted on the Contract with just under 80 per cent in favour of acceptance.

Under the 1948 Contract, GPs remained independent practitioners, in effect rather like a small business, paid on the basis of the number of patients registered with the practice and also receiving payments for specific activities such as out of hours visits and maternity care. The 1966 Contract saw, as we have described, the rise of the extended primary care team and the fall of uni-professional general practice. The 1990 Contract led to a renewed emphasis on capitation, perhaps at the expense at times of quality of care, although it also included financial encouragement for proactive work such as health promotion and health prevention and was an important catalyst in creating the multi-professional primary care team.

The nGMS Contract, is a practice based contract between the primary care organisation (PCO) and the practice, as opposed to a contract with each GP. In effect it breaks the formal link between a named doctor and a named patient and substitutes a contract between organisations, with, at the present time, unknown consequences for the doctor-patient relationship. There are far more centrally driven targets particularly within the Quality and Outcomes Framework, a financially incentivised quality framework consisting of 1050 points attached to over 140 evidence based indicators. This may theoretically encourage a better quality service with, for example, indicators related to the delivery of specific services including the provision of structured care reviews for people with serious mental illness and, from April 2006, two new indicators for depression. The Contract, may therefore ensure greater consistency in standards and services across the UK.

GPs can now decide to offer services at one of three levels:

- Essential services for those with acute and chronic illnesses which have to be provided by all practices
- Additional services including maternity and contraceptive services which will be offered by most practices
- Enhanced services including specialised care for people with depression which will be offered by some practices (although, at the present time, not as many as originally expected because of PCT cost constraints)

PCTs are obliged to provide alternative services for patients registered in practices that provide only essential services. This means that someone presenting with more than one problem may be able to see their regular GP for their sore throat, be directed to the neighbouring practice for contraceptive services and potentially have to go to a third health care setting to discuss mental health issues. Possible consequences of this new way of providing services include a lack of continuity and a potentially increased tendency to see people as having either a physical or a mental health problem. Badging some important aspects of primary care as an enhanced service also challenges the notion of GPs being 'specialists in generalism'.

The GP as sole gate keeper to services has also been threatened by the nGMS (where, for the first time in decades, GPs are no longer compelled to be responsible for out of hours care), and by the expansion of alternative access points such as NHS Direct and NHS walk-in centres. The slow creep of private primary health care providers, including Medicentre surgeries in some shops and railway stations, has also increased choice for those who can afford to pay although, one might argue, is in stark contrast with Aneurin Bevan's vision of a health service free at the point of access. However, on a more positive note, the nGMS enables new legal forms for the basic structure of primary care. The traditional partnership of doctors running a small business can be replaced by a variety of different entities and provides an opportunity to increase public and patient involvement in primary care though setting up practices as public interest companies or even as 'mutuals', based on the old building society model (Heath, 2004).

The high achievement across the UK in the Quality and Outcomes Framework, including the 90 per cent achievement of the mental health indicators for severe and enduring mental illness, also suggests that patients are being increasingly and consistently offered evidence based primary care. Although critics of the Framework suggest that performance related pay can lead to 'medicine by numbers' and a mechanistic approach to primary care, early indications suggest that the Framework is beginning to make a positive difference to patient health outcomes (personal communication).

The advent of Practice Based Commissioning

As primary care and PCTS become familiar with the new Contract, the next challenge on the horizon is that of operationalising Practice based commissioning. The idea that PCTs would extend indicative budgets to individual practices to commission a full range of services was initially raised in 1997 (Department of Health, 1997a). However it was brought firmly into the centre of the political arena in June 2004 when *The NHS Improvement Plan* (Department of Health, 2004a) indicated that from April 2005, GP practices that wished to do so would be given indicative commissioning budgets. This is seen by the Department of Health as consistent with the principles of greater devolution to the front line, and as ensuring that services are responsive to the needs of the locality.

Practice based commissioning should achieve universal coverage by December 2006. GP practices will take on responsibility from their PCTs for commissioning services that meet the health needs of their local population. Commissioning practices or groups of practices will have the following main functions:

- Designing improved patient pathways
- Working in partnership with PCTs to create community based services that are more convenient for patients

- Responsibility for a budget delegated from the PCT which covers acute, community and emergency care
- Managing the budget effectively

The evidence base suggests that practice based commissioning may be effective as part of a continuum of commissioning models (Smith *et al.*, 2004). However there are also concerns from mental health specialists that, unlike many other areas of the NHS, it is additionally difficult to attach a price tag to mental health services (indeed mental health services are excluded from the Payment by Results scheme introduced in April 2005 precisely because of this reason). Practice based commissioning also requires consistent quality of service delivery and good quality information about services to be able to offer patients a meaningful choice. Neither of these is as far advanced in mental health services as in other parts of the NHS (Sainsbury Centre for Mental Health, 2004).

The nGMS and the prospect of practice based commissioning are therefore, like previous policy, something of a mixed blessing. The wider patient population may receive better quality clinical services and ultimately be more involved in the development of primary care. However, if we 'oscillate our gaze' from the general to the particular, to the complex individual, the nGMS and the broader changes within the NHS may threaten the strengths of generalism and of continuity of care.

Primary care and mental health

The development of PCTs and the new NHS workforce have resulted in primary care exerting a significant influence over the shape and provision of

---

Figure 3.4	The National Service Framework Standards 2 and 3

Standard 2

Any service user who contacts their primary health care team with a common mental health problem should:

- Have their mental health needs identified and assessed
- Be offered effective treatments, including referral to specialist services for further assessment, treatment and care if they require it

Standard 3

Any individual with a common mental health problem should:

- Be able to make contact round the clock with the local services necessary to meet their needs and receive adequate care
- Be able to use NHS Direct, as it develops, for first-level advice and referral on to specialist help lines or to local services

Figure 3.5	Numbers of individuals with mental health problems per 1000 in different settings (after Goldberg and Huxley, 1992)
10/1000	People admitted to an inpatient unit such as a hospital ward
20–30/1000	People referred to Outpatients/CMHT for further care
130/1000	People identified by the GP as having a mental health problem
230/1000	People in the GP waiting room with a mental health problem
250/1000	Community as a whole

mental health services. Primary care now has specific responsibility for delivering standards two and three of the *NSF for Mental Health* (Department of Health, 1999a) (see Figure 3.4) and is also integrally involved in the delivery of the other five standards.

Despite these recent changes, mental health care has been a largely unacknowledged core part of the work of primary care for decades. The majority of people with serious mental illness and with common mental health problems are now registered with a GP and we know that only approximately ten per cent of people with a mental health problem (including up to 50 per cent of people with severe mental illness) are ever seen by secondary care mental health specialists (Kendrick *et al.*, 2000; Kingsland and Williams, 1997; see also Figure 3.5).

Mental health issues are the second most common reason for consultations in primary care (McCormick *et al.*, 1995) and are the sole reason for seeing the doctor in 20–25 per cent of consultations (Goldberg and Huxley, 1992). A more recent survey by the Mental Health After Care Association (1999) to nearly 2000 GPs in England found that they spent on average approximately 30 per cent of their time on mental health problems.

Mental health and physical health problems also frequently co-exist. People with chronic or recurring physical health problems, traditionally seen as the core work of primary care, often have higher rates of mental health problems than the general population. About one in five people who have a myocardial infarction (heart attack) go on to develop major depression (Lesperance *et al.*, 2002), further emphasising the potential role of primary care in diagnosing and treating mental illness. There is also a significant group of patients with medically unexplained symptoms, classically low back pain, who consult frequently and who often have significant mental health problems such as depression (Waxman *et al.*, 1999).

People with serious mental illness also often have poorer physical health and a lower life expectancy than the general population. The Sainsbury Centre for Mental Health (2003a) estimated the cost of premature mortality due to mental health problems as £1.8 billion. A person with schizophrenia can expect to live for 10 years less than someone without a mental health problem, mainly because of physical health problems (Allebeck, 1989). Deaths from infectious diseases, endocrine, circulatory, respiratory, digestive and genito–urinary system disorders are all significantly more likely for adults with serious mental health problems (Harris and Barraclough, 1998).

Primary care is frequently criticised for the standard of mental health care delivered, including a perceived failure to diagnose mental illness (particularly depression) (Docherty, 1997; Tiemans *et al.*, 1996) and inability to provide good physical health care for people with serious mental illness. However, as described above, primary care is a complex environment – a messy swamp of experiences and interpretations that rarely conform to text book definitions (Schon, 1983). Many GPs also have little formal training in mental health. One survey found that only one third of GPs had mental health training in the last five years, while ten per cent expressed concerns about their training or skills needs in mental health (Mental Health Aftercare Association, 1999). Detection and diagnosis can also be affected by the way patients present their problems. Some people are reluctant to talk about their mental health symptoms and, even within the lower stigma setting of primary care, are worried about the effects of divulging symptoms of mental illness. Even if they technically reach the cut off point for diagnosis on a screening questionnaire, from the patient's perspective a discussion of poor

Figure 3.6	Service users' views of the value of primary care

- In Faulkner and Layzell's (2000) study, a user-administered semi-structured questionnaire with 76 mental health service users in six geographical areas across the UK emphasised that satisfaction is increased by longer consultations, and by a GP perceived as caring and who demonstrated respect for the patient's viewpoint. Access and continuity of care were also centrally important to service users
- Kai and Crosland's study (2001) involving in-depth interviews with 34 service users with enduring mental illness found that participants valued an empathetic and continuing therapeutic relationship with professionals in primary care
- Lester *et al.*'s study (2003) with 45 users with serious mental illness in Birmingham found that longitudinal and interpersonal continuity of care, relative ease of access and option of a home visit were valued features of primary care. This was often contrasted with the difficulty of seeing a constant stream of new faces in secondary care mental health services, with painful life stories told and retold for staff rather than patient benefit
- Gask *et al.*'s (2003) study of the quality of care for service users with depression found that the ability to offer structured care and proactive follow up was important since non-attendance may signal deterioration rather than recovery and the illness itself may preclude the assertiveness sometimes required to negotiate access
- Lester *et al.*'s (2005) focus group study of forty-five patients with serious mental illness, 39 general practitioners and eight practice nurses found that where as health professionals perceived serious mental illness as a life long condition, patients emphasised the importance of therapeutic optimism and hope for recovery in consultations

housing and the need for a sick note may be a more pressing need than a discussion of symptoms. Worries such as tiredness and poor sleep may also be normalised and minimised and therefore not mentioned to the primary care team (Kessler *et al.*, 1999).

From the GPs' perspective, fewer formal diagnoses of depression than might be expected may also reflect a commitment not to medicalise unhappiness. GPs are also, in effect, gatekeepers between illness and non-illness. It might be argued that accompanying the patient on their journey and bearing witness to their distress is more important than reaching too quickly for a disease category, a computer template and a drug treatment.

The value of primary care from the service user perspective

There is, relatively speaking, little published about the views of service users with mental health problems on primary care, although a number of features, particularly access and interpersonal and longitudinal continuity of care, appear to be particularly valued (Freeman *et al.*, 2002) (see Figure 3.6).

The role of practice nurses in primary care and mental health

As described earlier in this chapter, the concept of a primary care team did not really become established until the 1970s. Indeed, the number of directly employed primary care based practice nurses remained very low until the mid-1980s. However, between 1982 and 1992, the numbers rose more than six-fold from 1515 to 9640 (NHS Executive, 1996), aided by incentives in the 1990 GP Contract. By 1995 there were 18,000 practice nurses in England, equivalent to almost 10,000 whole-time staff and, by 2001, to 11,163 whole-time equivalents (RCGP, 2002).

Mental health issues are a significant part of the workload of many practice nurses. Between 13–43 per cent of nurses feel that early identification of anxiety and depression is a routine part of their role (Thomas and Corney, 1993) and most spend more time responding to psychological problems than managing diabetes or asthma. Practice nurses also work with people with chronic physical illnesses who are often at particularly high risk of developing mental illness. Many practice nurses are also increasingly involved with people with serious mental illness (Kendrick *et al.*, 1998). A national survey of practice nurse involvement in mental health interventions found that 51 per cent were administering depots (injections of anti-psychotic drugs) at least once a month, 33 per cent were involved in ensuring compliance with anti-psychotic medication and 30 per cent with monitoring side effects of medication. Up to 56 per cent of practice nurses were also involved in counselling people with depression (Gray *et al.*, 1999).

Figure 3.7	Evidence based roles for practice nurses in primary care mental health

Problem solving: practice nurses trained to deliver six sessions of problem solving in primary care for patients with depression showed significant improvements on patient depression rating scales at 12 weeks (Mynors-Wallis *et al.*, 2000).

Telehealth initiatives: a randomised controlled trial involving practice nurse based telephone follow up for patients starting antidepressant medication was found to improve symptom resolution and increase user satisfaction with care (Hunkeler *et al.*, 2000).

Medication adherence: a randomised controlled trial evaluating two different methods of improving adherence with antidepressant medication found that, for people with major depression, practice nurse counselling significantly improved adherence to medication from 50–66 per cent at 12 weeks with the expected clinical benefits (Peveler *et al.*, 1999).

Self-help treatments: practice nurses may have a role to play facilitating skill acquisition for patient self-help for anxiety (Kupshik and Fisher, 1999).

Screening for co-morbidity: psychological morbidity in patients with chronic physical illness is more prevalent than in the general population. Practice nurses often know these patients very well and are ideally placed to make mental health assessments and offer psychological support to their patients, for example as part of asthma (Rimington *et al.*, 2001) and cardiovascular clinics (Sorohan *et al.*, 2002).

Practice nurse led walk in depression clinics: a clinic in primary care was well received by patients and had good medication adherence rates and follow up rates at four and six months (Symons *et al.*, 2002).

Despite this, few practice nurses have had specific training in mental health issues. Only two per cent of practice nurses have had dedicated mental health training and, in a survey published in 1999, up to 70 per cent of practice nurses reported receiving no mental health training at all in the previous five years (Gray *et al.*, 1999). It is therefore perhaps unsurprising that many practice nurses report a lack of confidence in their ability to talk to and treat people with mental health problems (Armstrong, 1997; Crosland and Kai, 1998). However, practice nurses do have considerable transferable experience, for example in running specialist clinics for patients with chronic physical health problems that incorporate systematic assessment of symptoms, treatment effects and side effects, the use of protocols for modifying management and proactive follow-up of non-attendees. There is also an evidence base demonstrating the value and effectiveness of practice nurse-led or nurse run interventions for people with mental health problems (see Figure 3.7).

The role of nurses in general and practice nurses in particular is currently undergoing a rapid re-evaluation and expansion. From being seen as the doctor's hand maiden, largely employed to undertake health promotion and prevention duties, practice nurses will have opportunities, under the nGMS

Contract, to become partners in a practice and to take on more advanced and specialised roles (Department of Health, 2003a; NHS Confederation, 2003b). They can extend their interests from the clinical to the business aspects involved in a practice and, with appropriate training, become sub or specialist providers of services such as mental health. This advanced role mirrors the general direction of change within the wider NHS, with traditional professional hierarchies challenged by a changing workforce, greater emphasis on continuing professional development and a clinical governance agenda that values quality and performance as much as primary qualification.

The new primary care mental health workforce

The NHS Plan (Department of Health, 2000a) heralded the development of a number of new roles to help develop and deliver better quality mental health services. A key component was the commitment that:

> One thousand new graduate primary care mental health workers, trained in brief therapy techniques of proven effectiveness, will be employed to help GPs manage and treat common mental health problems in all age groups, including children (Department of Health, 2000a, p. 119).

This role has since been developed through further guidance (Department of Health, 2001f, 2003b), with workers being based in a primary care setting, employed by the PCT and supervised by secondary care specialists. However, despite the strong policy imperatives, the evidence to support the PCGMHW role is limited (Bower, 2002; Bower and Sibbald, 2003) and there has, at the time of writing, been no large-scale evaluation of these workers' potential effectiveness. Despite this, primary care mental health

Figure 3.8	Potential roles and responsibilities of primary care graduate mental health workers

Client work: brief evidence based interventions such as anxiety management and CBT for people with common mental health problems. Information, assessment, screening and onward referral in partnership with the primary care team. Support for self-help, and mental health promotion.

Practice team work: to provide support for audit, development of a mental illness register, routine measures of outcomes, and for integration of service users and carers into mental health service systems.

Work in the wider community: liasing with primary care team members and statutory (housing, welfare and benefits) and non-statutory sector services (charitable and voluntary sector), as well as specialised services to provide effective services to patients including those with serious mental illness, who are managed in primary care.

needs to be strengthened and the new role of graduate primary mental health workers has significant potential to improve the delivery of primary care mental health for people with common mental health problems, as well as those with serious mental illness.

Although the exact nature of their role may depend on their professional background, the content of their training and PCT locality needs, many PCGMHWs will be involved in face-to-face client work including provision of cognitive behavioural therapy (CBT) and in developing the infrastructure of primary mental health care. They may also have a liaison role with both the voluntary sector and secondary care mental health professionals (see Figure 3.8) and be involved in new ways of treating people with depression.

The lack of clarity about these different roles, and the implied differing degrees of autonomy and job complexity, have raised concerns among some health professionals. PCGMHWs, for example, may be seen by some PCTs as an alternative to employing counsellors in primary care, a role that itself grew rapidly throughout the 1990s despite a relatively sparse effectiveness evidence base (Bower and Sibbald, 2003; Mellor-Clarke, 2000; NHS Centre for Reviews and Dissemination, 2001). However, PCGMHWs have a far smaller face-to-face role than counsellors and a potentially more significant referral facilitation and infrastructure role. If utilised effectively, they should be an adjunct to the primary care mental health team, not a threat or substitute for counsellors. It is however interesting to reflect that issues faced by primary care counsellors during the last decade such as the limited evidence base, lack of national consensus on what constitutes a counselling service in primary care and variations in service availability across the country (White, 2000) may be the very issues faced by PCGMHWs over the next decade if their own evidence base, roles and responsibilities are not addressed.

General Practitioners with Special Interests

The primary care workforce is, as we have seen, going through a rapid period of significant change including a re-evaluation of the number, roles and responsibilities of GPs themselves. The RCGP (2001) has estimated that there is a potential shortfall of up to 10,000 GPs in current workforce planning, influenced to some extent by the fact that more GPs are now salaried and are choosing to work flexibly, as GP assistants, associates and retainers. This trend is likely to continue, encouraged by the 2003 Contract, as doctors, like many other professionals, consider ways to balance work and family (Audit Commission, 2002a). This should in many senses be applauded as healthy practice and as better for patient care in the longer term. A further consequence of such changes is that as other members of the extended primary care team take on new roles and responsibilities, GPs will no longer automatically be the practice decision makers, but may be employed by a nurse partner to provide essential clinical services. Some GPs may alternatively opt to extend a particular aspect of their clinical role, providing additional more specialised clinical services as one of the new GPwSIs (Department of Health, 2003c).

Figure 3.9	Traditional models of mental health care at the primary/ secondary interface

1. Community mental health teams that provide increased liaison and crisis intervention.
2. Shifted outpatient clinics where psychiatrists operate clinics within health centres.
3. Attached mental health workers, usually community psychiatric nurses (CPNs), designated to work with those with mental health problems in a primary care setting.
4. The consultation liaison model where primary care teams are provided with advice and skills from specialist mental health services.

GPwSIs in mental health will have a clinical role in 'providing assessment, advice, information and treatment on behalf of primary care colleagues for patients with common mental health problems... in most cases working alongside other mental health providers ...and supporting the development of care pathways across the primary–secondary–community interface' (Department of Health, 2003c, p. 2). This new role may provide a mechanism for longer consultations and enable patients to see a GP with a greater knowledge base about mental health issues (including alternative treatments). They may encourage more seamless care between primary and secondary care teams. GPwSIs may also increase access to good quality mental health care for people who have been removed from their GP lists, something that seems to happen more frequently to people with mental health problems than the general population. However, by the very nature of being referred onto a GPwSI by their usual GP, continuity of care may be reduced, opportunities for taking a more holistic individual approach may be missed and the special nature of cradle to grave primary care may once again be eroded.

Creating a new model of primary mental health care

Primary care, as we have seen, now employs a mental health workforce of its own and is in a position to commission and run services. All these changes have meant adjustments in the way in which primary care now conceptualises itself and how other parts of the health and social care sector respond. This has provided a number of opportunities to re-examine how mental health services could be constructed and organised in primary care.

There are currently four main working models of mental health care at the interface of primary/secondary care, all translocated from secondary care services (Gask *et al.*, 1997) (see Figure 3.9). Although it could be argued that these models are part of a continuum that patients can access to meet varying needs at different points in their illness pathway, in practice, the variation in availability of locality based resources means that primary care practitioners are often only able to access one or at best two of the models described in Figure 3.9 at a single point in time.

Each of these models has particular strengths and weaknesses, yet none fully recognise primary care's central role in delivering good quality mental health care. For example:

1. The creation of community mental health teams often brings about a major increase in the rate of new patients referred, but the new clientele consists largely of patients with common mental health problems who might otherwise have been managed by their GP. There are also problems with non-attendance at community mental health team appointments (Killaspy et al., 2000) and the issue of 'inappropriate' referrals, where patients are seen on one occasion in secondary care and assessed as requiring a different type of response. Communication across the primary/secondary care interface can also be slow or incomplete, with missing information in referral letters and delayed clinic letters adversely affecting patient care (Killaspy et al., 1999).
2. The shifted outpatient model attracts similar referrals and has similar significant non-attendance rates as traditional outpatient appointments in a hospital setting (Murray, 1998). It also appears that both the community mental health team and shifted outpatient models lead to little improvement in GP mental health skills (Warner et al., 1993).
3. The impact of attached mental health professionals on referral patterns is still unclear. A Cochrane review of the effect of on site mental health workers in primary care found that the effect on consultation rates is inconsistent (Bower and Sibbald, 2003). Referral to a mental health professional reduces the likelihood of a patient receiving a prescription for psychotropic drugs or being referred to specialist care, but the effects are restricted to patients directly under the care of the mental health professional. Roles and responsibilities are also unclear with consequently less efficient working patterns (Corney, 1999).
4. The Cochrane review (2003) also concluded that consultation liaison interventions may cause short-term changes in psychotropic prescribing, but these are usually limited to patients under the direct care of the mental health worker.

The aspiration to achieve closer integration between primary care and community services should now enable the development of more integrated approaches to delivering primary mental health care. This direction of travel towards more integrated working reflects the growing emphasis on a partnership approach throughout health and social care. The extended role of the practice nurse and creation of GPwSIs (Gerada et al., 2002) and PCGMHWs, and the prominence given to the new workforce in primary care in *The National Service Framework for Mental Health – Five Years On* (Department of Health, 2004b) should also provide opportunities for developing a more integrated approach to primary care mental health.

Figure 3.10	The benefits of integrated primary mental health care

- It can improve adherence to medication and satisfaction with care. A US initiative, involving collaborative management by the primary care physician and psychiatrist, improved adherence to antidepressant regimens in patients with persistent depression (Katon *et al.*, 1999)
- It is the best way of improving the skills of primary care providers in dealing with the psychosocial aspects of care, with training through teamwork and a significant transfer of expertise between team members (Mauksch and Leahy, 1993)
- Integrated approaches appear to break even or be cost saving in the longer term (Blount, 1998)

Figure 3.11	Integrated models of service delivery

In South East London, a Mental Health Link programme has been set up to encourage general practices and associated community mental health teams to work together to develop a series of options for the configuration of shared care for people with long-term mental illness (Byng and Single, 1999). These include the placement of 'aligned caseload' link workers, guidance on setting up registers, databases and systems of recall, and an annual joint review of patients' notes to detect and address unmet mental and physical health care needs. Evaluation found significant reductions in relapse rates and increased practitioner satisfaction in the intervention practices, echoing US experiences of integrated care (Byng *et al.*, 2004).

The Workforce Action Team (Department of Health, 2001f) describes a fully integrated primary care liaison service in North Birmingham. The service was led by a consultant psychiatrist, who worked with a team of CPNs in primary care. The team screened urgent referrals, saw patients in GP surgeries and wrote in the notes rather than dictating letters to save time and improve informational continuity of care. GPs were also empowered to recognise and treat psychiatric illness and jointly manage patients.

What does an 'integrated approach' to primary care mental health look like?

An integrated approach is not one particular model of care but rather a way of working that acknowledges the importance of creating seamless patient pathways through the health system and which avoids the dichotomy of either physical or mental health when defining and treating a patient's problems. From a structural perspective, integrated care goes one step beyond collaboration to co-ordination and often co-location of care.

Figure 3.12	Factors affecting the success of integrated working

- New services are often championed by 'hero innovators' who are likely to move on and seek fresh challenges once a service is up and running (Georgiades and Phillimore, 1975). To be truly sustainable, new approaches to working need to be team owned, and not dependent on single individuals
- Change in working practices requires a commitment from primary care health professionals and PCTs to the issue. There is however already evidence to suggest that the *NSF for Mental Health* is being marginalised in some PCT agendas, unable to compete on an equal footing with other clinical priorities (Rogers *et al.*, 2002)
- New ways of working rely on secondary mental health workers being comfortable and valued within a primary care working environment (Katon *et al.*, 1996; Peck and Greatley, 1999). Secondary care skills and knowledge in key areas such as triage, risk assessment and delivery of specific psychological therapies need to be acknowledged and valued when new integrated approaches to care are debated

To be sustainable, an integrated approach needs to be underpinned by opportunities for health professionals from different backgrounds to train and learn together. It depends on good communication across the interface, particularly around criteria for referral and discharge (NICE, 2003; WHO, 2004). Work, largely from the US, suggests that a more integrated approach to care has a number of benefits compared to usual practice (see Figure 3.10).

Although the evidence base on the value of an integrated approach is still relatively sparse from the UK perspective, an increasing number of localities are beginning to commission and evaluate a range of more integrated models of delivering primary care mental health services (see Figure 3.11).

Barriers to partnership working

The emergence of a primary care agenda for the integration of mental health service delivery has sometimes been seen as more of a problem than an opportunity. Change, particularly if it impacts on professional roles and boundaries, can be perceived as threatening the power base of that individual or team and needs to be discussed in an open and non-confrontational way. The success of a more integrated approach to care will therefore depend on a number of factors (see Figure 3.12).

Conclusion

During the last 15 years, primary care has become increasingly central to the development and delivery of good quality NHS care. The emergence of PCTs has resulted in primary care exerting a significant influence over the shape and provision of services and has had a domino effect on the rest of the NHS. Traditional professional hierarchies are being increasingly challenged by a chang ing workforce, a greater emphasis on continuing professional development and the clinical governance agenda.

This quiet primary care revolution has seen the end of the monopoly over provision of independently contracted GPs, a radical change in access to primary care, a raft of new targets and, latterly, a renewed interest in primary care based commissioning. Primary care is set for even more change with structural reforms that include the rapid introduction of practice based commissioning, new strategic commissioning roles for a reduced number of PCTs and potentially a longer term divestment by PCTs of their responsibilities as community health service providers in favour of a mixed and contestable market. Change can, of course create opportunities, but may also lead to uncertainties for the primary care workforce which impact on patient care.

While mental health has always been a core part of primary care, this central role has only recently been recognised through policy imperatives around the new mental health workforce and opportunities to re-examine how mental health services could be constructed and organised in primary care (Department of Health, 2004b). However, in the rush for the new, it is important to remember that a key strength of UK primary care is the open access, cradle to grave approach, where the patient is seen as part of a complex network of family, friends, work and social life. As David Widgery, who was a socialist GP in the East End of London and political writer and activist, wrote prophetically in 1991 (p. 32):

> It is a process of decivilisation in which what doctors prided as a personal relationship between themselves and the patient, is now reshaped by the commodity process. Prevention for populations, service according to need, the family doctors' very idea of them- selves as people who had time to grieve with their patients, to share the joy of childbirth, the crisis of illness and the time of day in the corner shop, are swept away.

The nGMS and broader policy changes may mean that the patient popula- tion as a whole receives better quality clinical services and is ultimately more involved in the decisions over their care. However they may also constitute a threat to the very strengths of primary care: its generalism and, particularly, continuity of care.

Reflection exercises

1. Setting up a clinic for people with serious mental illness
Exercise for practice nurses, GPwSIs, PCGMHWs

The nGMS GP Contract suggests the provision of structured care for people with serious mental illness including the creation of registers and regular health reviews. However, such a chronic disease model may not necessarily be welcomed by all patients.

As a group, discuss the strengths and weaknesses of a more structured approach to care for people with serious mental illness including:

- The value of reviewing people when they are well and the effect this may have on the health professional/patient relationship
- The potentially ghettoising effect of a register and the effect on hope for recovery
- The implications in a broader sense of such an approach to notions of care or control for people with mental illness

2. Developing integrated working practices
Exercise for all workers

Undertake an analysis of the strengths, weaknesses, opportunities and threats (SWOT) in your working environment with regard to developing a more integrated approach to delivering mental health care.
Consider issues such as:

- The priority given to mental health in your locality
- Financial planning issues
- Local workforce capacity and training issues
- Role stereotypes and their effects on partnership working
- Cultural differences between different organisations
- Leadership capacity in mental health
- User and carer views on integrated care pathways

Suggestions for further reading

1. Chambers R., Boath, E. and Wakley G. (2001) *Mental healthcare matters in primary care.* Abingdon, Radcliffe Medical Press

   This book is a useful tool to help incorporate mental health into on-going professional development. It outlines how learning more about clinical mental health issues and reviewing current practice can be included in a personal development plan or practice learning plan.

2. Armstrong, E. (2002) *The guide to mental health for nurses in primary care.* Abingdon, Radcliffe Medical Press

   This is an easy to digest book with practical descriptions of the roles nurses can play in improving the care of people with mental health problems. It has disease specific and more generic chapters, for example, on health promotion and stigma.

3. Elder, A. and Holmes J. (2002) *Mental health in primary care.* Oxford, Oxford University Press

   This thought provoking four-part book is structured to reflect encounters in the consulting room, reflective practice, mental health thinking in the surgery and perspectives from secondary care (including chapters on postnatal depression, eating disorders, substance misuse and management of serious mental illness). There are beautifully written descriptions of the importance of using time, of bearing witness to patients' lives, of the importance of containment, of being a 'good enough' GP, of Balint's work on the function of the doctor as a drug, and gentle but pragmatic reminders of precipitating factors for burnout and ways to decrease the likelihood of this happening.

4. Nolan, P. and Badger, F. (2002) *Promoting collaboration in primary mental health care.* Cheltenham, Nelson Thornes

   Following on from the theme of integrated care, this edited book with chapters written by practitioners from both primary and secondary care provides practical guidance on how to break down barriers to collaboration and work effectively with colleagues across the interface.

4 Community Mental Health Services

In this chapter we discuss:

- The origins of community mental health care
- The development and roles of the generic CMHT
- The advent and impact of functionalised teams
- Alternative ways of providing community mental health services
- Social exclusion and mental health
- Positive practice in community inclusion

The origins of community mental health care

Although the term 'community' has been used in the English language since the fourteenth century (Williams, 1976), the precise origins of its meaning is difficult to pinpoint. It is similarly almost impossible to say, with any degree of accuracy, where the phrase 'community care' comes from. Titmuss claimed he had tried and failed to discover any precise social origin for the phrase but went on to reflect: 'Institutional policies both before and since the Mental Health Act of 1959 have without a doubt assumed that someone knows what it means' (1968, p. 105).

At the beginning of the twenty-first century, most people, including those with serious mental illness, are now cared for in the community. They are seen by locality based CMHTs rather than in outpatients in District General Hospitals and are likely to be treated in their own homes by specialised mental health teams when acutely unwell, rather than admitted to an inpatient ward.

There are multiple complex political and economic reasons under-pinning the development of community care (see Chapter 2 for a detailed discussion) and the move towards our current community based mental health care system has been slow and incremental. The rise of community care was probably heralded by the 1930 *Mental Treatment Act*, which enabled voluntary treatment in 'Mental Hospitals' for the first time and legitimised local authority spending on outpatient care. Perhaps the next significant step was the move by a handful of 'Mental Hospitals' just after the Second World War, towards an 'open door' rather than a locked ward system. At approximately the same time, a small number of hospital based nurses were seconded to work within the wider community as prototype CPNs and the first mental health day hospital was opened in London in 1946 (Bierer, 1951).

CPN practice, as we might recognise it today, began at Warlingham Park Hospital (Croydon) in 1954. Dr Rees, the Physician Superintendent, decided that a pragmatic method of relieving pressure on hospital beds would be to develop a psychiatric nursing service within the community. Two outpatient nurses were therefore seconded to work in the community, initially for a six-month trial period, although Lena Peat, one of the first two nurses, recalls that she in fact stayed for 23 years (Peat, 1979)! Gradually, as the role spread to other hospitals and settings, CPNs became responsible for the administration of depot (injectable) medication in the community, running clubs in day hospitals, checking up on patients who failed to keep appointments and providing support to relatives (Royal College of Psychiatrists, 1997). Some CPNs also became involved in delivering forms of psychosocial care including family therapy and CBT.

This new extended nursing role initially met with a mixed response. White and Brooker suggest:

> The Regional Health Authority disclaimed knowledge of the development, provided no extra funds and refused to recognise that the nurses who worked outside the hospital were part of the official establishment. In some situations, District Nurses insisted that only they could administer drugs to patients in their homes resulting in two nurses visiting the same patient. Some General Practitioners welcomed the assistance of the psychiatric nurses while others would have nothing to do with them. Even consultant psychiatrists were divided (2001, p. 62).

The 1959 *Mental Health Act* made two key provisions that helped to establish community mental health services. First, it required outpatient follow up for patients who had been detained (sectioned) and therefore, in some sense, began to recognise the importance of continuity of care. Secondly, the Act legislated for the involvement of social workers in the care of people with mental illness.

As the process of asylum closure continued during the 1960s and 1970s, day hospitals and inpatient units in District General Hospitals became the central planks of community reprovision for people with serious mental illness (Burns, 2004). The process was, however, much slower than the policy makers and planners might have hoped. Between 1962 and 1970, the time period over which the *Hospital Plan* (Ministry of Health, 1962) proposed a 43.4 per cent reduction in asylum beds, the actual reduction was 14.8 per cent (Maynard and Tingle, 1975).

As we discussed in Chapter 2, the move towards community care was accompanied by concerns about the potential negative consequences of moving people out of long-stay wards into community accommodation.

Figure 4.1	The outcomes of the TAPS project

- Nearly 80 per cent of people were discharged to staffed houses and two thirds were still living in their original residence at the end of the five years
- 72 patients were considered to be too difficult to place in standard staffed homes and were transferred to high-staffed facilities. However, 40 per cent of this group were subsequently transferred to standard community homes by the end of the five years
- Reprovision did not increase death or suicide rates
- Four patients were estimated as lost to follow up because of homelessness, giving a 'vagrancy' rate of 0.6 per cent over the study period
- There were 24 recorded criminal incidents committed by 18 patients
- Psychiatric symptoms and social behaviour problems remained unchanged overall. The community homes were much less restrictive than the hospital wards with an average of 10 rather than 26 rules. Eighty four per cent of patients wished to remain in their home. Although social networks did not enlarge, patients increased the number of people they could confide in
- Perhaps the biggest issue was that of readmission. The reprovision plans for the hospital closure included a reduction in beds in general hospitals which meant that, at times, there were no beds available for people in crisis. When admitted, many patients also found wards in general hospitals noisy, crowded and non-therapeutic
- The overall readmission rate was 38 per cent. Of these, one third of people remained in hospital for over one year, often because of a lack of rehabilitation services. These patients technically became long-stay patients once again
- Overall, there was little difference between hospital and community costs. Coupled with the outcome findings, the economic evaluation suggests that community based care is more cost effective than long-stay hospital care

(Leff *et al.*, 2000)

Perhaps the most influential and certainly the most detailed study of the outcomes of deinstitutionalisation from the NHS perspective was the Team for the Assessment of Psychiatric Services (TAPS) project. Established in May 1985 with the explicit purpose of evaluating the national policy of replacing psychiatric hospitals, (in this case, Friern and Claybury Hospitals in North London), with district based services, the study followed up 630 people who had been inpatients for a period of five years, giving a comprehensive picture of life and care in the community (see Figure 4.1).

In parallel with the deinstitutionalisation agenda, multi-disciplinary CMHTs began to be established across the country throughout the 1980s. CMHTs usually consisted of CPNs, psychiatrists, occupational therapists and psychologists with some form of integration with social services. A generic catchment area CMHT became available to over 80 per cent of the population by the early 1990s (Johnson and Thornicroft, 1993). The number of

CPNs therefore increased from 717 in 1975 to 4351 in 1990 (White, 1990) and indeed now numbers over 9000. CMHTs were tasked with assessing and treating any adult patient referred to them, and support and advise local GPs. In fact, by 1993, CPNs were taking over 40 per cent of their referrals from primary care professionals (White, 1993). However, this also meant that CPNs and CMHTs began to focus on people with common mental health problems as well as people with serious mental illness.

In the last decade, the community mental health debates have increasingly centred on the need for more specialised community based mental health teams such as assertive outreach, crisis intervention/home treatment and early intervention teams. The findings from the TAPS project and the increasing recognition of so-called 'revolving door' patients (see Chapter 5) have also highlighted the effects of inadequate reprovision of beds for people who are 'difficult to place' and for the 'new long stay' patients. The wider social inclusion agenda, particularly for people with serious mental illness, has also become a more prominent issue, since living within and being part of a community are very different outcomes. We explore these issues in more detail later in this chapter.

The development and roles of the generic CMHT

Since the 1980s, multi-disciplinary generic CMHTs have been the main vehicle for delivering co-ordinated comprehensive community based mental health services (Kingdon, 1989). A major tension, almost from inception, has been the caseload balance of people with short-term more common mental health problems and those with serious and more enduring mental illness (Sayce et al., 1991). The relatively disappointing effectiveness and cost effectiveness outcomes in studies of CMHTs in the late 1980s (Gournay and Brooking, 1994, 1995; Patmore and Weaver, 1991) and the fierce criticism in some quarters about CPNs' lack of appropriate training in treating people with common mental health problems helped convince policy makers in the 1990s that CPNs and CMHTs should focus on people with serious mental health problems. This move was further reinforced by the wider policy debate about care or control in the community (see Chapters 2 and 6) (Department of Health, 1994; Department of Health, 1998a), risk management and the introduction of the CPA (Department of Health, 1990a) (see Figure 4.2).

Tensions over the most appropriate client groups for CPNs and for CMHTs were also increased by the advent of fund holding in the early 1990s, which enabled some practices to employ their own CPN and to then determine their role in mental health care provision (Monkley-Poole, 1995). CPNs were therefore left in a difficult position, torn between the different needs of client groups, employers and policy imperatives (Secker et al., 2000). This tension looks set to be increased by the advent of Practice Based Commissioning, with some practices no doubt keen to commission CPN services once again.

Figure 4.2	The Care Programme Approach

- CPA, introduced in 1991, became the cornerstone of the US influenced 'case management' approach to care for people accepted by specialist mental health services. Outside mental health services, this type of care co-ordination was known as 'care management' and tended to fall under the remit of social workers rather than the NHS (Means *et al.*, 2003). Hardly surprisingly, this overlap has led to a degree of confusion and duplication of effort
- Led by health workers, CPA obliged health and other agencies to assess the individual needs of service users, construct care plans to meet these needs, identify a key worker to oversee each individual plan of care and undertake a regular multi-disciplinary review of care, including issues of risk
- Revised guidance (Department of Health, 1999b) heralded the integration of CPA with care management to form a single care co-ordination approach, with health and social services jointly identifying a lead officer
- CPA is now divided into two levels – standard and enhanced
- It is interesting to note that a Cochrane review (Marshall *et al.*, 1998) of case management for people with 'severe mental disorders' found no evidence that case management improves outcome on any social or clinical variable other than ensuring that more people remain in contact with psychiatric services (one extra person remains in contact for every 15 people who receive case management)
- Evidence also suggests that, from a users' perspective, very few receive a copy of their care plan or know what is in it, and some users do not know who their key worker is (McDermott, 1998)
- CPA does, at face value, appear to systematically assess health and social care needs, formulating a care plan, appointing a key worker and ensuring a regular review. However Took (2002) argues that CPA is largely driven from a professional rather than user perspective and is focused on aspects of mental health and social needs that seek to keep people safe and well rather than adopting a holistic approach that seeks to help someone recover from mental illness on their own terms

The evidence base on the effectiveness of CMHTs is largely descriptive and relatively difficult to interpret because of variations in team structures and functions. As Burns suggests 'they (CMHTs) evolved by word of mouth as clinicians tried to find ways of dealing with a changing health care system and rising expectations within fixed resources. As a result there have been many blind alleys along the way and enormous local variation in how they are managed, staffed and function... A consequence of this is that the "feel" of CMHTs can vary enormously even if their core activities are fairly uniform' (2004, pp. 49–50).

However, the evidence suggests that, at least in comparison with a traditional psychiatric service in a District General Hospital psychiatric unit, CMHTs provide better quality care at both two and four years after referral

(Gater *et al.*, 1997). Generic CMHT management also appears more effective than standard non-team hospital-oriented care for people with serious mental illness, particularly in terms of accepting treatment and also in possibly reducing hospital admissions (Tyrer *et al.*, 2000).

CMHTs have, however, also been criticised for having over-ambitious aims, and a tendency to neglect people with the most challenging health and social care needs (Patmore and Weaver, 1991). Their role in providing assessment and management of people with a range of needs and in integrating the health-led CPA with social services-led care management has meant that community mental health managers have had a difficult brokering role, often with no additional resources (Onyett *et al.*, 1997). The Sainsbury Centre for Mental Health (1998a) report, *Keys to Engagement*, also noted that members of CMHTs frequently have caseloads that are too high to allow sufficient contact time to work effectively with people with serious mental illness.

The advent of functionalised teams

Recently this notion of a generic CMHT responsible for all aspects of care for people with common mental health problems referred from primary care and also people with serious mental illness and more complex needs has been reassessed. Evidence from evaluations of service models in North America (Stein and Test, 1980) and Australia (Hoult, 1986) and successful remodelling of the community mental health services in North Birmingham have been influential in the thinking and development of *functionalised* mental health teams in the UK. Functionalised teams are, in essence, specialist teams organised to provide for the needs of particular patient groups. This approach has been reinforced by the *NSF for Mental Health*, *The NHS Plan* and a number of team specific Policy Implementation Guides (Department of Health, 1999a, 2000a, 2001g). *The NHS Plan*, for example, heralded the creation of 220 assertive outreach teams, 335 crisis resolution teams and 50 early intervention teams by 2004, with the *Mental Health Policy Implementation Guide* (MH-PIG) describing the more detailed team structure and functions.

The MH-PIG on CMHTs states that 'Community Mental Health Teams will continue to be the mainstay of the system. CMHTs have an important and indeed integral role to play in supporting service users and families in community settings. They should provide the core round which newer service elements are developed' (Department of Health, 2002g, p. 3). Although the guidance is not prescriptive about the relationships between CMHTs and the newer functionalised teams, it suggests that 'mutually agreed and documented responsibilities, liaison procedures and in particular transfer procedures need to be in place when crisis resolution, home treatment teams, assertive outreach teams and early intervention teams are being established' (2002g, p. 17; see also Figure 4.3). CMHTs in future are therefore envisaged as the central hub of mental health care, liaising with the more specialised teams as well as with primary care.

Figure 4.3	The roles and responsibilities of CMHTs

1. Giving advice on the management of mental health problems by other professionals – in particular advice to primary care and a triage function enabling appropriate referral
2. Providing treatment and care for those with a time-limited disorder who can benefit from specialist interventions
3. Providing treatment and care for those with more complex and enduring needs

(Department of Health, 2002g)

The roles and responsibilities of functionalised teams

Assertive Outreach

Assertive outreach teams (AOTs) are the best developed, described and most evidence based of the functionalised teams. They were first established in the late 1970s in Madison, Wisconsin, as the Programme for Assertive Community Treatment (PACT) (Stein and Test, 1980). This programme was essentially a form of intensive case management, with patients with serious mental illness who seemed likely to need an admission allocated either to intensive case management and given intensive help with social functioning and clinical care, or to standard treatment. A service evaluation found that patients in the PACT group were less likely to require inpatient admission, had improved clinical and social functioning and were more satisfied with their care. The service was also judged to be cost effective (see Figure 4.4).

The funding for the original PACT ran out after 14 months and the significant gains were lost almost as quickly as they were established, indirectly confirming

Figure 4.4	The core components of PACT

The core components of PACT/AOTs were and continue to be:

- Assertive follow up
- Small caseloads (ideally 10:1)
- Increased frequency of contact (capacity to visit daily)
- An emphasis on medication
- Assertive engagement (tenacious, creative and innovative rather than aggressive)
- Support for family and carers
- Emphasis on relapse prevention
- Crisis intervention
- Availability 12 hours a day, seven days a week

the effectiveness of the programme. The programme was also replicated by a group in Australia (Hoult, 1986) with similar positive outcomes.

In the UK, the PRiSM (Psychiatric Research in Service Measurement) study was the first large-scale attempt to explore how community teams functioning in different ways might lead to different service outcomes (Thornicroft *et al.*, 1998a). PRiSM compared two contrasting service models for patients with psychosis: a standard generic CMHT and a more intensive two-team approach that incorporated a psychiatric acute care and emergency team and a psychiatric assertive continuing care team. The main study conclusion was that: 'On balance the results weigh slightly in favour of the two-team model for acute and continuing care in terms of clinical effectiveness, but the general model is almost as effective and is less expensive' (Thornicroft *et al.*, 1998b, p. 423).

However, the results caused controversy when published, not least from proponents of functionalised models (Sashidharan *et al.*, 1999). Marshall *et al.* (1999) also suggested that the PRiSM study had a number of flaws and in particular criticised it for evaluating a mixture of models of care. A Cochrane Review of assertive community treatment (ACT) for people with severe mental disorders (Marshall and Lockwood, 1998) also found that, compared to standard community care, patients receiving ACT were more likely to remain in contact with services, less likely to be admitted to hospital, spent less time in hospital and had better clinical and social outcomes in terms of accommodation, employment and satisfaction. The review also concluded that, when targeted on high users of inpatient care, ACT can substantially reduce the costs of hospital care. On balance, therefore, despite the equivocal outcomes of PRiSM, the evidence base for the value of an AOT approach is still relatively strong.

The MH-PIG (2001g) suggests that AOTs are most appropriate for patients with:

- Severe and persistent mental disorder associated with a high level of disability
- A history of high use of inpatient or intensive home based care
- Difficulty in maintaining lasting and consenting contact with services
- Multiple complex needs including self harm, homelessness and substance misuse

This group has been estimated to be about 15,000 people at any one time in the UK (Sainsbury Centre for Mental Health, 1998a).

Although the AOT model has been well described, there are still a number of uncertainties over how best to apply the core principles. A recent report from the Sainsbury Centre for Mental Health (Chisholm and Ford, 2004, p. vi) suggested that

> Setting up AO teams means changing not merely structures and processes but cultures and attitudes within mental health services.

Such a paradigm shift takes time and resources – it cannot be achieved overnight. It relies on an acceptance of the need for changes, good project management and a shared understanding of how services will be improved.

There are also potential tensions between fidelity to the AO model and individualised care and local flexibilities, and between assertive treatment and individual patient civil rights. As Burns suggests 'Assertive outreach teams… need to maintain a broad psychosocial approach to their patients while not losing sight of the central importance of evidence based medical practice. In short, their research based and prescribed approach is both their greatest strength and their Achilles' heel' (2004, p. 101).

Crisis Resolution (CR) and Home Treatment (HT) teams

CR teams have been in existence in the US and Australia since the 1980s. Just as the terminology with assertive outreach can be confusing, (PACT/ACT/AOT), the terms 'home treatment' and 'psychiatric emergency team (PET)' are sometimes used rather than 'crisis resolution'. Essentially, however, these services offer an alternative to inpatient care for people experiencing an acute mental health crisis.

There have been two powerful drivers for developing CR/HT teams. Service users and carers have clearly asked for services to be available 24 hours a day, 7 days a week (Minghella et al., 1998), echoing the emphasis on quick response times (e.g. pain to needle time in chest pain) within the wider NHS. CR/HT have also been seen as a mechanism to reduce reliance on the ever decreasing supply of inpatient beds.

Overall, the evidence suggests that CR/HT services may achieve reduced admissions and bed use, better service retention and equal clinical outcomes to inpatient care (Johnson et al., 2005). The services are also generally preferred by patients and relatives (Minghella et al., 1998; Smyth and Hoult, 2000). Some, however, have suggested that such positive findings may reflect the commitment and charisma of the 'hero innovators' of home treatment and may be more difficult to replicate in every day practice, particularly in rural areas (Burns, 2004; Coid 1994; Owen et al., 2000).

The MH-PIG (Department of Health, 2001g) states that CR/HT should be targeted at adults (16–65 years old) with severe mental illness (schizophrenia, bipolar affective disorders, severe depressive disorder) with an acute psychiatric crisis of such severity that, without the involvement of the CR/HT team, hospitalisation would be required (see Figure 4.5).

Teams are meant to cover approximately 150,000 people and have a case load of 20–30 service users shared between a multi-disciplinary team of around 14 people. The intensity of the service means that there is team but not necessarily health professional continuity of care. Although the guidance suggests patients should stay in contact with the team for three to four weeks, in practice it appears this may be as long as three to six months (Burns, 2004). The most noticeable rhetoric/reality gap for CR/HT teams

Figure 4.5	Core components of CR/HT teams

A CR/HT team should be able to:

- Act as a gatekeeper to mental health services, rapidly assess individuals with acute mental health problems and refer them to the most appropriate services
- For individuals with acute severe mental health problems, for whom home treatment would be appropriate, provide immediate multi-disciplinary community based treatment 24 hours a day, 7 days a week
- Remain involved with the person until the crisis has resolved and the service user is linked into on-going care
- Have an assertive approach to engagement
- If hospitalisation is necessary, be actively involved in discharge planning and provide intensive care at home to enable early discharge
- Provide a time limited intervention

(Department of Health, 2001g, pp. 11–12)

however, is the significant number of people on the caseload with problems other than acute mental health crises. Chisholm and Ford's report on CR/HT teams (2004) found that a significant minority of patients had mild or moderate mental health problems, drug or alcohol problems and/or personality disorders and recurring psychosocial crises. Whilst acknowledging that these patients' needs are genuine, the challenge within an integrated comprehensive mental health system is to meet these in the most appropriate and cost effective way, which may not necessarily be via CR/HT.

Early Intervention Services

Early Intervention Services (EIS) have been a feature of health care in Australia, Scandinavia and the US for over a decade. They have, however, only relatively recently become part of the landscape of UK mental health care. The policy imperative for EIS for young people with first episode psychosis has been driven by user and carer dissatisfaction with existing poor quality services (Rethink, 2003a), health professional concerns about the state of services, and a growing evidence base that links long duration of untreated psychosis (DUP) with poorer long-term prognosis (Norman and Malla, 2001). Evidence has also emerged in the last decade that the early phase following the onset of a first psychotic illness could be conceived of as a 'critical period', influencing the long-term course of the illness. Providing timely and effective interventions at this stage might therefore alter the subsequent course of the illness and have a disproportionate impact relative to later interventions (Birchwood et al., 1998).

Evidence also suggests that patients' needs during the early phases of the illness differ from those of individuals with longer-standing illness and therefore require different treatment options (Norman and Townsend, 1999). Young people have to deal with the initial personal trauma of psychosis in addition to the normal anxieties associated with adolescence and young adulthood and have high hopes of returning to a normal level of functioning. Engagement, or the formation of a 'therapeutic alliance', is therefore crucial and can be fostered by developing youth sensitive services in as flexible a way as possible.

Most of the EI evidence so far has concentrated on justifying the need to provide services at an earlier stage in the illness. The evidence base for the effectiveness of EIS themselves is still emerging and to that extent policy implementation has preceded a cast iron evidence base. However data from the Lambeth Early Onset trial shows statistically significant differences in terms of relapse and re-hospitalisation for young people in contact with the EIS compared to standard care delivered by the CMHTs (Craig *et al.*, 2004). Early results from the OPUS trial, a large randomised clinical trial of integrated treatment versus standard treatment for patients with first episode psychosis, also suggests that integrated treatment improves clinical outcomes and adherence to treatment at one and two year follow up (Peterson *et al.*, 2005).

The MH-PIG (Department of Health, 2001g) states that EIS should be targeted at people aged between 14 and 35 with a first presentation of psychotic symptoms during the first three years of psychotic illness. Key feature of EIS in the MH-PIG are shown in Figure 4.6.

Despite this, there are still concerns about the speed with which EIS are being developed (Bradshaw and Everitt, 1999), the core components of an EIS and, indeed, the need for a separate EIS at all (Burns, 2004; Pelosi and Birchwood, 2003). However, on-going research should provide good quality evidence on the key components of EIS, the effects of variations from the

---

Figure 4.6	Key features of EIS

EIS should be able to:

- Reduce the stigma associated with psychosis and improve professional and lay awareness of symptoms of psychosis and the need for early assessment
- Reduce the length of time young people are undiagnosed and untreated
- Develop meaningful engagement, provide evidence based intervention and prioritise recovery during the early phase of illness
- Increase stability in the lives of service users, facilitate development and provide opportunities for personal fulfilment
- Provide a user centred service i.e. a seamless service available for those from 14–35 that effectively integrates child, adolescent and adult mental health services and works in partnership with primary care, education, social services and youth services
- At the end of the treatment period, ensure that care is transferred thoughtfully and effectively

(Department of Health, 2001g, pp. 46–7)

MH–PIG on outcomes and the essential factors in successful implementation from the viewpoint of service commissioners, providers, users and carers.

Alternative service provision within the community

As we discuss in Chapter 5, users frequently report negative inpatient experiences. Hospital beds are also a relatively scarce and expensive form of service provision. Yet government policies that emphasise patient choice mean that alternatives to inpatient wards, and indeed to the essentially medical model of the CR/HT team, are needed. Against this background, there are a small but growing number of alternatives to inpatient units, although few have been subject to rigorous evaluation or are widely available. Within a whole systems approach, users and their families, who particularly since *The NHS and Community Care Act* (1990) have shouldered the main responsibility for everyday care in the community, should ideally be offered a number of alternatives to acute admission, including CR/HT teams, user-led crisis houses, day hospitals and half way hospitals/community inpatient units (see Figure 4.7).

A further hopeful development in community services is the advent of direct payments. Under the *Community Care (Direct Payments) Act* 1996, social services departments can make cash payments to a range of different

Figure 4.7	Some alternatives to inpatient care

User-led crisis houses
There are a small number of user-led crisis houses in England, staffed or managed by service users or people with experience of crisis. An evaluation of three such houses by the Sainsbury Centre for Mental Health (2002a) found that in Anam Cara (Soul Friend in Celtic) in Birmingham, 100 per cent of those interviewed felt the service met all their needs, and that it was more cost effective than inpatient care. Users particularly valued support from recovery guides with similar experiences and the non judgemental atmosphere of the house.

Day hospitals
Evidence suggests that up to 40 per cent of people in need of hospital admission could be treated successfully in a day hospital setting with few differences in clinical or social outcomes (Creed *et al.*, 1990) and that the costs associated with day hospital care are less than inpatient care (Creed *et al.*, 1997).

Community inpatient units
Community inpatient units or halfway hospitals provide a service for patients who require admission but not the high intensity of supervision that an acute ward would provide. They can also act as a support facility between the acute ward and the community to enable respite in a therapeutic environment for people with acute mental illness (Boardman and Hodgson, 2000).

user groups in lieu of directly provided social services. At the time of writing there are over 12,000 people receiving direct payments across the country, and the policy has recently shifted from being discretionary (local authorities can make payments if they choose) to being compulsory (authorities must make payments to people who are able to consent to and manage a payment). To date, the considerable research in this area suggests that direct payments give recipients greater choice and control, are more cost effective than directly provided services and lead to greater user satisfaction, a more creative use of resources, greater continuity of care and fewer unmet needs (see Glasby and Littlechild, 2002 for a summary). However, direct payments have yet to make a significant impact on mental health services in many areas. In 2000 there were no mental health direct payment recipients in Scotland at all, while in 2003 in England only five local authorities had ten or more direct payment recipients with mental health problems (and 57 per cent had no recipients with mental health problems at all) (Spandler and Vick, 2004; Witcher *et al.*, 2000). Although there are a number of well-known barriers to the implementation of direct payments in mental health (see Figure 4.8), there are grounds for optimism. From April 2004, the number of direct payment recipients is a performance indicator for social services departments, so they will have a greater interest in increasing the number of people receiving such payments. At the same time, government policy also appears to be shifting, and the assumption is now that everyone will receive a direct payment unless there are good reasons for them not to. This contrasts strongly with the past, where we have assumed that everyone will receive a direct service.

Figure 4.8	**Direct payments and mental health**

Barriers to direct payments for people with mental illness include:

- The emphasis of the 1996 Act on the needs of people with a physical impairment
- A lack of information for users, carers and staff
- Low expectations of social services due to previous poor experiences
- A tendency for people with mental health problems to have contact with the NHS (where direct payments are not available) rather than with social services
- Difficulties which people with mental health problems may have managing money when ill and an awareness of being perceived as people not trusted to take care of themselves

(Glasby and Littlechild, 2002; see also Ridley and Jones, 2002; Spandler and Vick, 2004). Further information is also available from the National Centre for Independent Living (www.ncil.org.uk)

Social exclusion and mental health

Community based mental health services have enabled literal care in the community. However, as Prior (1993) suggests, people are not accepted 'more openly and readily by the community at large simply because they have a new mailing address' (p. 192). The significance of moving beyond the meaning of community as acknowledged in communitarian theory (see Chapter 2) is that people with mental illness who are often in most need of community care may be just those who are most excluded from participating in communities of interest. Indeed there is plenty of evidence to suggest that people with mental health problems are multiply excluded and that the situation is particularly difficult for people with serious mental illness. In this final part of the chapter, we therefore look at the nature, origins and realities of social exclusion and argue that it is not enough to be treated in the community where the meaning is simply geographical (*out* of hospital), but that people also need to be *included within* society as part of a community of interest.

Sayce has described social exclusion as:

> ...the inter-locking and mutually compounding problems of impairment, discrimination, diminished social role, lack of economic and social participation and disability. Among the factors at play are lack of status, joblessness, lack of opportunities to establish a family, small or non-existent social networks, compounding race and other discrimination, repeated rejection and consequently restriction of hope and expectation (2001, p. 121).

On virtually any indicator of social exclusion, people with serious mental illness are amongst the most excluded in British society (Office of the Deputy Prime Minister (ODPM), 2004; Sayce, 2001). Part of the difficulty in teasing out what we mean by, and how we can address, issues of social exclusion within the context of mental illness, is that many of the precipitating factors for social exclusion such as unemployment, lack of social networks and poverty can be both a cause and a consequence of mental illness.

Stigma and negative stereotyping and attitudes all have a significant role to play in the generation of discrimination and prejudice (see Figure 4.9). The Department of Health has been tracking popular attitudes to mental health since 1993 and, although certain aspects of the British public's attitudes have become a little more positive over the past decade, there are still many examples of negative stereotyping (see Figure 4.10).

Link and Phelan (2001) have suggested the following process of exclusion for people with mental illness: we label a person as different, but then, at least in the context of mental illness, associate that label with negative attributes (that is, we negatively stereotype the person as being dangerous or incompetent). We then separate out 'them' from 'us' and so differentiate ourselves from people we perceive as 'other' (see Figure 4.11). Finally, 'they' become the thing that they are labelled, so they become not a person with

Figure 4.9	Key concepts in social exclusion and mental health

- 'Stereotype' describes the picture in people's heads of various social groups, and can be positive or negative
- 'Stigma' refers to socially constructed negative stereotypes related to the characteristics of a person
- An 'attitude' is a psychological tendency that is expressed by evaluating a particular issue in a positive or negative way
- 'Discrimination' is being treated unfairly or denied opportunities
- 'Prejudice' is public fear, misunderstanding and intolerance

Figure 4.10	Attitudes towards people with mental illness

- In 1993, the Department of Health survey found that 30 per cent of people thought anyone with a history of mental problems should be excluded from public office and that 43 per cent thought that most women who were once patients in a mental hospital could not be trusted as babysitters. However, 92 per cent of people agreed that we need to adopt a far more tolerant attitude toward people with mental illness in our society (Department of Health, 1993)
- In 1997 (Department of Health, 1997b), the survey found strong support for community care services but only 13 per cent of people would be happy if their son or daughter were going out with somebody with schizophrenia
- In 2000, just under 20 per cent of respondents were frightened to think of people with mental illness living in residential areas (compared to 25 per cent in 1997). However, 90 per cent also agreed that we need to adopt a far more tolerant attitude towards people with mental illness in our society and 92 per cent believed that virtually anyone can become mentally ill (Department of Health, 2000b)
- In 2003, only 83 per cent of people agreed that we need to adopt a far more tolerant attitude toward people with mental illness in our society (Department of Health, 2003d)

Figure 4.11	The otherness of mental illness

There is a vast and very complicated unwritten constitution of conduct which allows us to move with confidence through public spaces, and we can instantly and by a very subtle process recognise someone who is breaking that constitution. They are talking to themselves; they are not moving at the same rate; they are moving at different angles; they are not avoiding other people with the skills that pedestrians do in the street. The speed with which normal users of public places can recognise someone else as not being a normal user of it, is where madness appears.

(Miller in Laurance, 2003, p. 43)

schizophrenia, but a 'schizophrenic'. This leads to a loss of status and discrimination, and then, quite quickly, to exclusion

The realities of social exclusion

The reality of social exclusion for many service users is that of multiple interlocking factors that can impact on every aspect of life (see Figure 4.12). People with mental health problems also have fewer social networks than average, with many of their contacts related to health services rather than sports, family, faith, employment, education or arts and culture. One survey found that 40 per cent of people with on-going mental health problems had no social contacts outside mental health services (Ford *et al.*, 1993). Fear of stigma and discrimination can also lead to severe loss of confidence.

Perhaps the biggest issue for people with mental health problems is that of unemployment and the consequent risk of financial hardship. In the general working age population, 70–90 per cent of people are economically active. However, in England, only 24 per cent of people with mental health problems are currently in work, the lowest employment rate of any group of people (see Figure 4.13). People with mental health problems also earn only two-thirds of the national average hourly rate (ONS, 2002). The costs to society of workforce exclusion are also considerable. Recent statistics show that people with mental health problems constitute 34 per cent of Incapacity Benefit claimants (Department for Work and Pensions, 2002).

Studies show a clear interest in work and employment activities amongst users of mental health services with up to 90 per cent wishing to go into or back to work (Grove and Drurie, 1999). In 2001, however, fewer that four in ten employers said they would consider employing someone with mental health

Figure 4.12	Social exclusion and mental illness

- People with mental health problems have more than double the risk of losing their job than those without (Burchadt, 2003)
- People with mental health problems are nearly three times as likely to be in debt (Meltzer *et al.*, 2002)
- It has been estimated that someone with a serious mental illness is four times more likely than an 'average' person to have no close friends (Huxley and Thornicroft, 2003)
- One in four tenants with mental health problems have serious rent arrears and are at risk of losing their homes (Shelter, 2003)
- People with mental health problems have, until recently, been barred from being school governors and ineligible for jury service (ODPM, 2004)
- People with a severe mental health problem are three times more likely to be divorced than those without (Meltzer *et al.*, 2002)

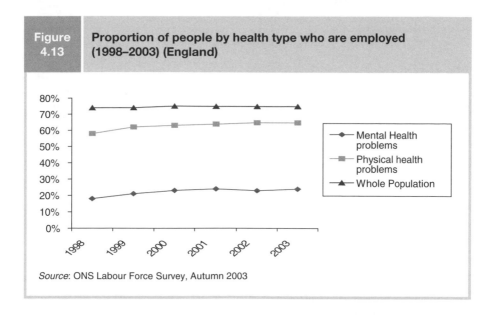

Figure 4.13 Proportion of people by health type who are employed (1998–2003) (England)

Source: ONS Labour Force Survey, Autumn 2003

problems (ODPM, 2004). Read and Baker (1996) found that 34 per cent of people with mental health problems had been dismissed or forced to resign from their job, and that almost four in ten people with mental health problems felt they had been denied a job because of their previous psychiatric history.

Employment also provides latent benefits such as social identity and status, social contacts and support, a means of occupying and structuring time and a sense of personal achievement (Shepherd, 1998). Lack of work, therefore, exacerbates the paucity of available social contacts and networks.

Positive practice in community inclusion

The test of a good society, we would suggest, lies in the care and support it offers to its most disadvantaged members. The importance of tackling social exclusion, particularly for people with mental illness, is becoming increasingly widely recognised. Standard One of the *NSF for Mental Health* (Department of Health, 1999a) acknowledged the importance of combating stigma and *The National Service Framework for Mental Health – Five Years On* (Department of Health, 2004b) also highlights the need to 'tackle social exclusion in people with mental health problems, improving their employment prospects and opposing stigma and discrimination' (p. 1). The Royal College of Psychiatrists and voluntary sector organisations continue to campaign for better understanding of mental health issues. NIMHE have also included social inclusion as an important strand of their work programme. Indeed the Social Exclusion Unit report (ODPM, 2004) on mental health and social exclusion has proposed a 27-point action plan involving a range of government departments and other organisations in a concerted effort to challenge attitudes and significantly improve opportunities and outcomes

Figure 4.14	Encouraging community inclusion

- Mechanisms that appear useful in changing public attitudes towards people with mental illness include encouraging contact between users and non-mental health service users in a positive way, for example by employing users and ex-users as staff in mental health services; ensuring users have training and support to speak to the media; targeting young people in particular with images and labels that they don't necessarily associate with mental illness and challenging negative attitudes
- Training and employment opportunities are also a key part of promoting social inclusion. People with long-term mental health problems can work effectively given the right support and adjustments (for example, someone to talk to or a quiet space). Prevocational training (a period of preparation before entering competitive employment) and supported employment (placement in competitive employment while offering on the job support) are both ways of helping people with severe mental illness obtain work. A systematic review of the evidence in this area found that supported employment is more effective than prevocational training in helping people obtain and keep competitive employment (Crowther *et al.*, 2001) and there is also some evidence that supported employment is cost effective (Grove *et al.*,1997)
- The government's *Pathways to Work* initiative, which promotes employment for people receiving Incapacity Benefit, includes a *Choice Package* that aims to help people manage the symptoms and effects of their illness so they are better able to find work. Pilots of the initiative have tested the impact of specialist personal advisers and help for people to manage their condition better in a work environment (ODPM, 2004)
- Initiatives like the Support Time and Recovery workers (Department of Health, 2003e) and PCGMHWs (Department of Health, 2003b) offer positive examples of developing jobs where lived experience of mental illness is a positive asset rather than a gap on the curriculum vitae

for people with mental illness (see Figure 4.14). The White Paper *Choosing Health: making health choices easier* (Department of Health, 2004c) also highlighted the need to work with non–government organisations in the voluntary and community sector and deliver services in settings where people live their lives. *Choosing Health*, in particular, adopts a broad definition of community, beyond that of traditional communitarianism, in talking about the potential of community action:

> Individuals belong to a range of overlapping communities – their local neighbourhood or state, a faith or age group, communities relating to common interests or social networks…communities are vital in improving health and can play a significant role in promoting individual self-esteem and mental wellbeing and reducing exclusion (Department of Health, 2004c, pp. 78–9).

Conclusion

Community mental health care has developed in a piece-meal fashion, influenced by a range of factors including economic constraints, difficulties in partnership working between health and social care and public concerns over safety. The closure of asylums and the development of mental health teams within the community 'have occurred unevenly across the country…in no instance however has a psychiatric hospital simply withered away because all its functions were replaced by a network of community services' (Leff, 1997, p. 189).

To make a difference at an individual level, a range of adequately resourced generic and more specialised community based mental health teams are required, staffed by well trained people who understand their remit and share a common approach within a healthy team culture. Separate teams also need to have clear lines of communication and referral pathways. New teams require additional finances, not redistribution of existing monies, since siphoning off resources from established teams to set up newer teams may not only create resentment but also mean that the 'forgotten generation' (people with serious mental illness who do not meet the inclusion criteria of new teams) may be left more isolated and excluded. The development of acceptable, appropriate, accessible and effective user centred services is therefore complex and requires all key stakeholders to understand each others' position and work together in partnership.

Many people now living in the community who might, in previous generations, have lived within long-stay institutions, have not necessarily been able to access adequate health or social care or housing or employment opportunities. Geographical inclusion (physically living in the same street) does not mean an individual automatically participates in the social life of that community or in the activities of wider society. Public concerns and policy focused on risk and safety rather than on quality of life for individuals have exacerbated social exclusion. Good community mental health care requires individuals as well as wider society to recognise these inequalities and work towards a culture of inclusion.

Reflection exercises

1. Alternatives to inpatient care
Exercise for community based staff

Think about the alternatives that currently exist for patients who are referred to you with an acute mental health crisis. Consider what options you are able to offer the patient and their family.

- Are these options the ones you would choose for yourself or a close family member?
- If not, reflect on why not
- As a wider group, discuss the type of provision you would like to see made available to people who live in your team's catchment area

2. Stereotypes of mental illness
Exercise for all staff

It is all too easy to take on board and even help disseminate negative stereotypes of people with mental illness, often through the things we don't do and behaviours we see or hear about, but don't actively challenge.

- As a group, look on the web and in local and national newspapers for stories that both increase and challenge stereotypes of mental illness
- What is the ratio of negative to positive stories about people with mental illness?

You might want to look at the way in which the boxer Frank Bruno's episode of mental illness was reported in one newspaper in September 2003, and the media reaction to both the event itself and the public's response (http://society.guardian.co.uk/mentalhealth/story/0,8150,1060499,00.html)

You might also find the Media Action Group for Mental Health website (http://www.sanityfair.org.uk/media_action_group.htm) helpful and thought provoking.

What can you, as an individual, do to help dispel myths and disseminate the realities of mental illness?

3. Promoting social inclusion
Exercise for all staff

Think about the ways in which your organisation and you as an individual can promote access and inclusion for people who use your service.

- What skills do you think are key to building a positive and affirming relationship with your service users and patients?
- What strategies can you use and what resources can you call on or direct people towards to help them feel more included within their local community?

Suggestions for further reading

1. Burns, T. (2004) *Community mental health teams: a guide to current practices.* Oxford, Oxford University Press

     This book, written by Professor Tom Burns (who has a long and distinguished career as both a researcher and consultant psychiatrist), describes a personal view of the current state and future challenges facing the generic CMHT with the newer functionalised teams.

2. Hannigan, B. and Coffey, M. (eds) (2003) *The handbook of community mental health nursing.* London, Routledge

     This edited collection from leaders in the field is a comprehensive and easy to read resource for practising community mental health nurses. It includes chapters that contextualise the area, as well as interesting and thought provoking contributions on a broad range of issues including ethics and the law.

3. Leff, J. (ed.) (1997) *Care in the community: illusion or reality?* Chichester, John Wiley and Sons

     This book describes the evolution of the policy of community care and the findings of the TAPS study. It also discusses the implications of the study for future community mental health care developments.

4. The *Mental Health Policy Implementation Guidance* describes the functions and standard operating procedures for different mental health teams, and can be downloaded free of charge from: www.dh.gov.uk/ PublicationsAndStatistics/Publications/PublicationsPolicyAndGuidance/

5. ODPM (2004) *Mental health and social exclusion.* Social Exclusion Unit Report. London, ODPM

     This excellent, evidence based practical report can be downloaded free of charge from www.publications.odpm.gov.uk

6. For direct payments, Spandler and Vick's (2004) *Direct payments, independent living and mental health: an evaluation* reports findings from a national development project to increase the number of direct payments made to people with mental health problems. This contains a wealth of detailed but accessible analysis about barriers to direct payments, the benefits of payments and possible ways forward.

5 Hospital Mental Health Services

In this chapter we discuss:

- The importance of hospital services
- The centrality of acute care to the NHS
- Trends and pressures in acute psychiatric care
- The hospital stay
- Hospital discharge
- Grounds for optimism?

The importance of hospital services

When someone becomes ill and is admitted to hospital, it can provoke a range of emotions. Some people may have had a sudden medical emergency and know little about their admission. When they wake up and find themselves in hospital, they may be disorientated and confused, not certain where they are or what is happening to them. Some people may have been feeling unwell for some time. They may have sensed that something was wrong, but were too scared to contact the health service and ask for help. Perhaps they thought that if they left the problem alone for long enough, it would go away. For them, hospital might be intimidating (with fear of the unknown) but also a relief (knowing that they are finally going to get the care and attention they may need). However, some people might not want to be in hospital at all and are only there because they feel they have little choice. As they became ill, it may have been that hospital was the only option; on some occasions, people may have felt pressured to go to hospital by family or friends. These people might be worried about what the future will hold and scared of potential pain or discomfort. They may be missing their family and friends, their home, their children, their pets, and want to get out as soon as possible.

Once admitted, the experience of being in hospital can vary significantly. Some hospitals are purpose-built, open and light, well equipped and pleasantly designed with gardens, shops, a homely atmosphere and plenty of things to do. Others may be in outmoded buildings which are dirty, dark and unappealing. They may be hot and noisy, and it can be difficult to sleep.

Some hospitals may have mixed sex provision, which might make some people feel uncomfortable. On some wards, there may be a regimented routine and some patients can quickly adopt a dependent 'sick role' (Parsons, 1964), not getting dressed and lying in bed all day. Sometimes, life in hospital can be very boring with little to do and nowhere to go. Often the quality of the individual's experience can depend on the staff they meet: workers who are very committed, highly skilled and friendly are likely to make hospital much more enjoyable and make patients more confident in the treatment they will receive. However, the opposite can also be true: staff who do not seem very motivated or competent and who lack empathy or interpersonal skills can make patients feel worried about their treatment and may be experienced as 'bossy' or unsympathetic.

When the time comes to leave, there can be a mixture of thoughts and feelings. Some people may feel completely recovered and cannot wait to go home. Others may still be feeling unwell and will be uncertain about how they will manage at home. For them, leaving hospital may be a traumatic experience as they try to build up the confidence and courage to adapt to life in the community after all the support and services available in an acute setting. For those with on-going needs, they may be medically fit for discharge but could still need on-going support from community services. This is particularly the case with frail older people, and there is a large body of evidence to suggest that some people have a very variable experience of the discharge process. While many go home with no problems, there is substantial research highlighting the difficulties which some older people can face. These include (summarised in Tierney *et al.*, 1994, pp. 479–80):

■ Poor communication between hospital and community
■ Lack of assessment and planning for discharge
■ Inadequate notice of discharge
■ Inadequate consultation with patients and their carers
■ Over-reliance on informal support and lack of (or slow) statutory service provision

In some cases, the support people need in the community is not available (for example, if there is a funding shortage or no spaces left in a particular service) and they have no choice but to wait in an acute bed until the necessary provision materialises. This is often known as 'bed blocking', although this term is now avoided in favour of more neutral concepts such as 'delayed hospital discharges' or 'delayed transfers of care'. As Victor (1991, p. 123) explains:

> The whole notion of bed blocking seems to imply that older people enter hospital and then wilfully continue to occupy a bed which, in the view of staff, they no longer require. Older people (or indeed patients of any age) do not become bed blockers of their own intent. Rather where such cases do occur it is because the health and social care system cannot provide the type of care they need.

In recent years the problem of delayed hospital discharges has become an increasing political priority at a local and national level, and the government has introduced a range of different initiatives in response (from increased investment to good practice guidance and from new forms of service provision to a new government team to improve discharge practice) (see, for example, Department of Health, 2003f; House of Commons Health Committee, 2002). Often, delayed discharges are caused by a range of factors, including (Glasby *et al.*, 2004):

- Factors within the control of social care (such as funding shortages and lack of capacity)
- Factors within the control of acute hospitals (such as internal hospital delays, waiting for test results or the timing of consultant ward rounds)
- Factors outside the control of social care or hospitals altogether (such as waiting for community health services, housing and the decisions made by service users and carers)

As a result, there is increased recognition of the need for a range of different agencies to work together to ensure timely and well co-ordinated discharge from hospital.

In all these circumstances and for all these reasons, the process of hospital admission, hospital stay and hospital discharge can be life-changing events for many people and have the capacity to drastically improve someone's health or to cause significant stress and anxiety. If this is true of general hospitals, it is particularly the case in mental health services where service users being admitted to hospital may be feeling especially vulnerable and distressed and where hospital buildings may be particularly run down. As the Sainsbury Centre for Mental Health (1998b, p. 9) observes:

> If and when people with severe mental health problems can no longer manage to live in the community... they, their relatives, and society expect care to be available in a therapeutic and humane place. In practice, this means admission to an acute psychiatric ward and inevitably losing some degree of freedom and privacy. Most people suffering from a severe mental illness will have been in hospital at some stage in their lives. A considerable proportion will have been admitted against their will under the Mental Health Act because they were judged to be a danger to themselves or others. At the point of admission people become patients, and will be in a severe state of crisis, both personally and mentally. Imagine being transported to a frightening unknown place, possibly in an ambulance or police car, while suffering from deep despair or confusion. It is unlikely that at any point in their life anyone could feel more vulnerable, and would be more in need of high quality and sensitive care.

The centrality of acute care to the NHS

In the UK (and in many other countries), hospitals and hospital beds are a central feature of the health system:

- Because they provide so many specialist services to those with significant health problems, hospitals tend to have sophisticated equipment and to be very expensive to run
- Because they provide 24–hour care, they have to be well-staffed
- Because they cater for so many people, they tend to be in large and sometimes very imposing buildings
- Because they care for people in need, they are often popular and inspire strong local loyalty. An example of this comes from the Wyre Forest where proposals to down–grade a local hospital led to the election of a new MP from the 'Health Concern' pressure group (Thorne, 2001; Timmins, 2001)
- Because society and technology both evolve so quickly, hospital buildings can quickly get out-of-date. Because they are so expensive to build, however, they tend to be used over a long period of time, even when they may feel a little outmoded

As a result of this, hospitals tend to be expensive, resource–intensive places. Despite the recent emphasis on primary and community care (see Chapters 3 and 4), therefore, acute hospitals continue to consume a large proportion of the health budget and to employ a significant number of staff. For example, the gross cost of hospital services in the UK was £26.1 billion in 2000 (46 per cent of NHS resources) with a workforce of around one million people (Yuen, 2003). In mental health, exactly the same is true. Despite the emphasis on primary care based mental health and community services, acute mental health inpatient services receive a significant proportion of the mental health budget and employ a large number of staff (see Figure 5.1). Like acute general hospitals, mental health inpatient services tend to be in large, imposing buildings, which can date very quickly.

Figure 5.1	Acute mental health care

- Mental health inpatient care consumes some £800 million per year, representing 25 per cent of the total health and social care budget for mental health
- In England, there are 14,000 beds on 521 wards
- There are 138,000 admissions per year (occupying 4.3 million bed days)
- Inpatient care employs 15,000 staff: 12,223 nurses, 425 occupational therapists and 911 doctors

(Sainsbury Centre for Mental Health, 2002b, p. 2)

Despite these similarities, the key difference between general and mental health hospitals seems to be their popularity – while acute general hospitals are often crucial parts of their local communities, mental health services can be extremely unpopular due to negative stereotypes about people with mental health problems and the risk of violence (see Chapter 6). This is sometimes known as 'nimbyism' and applies also to community services (I know people with mental health problems need hospital services, but '*not in my back yard*').

Trends in acute psychiatric care

Traditionally, services for people with mental health problems have been dominated by institutions, with many people being placed in long-stay hospitals or asylums. As discussed in Chapter 4, however, this emphasis on institutional care has been replaced in the second half of the twentieth century with a recognition of the need to care for more people in the community, either in their own homes or in community-based settings which are as homely as possible. As a result of this, the number of hospital beds for people with mental health problems has fallen considerably (both in the UK and elsewhere). In 1954, there were 154,000 residents in UK mental hospitals. By 1982, this figure had fallen to 100,000 and, by 1998, to under 40,000. Another way of looking at this is that the number of psychiatric beds per 100,000 population has fallen from 131.8 in 1990 to 62.8 in 2001 (Priebe *et al.*, 2005). In some countries the degree of the deinstitutionalisation has been even greater. For example, in Italy between 1968 and 1978, the asylum population fell from 100,000 to 50,000. In the US, although relatively few psychiatric hospitals have been closed (26 in 17 states since 1970), there has been a similar dramatic reduction in the number of inpatients over the last four decades from 560,000 people in 1955 to 77,000 in 1995 (see Goodwin, 1997; Rogers and Pilgrim, 2001; Centre for Mental Health Services, 1995 for all statistics quoted).

However, this does not necessarily mean that the number of hospital admissions has been decreasing in the UK. On the contrary, the number of admissions has increased from 155,000 in 1964 (347 per 100,000 population) to 192,000 in 1984 (409 per 100,000 population) and 224,000 in 1993–94 (462 per 100,000 population) (Payne, 1999, p. 247). More recently there have been indications of a new process of 'reinstitutionalisation' (see Chapter 2) with an increase in certain types of bed. However, the overall trend for many years has been one of decline, with the number of hospital beds falling at the same time as admissions were increasing. As is also the case for other user groups, this has been achieved by:

- A reduction in the length of hospital stay (see Figure 5.2)
- Changes in community services to work with people with increasingly high level needs. In older people's services, this is often described in terms of people being discharged from hospital 'quicker and sicker' (Neill and Williams, 1992, p. 17), with community services having to support a growing number of people who would previously have been cared for in an acute setting

Figure 5.2	The importance of hospital services

Many recent studies have highlighted the enormous pressures currently facing acute psychiatric wards. There has been a dramatic decline in hospital beds for mental health care since their peak at 155,000 in the mid-1950s. The number of available beds in NHS hospitals has more than halved in the last decade or so to around 37,000... At the same time demand has been rising. Throughput in mental health beds has more than doubled... Referrals of patients appear to be rising while at the same time the severity of problems of people treated in hospital has also increased... [Thus], studies have reported increasing numbers of patients on wards with drug or alcohol abuse problems, people referred by court diversion schemes (aimed at keeping mentally ill people out of the prison system) and people needing accommodation in low or medium secure units.

(Sainsbury Centre for Mental Health, 1998b, p. 10)

Hardly surprisingly, this puts extra pressure on hospital services (to treat and discharge people as quickly as possible) and on community services (to support people with increasingly significant and complex needs). This not only means that community services have a heavier caseload, but that those people who are admitted to hospital are likely to have particularly severe needs and that the whole service becomes increasingly intensive in its focus. This has a number of implications which are discussed in further detail throughout the remainder of this chapter. As Quirk and Lelliott (2001, p. 1567) observe: 'the emergent picture is that:

■ The reduction in bed numbers has created a 'concentrating' effect whereby the threshold for admission has increased...
■ High bed occupancy rates mean that quality of care is compromised. Some people have to be admitted to distant hospitals with subsequent loss of continuity; nurses spend most of their time managing crises rather than giving care
■ Because of the concentrating effect, wards are disturbed places where 'violence breeds violence'...
■ Unavailability of beds compromises the quality of community care which requires easy access to beds for short-term management of crises or for respite'

Interestingly, however, the statistics above do not tell the full story. As Payne (1999, p. 248) explains, some of this increase in psychiatric admissions is actually the same people being admitted and re-admitted to hospital:

The pattern for many patients, however, is one of admission to psychiatric hospital and discharge which is then followed by subsequent readmission at a later date. If one compares figures for first admissions...

with figures for total admissions it is clear that the vast majority of the increase in psychiatric admissions… is accounted for by the readmission of those who have already been treated as in-patients and discharged from hospital – the phenomenon of the so-called 'revolving door'.

Although the concept of the 'revolving door' admission is discussed in more detail below, it is significant to note that these trends within mental health can also be seen in services for other user groups. As an example, the Audit Commission (1997, 2000a) describes a 'vicious circle' in services for older people (see Figure 5.3) in which the number of hospital admissions is rising, lengths of hospital stays are declining, opportunities for rehabilitation are reduced, there is an increased use of expensive residential/nursing home care and less money for preventative services, thereby leading to more hospital admissions. As a result, there are concerns that older people could be discharged from hospital too quickly, only to be readmitted again at a later stage when their initial medical problems recur or due to a breakdown in hastily assembled community support arrangements (see, for example, Glasby, 2003).

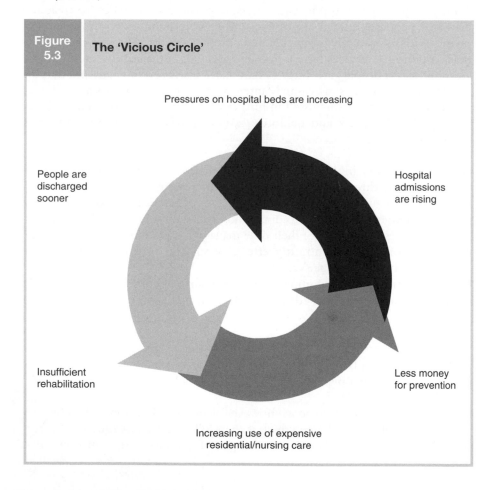

Figure 5.3 The 'Vicious Circle'

Pressures on hospital beds are increasing

People are discharged sooner

Hospital admissions are rising

Insufficient rehabilitation

Less money for prevention

Increasing use of expensive residential/nursing care

Pressures on acute care

Hardly surprisingly, one of the main results of the decline in the number of psychiatric beds and rising demand has been a significant increase in pressure on hospital services. In response, the tendency has been for mental health services to seek to treat more people with fewer resources by increasing bed occupancy rates (more people seen per bed). This can be done using a variety of tactics, all of which are 'unsatisfactory' (Quirk and Lelliott, 2001, p. 1566):

- Transferring patients to hospitals outside the local area (a practice tradi-tionally known as extra-contractual referrals or ECR, sometimes referred to as Out of Area Transfers or Individual Patient Placements)
- Maintaining waiting lists, with people needing inpatient care waiting in settings such as general medical wards, community settings, prison or police cells
- Sending some patients home on short-term leave (sometimes prematurely and often at short notice) in order to free up beds for others

As a result of this, the bed occupancy rate (when all those in the above cate-gories are added in) can frequently exceed 100 per cent (see Figure 5.4) and can reach levels as high as 153 per cent (quoted in Quirk and Lelliott, 2001). This is particularly the case in London, where, in January 1999, there were 241 patients on leave (123 of these with an urgent need for a hospital bed) and 80 people in ECR beds, with a further 88 people in other types of bed, at home/in the community or in prison/police cells (Audini et al., 1999). Clearly, the implications of such pressure on beds can be extremely serious. For example:

- Quality of care can be compromised by admitting patients to hospitals at a long distance from their homes, discharging or sending people on leave early and not admitting other patients
- The use of ECRs is not only unpopular with service users, but is also very costly, diverts money away from community services and disrupts continuity of care
- Sending people out on leave can also can create significant administra-tive difficulties for hospital wards as patients can sometimes return at any time, making it difficult to use temporarily vacant beds for other people requiring admission

Despite immense pressure on existing beds, the answer may not necessarily lie in expanding hospital services. This is the result of a number of factors:

- Occupancy rates are not uniform throughout the country, and the evidence suggests that pressures are particularly strong in the south of England (especially London) and in inner-city areas (see, for example, Audini et al., 1999; Greengross et al., 2000; Shepherd et al., 1997). As a

Figure 5.4	Bed occupancy

In Dewsbury, two adult mental health wards often have bed occupancy rates exceeding 120 per cent (Auckland *et al.*, 2000).

Regular surveys of 13 inner London psychiatric trusts undertaken by the Royal College of Psychiatrists have found that average occupancy rates have always been above 100 per cent during each of the seven censuses conducted between 1994 and 1999 (Audini *et al.*, 1999). Crucially, the study distinguishes between three different ways of calculating occupancy rates:

- 'True' occupancy – all people registered as inpatients plus those awaiting admission. In January 1999, this rate was 128 per cent
- 'Ward' occupancy – the total number registered as inpatients. In January 1999, this rate was 112 per cent
- 'Minimum' occupancy – people registered as inpatients minus those on leave who were thought not to need a bed kept available, plus those for whom a bed is required but who are placed elsewhere because no acute bed is available locally. In January 1999, this rate was 112 per cent

As a result, the researchers conclude that 'between 1994 and 1999 there were consistently more patients requiring acute inpatient care than there were beds available. This leads to poor quality care and is not cost effective' (p. 593). To reduce bed occupancy rates to a more manageable level of 85 per cent, the authors calculate that a further 14 beds or community alternatives will be required per 100,000 population.

A 'national visit' carried out by the Mental Health Act Commission to 199 adult psychiatric inpatient units in England and Wales found that occupancy rates were 86 per cent if patients on overnight leave were excluded, but rose to 99 per cent when such patients were included (Ford *et al.*, 1998).

A national survey of 173 mental health trusts found that around 70 per cent are often or sometimes over-occupied and that just under 40 per cent often or sometimes have to use ECRs (Greengross *et al.*, 2000).

Bed occupancy in a study of 11 different sites across England ranged from 73 to 136 per cent (Higgins *et al.*, 1999). Nine sites reported occupancies above 85 per cent, with five having occupancies of 100 per cent or more.

A Social Services Inspectorate report found high occupancy levels, particularly in London, and high levels of demand from people who have a mental health problem and misuse substances (Watson, 2001).

result, it may be that local agencies may need to reassess the level of their provision with a view to increasing bed availability in some areas, but not in others.

- There is evidence to suggest that some admissions to hospital may be inappropriate. In North Cheshire, for example, 35 out of 520 people were admitted to hospital as a result of social problems (Cawley *et al.*, 1997), while national research undertaken by the Sainsbury Centre for

Figure 5.5	Revolving door admissions

In one London health authority, researchers studied the process of care for a sample of 100 consecutive discharges from acute wards in two mental health trusts (Minghella and Ford, 1997). Overall, three-quarters of the sample had been in hospital before and many were readmitted after the research was completed. Despite this, around half did not have a recorded care package or had a package which broke down prior to admission.

Elsewhere, a national study of acute care found that: '89 per cent of admissions were classified as emergencies. However, 40 per cent of the patients had previously been admitted to the same service in the last 12 months, 20 per cent within the last 90 days and 13 per cent within the last six weeks, confirming the so-called "revolving door" of mental health care. This high rate of people returning to acute care in a crisis indicates the difficulties community services experience in preventing admission or finding alternative forms of care for people with mental health problems.'

(Sainsbury Centre for Mental Health, 1998b, p. 16)

Mental Health (1998b) found that one in ten people were admitted for social reasons or for respite care. Elsewhere, a systematic review of the appropriateness of acute bed use cites two studies which suggest that just under one-third of admissions may be inappropriate (McDonagh *et al.*, 2000). Key factors contributing to inappropriate admissions may include inadequate assessments undertaken by junior and non-specialist staff in Accident and Emergency (A & E) and general wards, inadequate community services and a lack of alternatives to hospital outside office hours (Auckland *et al.*, 2000; Minghella and Ford, 1997). As noted above, moreover, other patients may experience 'revolving door' admissions to hospital due to breakdowns in community services or as a result of services treating outward symptoms of mental illness rather than tackling the underlying causes (see Figure 5.5). Taken together, findings such as these suggest that it may be possible to reduce the number of hospital admissions by making more accurate initial assessments of people's needs and by developing community-based alternatives to inpatient care.

The hospital stay

Once in hospital, some people will receive high quality services that meet their needs. Despite this, many accounts of inpatient care suggest that some service users have very poor experiences of hospital services, with few people having 'anything good to say about acute hospital care' (Royal College of Psychiatrists, 2002). In 2000, moreover, a national survey carried out by Mind revealed a series of extremely worrying findings

Figure 5.6	Mind national survey

In 2000, the mental health charity Mind published the results of a national survey of 343 people with experience of hospital services:

- More than half (56 per cent) of patients said that the ward was an un-therapeutic environment
- Just under half (45 per cent) said that ward conditions had a negative effect on their mental health
- Just under half (45 per cent) said they found the atmosphere on wards 'depressing' and bleak
- Almost a third (30 per cent) of patients said that they found the atmosphere on wards unsafe and frightening
- Just under a third (30 per cent) said illegal drugs were being used on the wards. Two-thirds of these patients (66 per cent) said that drugs were easily available to patients
- Almost two-thirds (64 per cent) of patients who needed an interpreter did not get one
- More than half (57 per cent) said they didn't have enough contact with staff. Only 35 per cent said they did
- The vast majority (82 per cent) of patients who said they didn't have enough contact with staff said that they spent 15 minutes or less with staff each day
- Almost 1 in 6 (16 per cent) of patients said they had experienced sexual harassment on the ward. 72 per cent of those patients who complained said that no action was taken to prevent it happening again
- Almost two-thirds (60 per cent) of patients had problems getting a restful night's sleep
- Just under half (45 per cent) of patients said they didn't have enough access to food, and 31 per cent said they didn't have enough access to drinks
- A quarter (26 per cent) of patients said the toilets weren't clean

(Baker, 2000, p. 6)

(see Figure 5.6), which paint 'a grim picture of life on many psychiatric wards – a depressing environment, unsafe, dirty, with illegal drugs easily available, minimal contact with staff, not enough to do and not enough access to food, drink, bathing facilities, interpreters if needed, telephones and fresh air' (Baker, 2000, p. 31).

Unfortunately, many of these findings are mirrored in other studies, suggesting that they may not be unique to the Mind survey. Thus, the Social Services Inspectorate suggests that users often experience inpatient wards as stressful rather than therapeutic environments (Watson, 2001), while social work trainees in Merseyside observing psychiatric wards are very critical of the quality of care provided (see Figure 5.8). Similarly, Goodwin *et al.*'s (1999) analysis of the views of 110 inpatient mental health service users identifies a number of key criticisms, including inadequate buildings, poor food, insufficient access to telephones, a lack of control, a lack of respect showed by staff to patients and a lack of information (see Figure 5.7). Inpatient stays may also be particularly difficult for young people, who should not be placed on adult wards unless there are exceptional circumstances. However, monitoring suggests that this often does not happen, with young people placed on adult wards, sometimes from a very young age, with no programme of suitable activities. Hardly surprisingly, this can lead to 'boredom and frustration that cannot assist with recovery' (Healthcare Commission, 2004, p. 79).

Other recurring issues from the literature include:

- High levels of staff vacancies and the use of workers employed on a casual basis (Ford *et al.*, 1998)
- Staff dissatisfaction with rapidly increasing administrative duties and reduced contact with patients (Higgins *et al.*, 1999)
- Widespread boredom amongst patients (Warner *et al.*, 2000a)
- Disempowering regimes that promote a culture of infantilisation (Barnes *et al.*, 2000)
- A lack of involvement from community services (Sainsbury Centre for Mental Health, 1998b)
- A lack of information for users and carers (Watson, 2001)
- The difficulty of reconciling the needs of smokers and non-smokers (Goodwin *et al.*, 1999)

Figure 5.7	Acute care: users' views

'X ward was very dull and in need of redecoration – when I first entered the ward it gave me the feeling I wanted to turn back and go home. Not a homely feeling but a cold feeling, I couldn't relax. I felt more depressed going into hospital.'

'I don't think I have much influence. I will tell them how I feel but I don't expect they will pay me much attention.'

'The ward staff are very helpful if they've got the time but, like all hospitals, they haven't always got the time to sit and talk and listen and when you're mentally ill that's what you want.'

'The gentleman I'm under goes in for telling you rather than asking you. I can't ask him questions. He doesn't put you at ease.'

'The staff don't help you. They just sit around talking and eating and drinking and smoking. I wish the staff would talk to me more. They hear me crying and don't help me.'

(Goodwin *et al.*, 1999, pp. 45–50)

Figure 5.8	Users' experiences of hospital

Users in a Social Services Inspectorate inspection had a negative experience of hospital services due to (Watson, 2001, p. 14):

- Delays in admission caused by limited bed availability
- Shortage of beds leading to patients sleeping on other wards and having no personal space
- Women service users having insufficient privacy on mixed sex-wards
- Users from minority ethnic backgrounds who spoke to no-one with knowledge of their language, religion or culture during their inpatient stay
- The disruptive behaviour of other patients which sometimes led to the police being called, for example, to search for illicit drugs
- Lack of daytime occupation, boredom and no access to quiet areas

In Merseyside, social work students observing local psychiatric wards highlighted the following issues (Walton, 2000):

- *Institutional aimlessness*: Patients are often bored, do little other than watch TV and are regularly moved round by cleaning staff. Ward routines have become ends in themselves and the physical atmosphere is debilitating. The limited activities on offer are seen as being very patronising, but users take part to try to demonstrate that their mental health has improved and secure an early discharge
- *Poor staff-patient relationships*: Most staff time is spent on administrative tasks, talking to each other in the office and watching patients rather than engaging with them
- *Narrow approaches to mental health*: Staff see patients as being 'ill' and pay little attention to users' social backgrounds. As a result, the presenting problem is often seen as the issue to be addressed with no consideration of the factors that may have caused this problem in the first place. There is an almost total reliance on psychiatric drugs as the solution to mental health problems
- *Indifference to civil and human rights*: Staff tend to treat all patients the same way irrespective of whether or not they have been admitted as compulsory patients. Some people have little knowledge of the law and have had no training at all in this area. Ward routines are very rigid and some are unnecessarily stressful (such as denying people drinks outside set times even though dry mouths are a common side-effect of medication or the oppressive nature of ward rounds, with patients unable to contribute due to the large number of professionals that come to see them)

Negative experiences have also been identified by the Sainsbury Centre for Mental Health (1998b, p. 35):

A total of 112 patients were interviewed at or around the time of discharge about aspects of the care and environment on their ward... More than half (55 per cent) had no separate bedroom. Nearly three-quarters (71 per cent) did not have a secure locker for their belongings. Nearly half (47 per cent) had no quiet area where they could take visitors. 20 per cent felt washing facilities were not private. There were also concerns about hygiene – 22 per cent were unhappy at the cleanliness of the ward – and food – 28 per cent did not like the food while 37 per cent did not judge mealtimes to be pleasant and enjoyable. Most worryingly, nearly a third (32 per cent) did not feel safe on the wards.

Figure 5.8	Users' experiences of hospital *(continued)*

Despite these findings, service users can be very clear about what they want from hospital services. As an example, Mac Gabhann's (2000) study of patients' views suggests that service users value:

- Support and understanding
- Being able to talk and be listened to
- Being away from home pressures
- A sense of safety/sanctuary
- Freedom and choice
- Feeling part of a friendly community

To achieve these goals, patients wanted nurses to be more flexible to individual needs, to respect and invest in relationships and to spend more time with patients. Similar findings are also echoed by Quirk and Lelliott (2001), who suggest that service users value nursing staff who are active listeners and 'humane' qualities such as tolerance, respect and empathy.

Hospital discharge

Although hospital discharge can be problematic for other user groups such as older people, it is also a central concern in acute psychiatric inpatient services. In 1999, for example, a Department of Health funded study of acute psychiatric nursing care found that the pressure on beds meant that patients were discharged from hospital before they had sufficiently recovered and were often quickly readmitted after their community services broke down (Higgins *et al.*, 1999). At the same time, research by the Sainsbury Centre for Mental Health (1998b) indicates that discharge arrangements were often dealt with in an *ad hoc* way during ward rounds, with only one-third of patients receiving a formal or separate meeting to plan for leaving hospital. Most patients had very little notice of their discharge and had little involvement in discussions about their futures. Involvement from carers and community staff was also limited (Sainsbury Centre for Mental Health, 1998b, p. 6):

Discharge is often unplanned with inadequate involvement of community staff, patients and carers... Only 34 per cent of patients had a discharge planning meeting and most patients had no idea that they were to be discharged until a few days before they left, and had little involvement in discussions about their future.

Although some patients may be discharged from hospital prematurely, others may remain in hospital much longer than they need to because of a lack of community services. In 1999, a review of alternatives to acute psychiatric beds found that between 20 and 60 per cent of patients could be better placed (although the latter figure was produced by a study outside the UK) (Bartlett *et al.*, 1999). The following year, a systematic review of the appropriateness of acute bed usage found that between 24 and 58 per cent of days of care were not considered appropriate (McDonagh *et al.*, 2000). In both studies, key factors contributing to delayed discharges were found to include a lack of housing, a lack of community services (such as group homes), a lack of rehabilitation services and, in a small number of cases, the need for higher levels of care. Similar findings have also been produced by a range of other commentators, suggesting that a substantial number of people would be able to leave hospital if community alternatives were more readily available (see Figure 5.9).

Figure 5.9	Delayed hospital discharges	
Study	**Rate of delayed discharge**	**Causes/possible alternatives**
Fulop *et al.* (1992)	37%	Lack of accommodation and long-stay hospital care
Lelliott and Wing (1994)	61%	Lack of continuing care provision, rehabilitation, supported group homes or low-staffed hostels
Fulop *et al.* (1996)	23%	Professional support in the patient's home, housing/more appropriate housing, group homes, rehabilitation
Koffman *et al.* (1996)	24%	Residential and/or nursing home care, total dependency psychiatric care, community services (such as day care or home care), housing
Connolly and Ritchie (1997)	54% in 1994 46% in 1995	Some patients with stays of three months or more could have been discharged to other NHS services (for people with complex needs), supported accommodation or mainstream housing
Beck *et al.* (1997)	42%	Of patients with stays of at least 60 days, some could have been discharged to alternatives such as a non-acute low-level observation inpatient facility, the patient's own home, a group home, day hospitals and support by a CPN

Figure 5.9	**Delayed hospital discharges (*continued*)**	
Minghella and Ford (1997)	10%	Problems finding suitable accommodation (including forensic care)
Shepherd *et al.* (1997)	27%	Lack of supported housing/rehabilitation services, secure accommodation and specialist services
Sainsbury Centre for Mental Health (1998b)	19% (after 1 week)	Lack of accommodation, home based support and rehabilitation, and patients requiring higher levels of supervision
Bartlett *et al.* (1999)	Systematic review	A spectrum of provision is required, including support at home as well as residential care staffed by specialist nurses
McDonagh *et al.* (2000)	Systematic review	Delayed discharge could be reduced by services such as more appropriate housing/ housing plus support, group homes, rehabilitation and services with higher levels of supervision
Paton *et al.* (2004)	46%	Insufficient specialist resources for placement or return home, lack of money to finance placements, no alternative to acute ward and users and carers refusing placements/ refusing to pay for care

Grounds for optimism?

To date, much of the research on inpatient services has been extremely negative and raised serious concerns about quality of care. While these are significant issues, it is important to emphasise that there have been a number of national initiatives to improve acute care. At a local level, there is also a range of activities underway to tackle some of the problems identified in this chapter, and these should not be overlooked. As Quirk and Lelliott (2001, p. 1571) observe:

[Research to date has] generated much useful information about what happens on acute psychiatric wards... However, such accounts are limited by the fact that they tend to present an unremittingly bleak picture of life on the wards – something that is unlikely to be the case for all the patients all of the time and across all wards.

One example is the Sainsbury Centre for Mental Health's *Acute Solutions* Project (Sainsbury Centre for Mental Health, 2002c). Launched in November 2001 in partnership with the Department of Health, the Royal College of Psychiatrists, the Royal College of Nursing and the NHS Confederation, the aim is to develop a generalisable model of care that users experience as both safe and therapeutic, and where staff strengthen their skills and experience and have improved morale (see Figure 5.10 for examples of other initiatives). At a national level, moreover, the Department of Health's acute inpatient care provision guidance acknowledges that problems exist within acute care, that inpatient services have not received the same emphasis as community services and that this needs to change (Rooney, 2002, p. 3):

> Too often acute inpatient services are not working to everyone's satisfaction. A range of reports and surveys and the reported experience of service users and staff have clearly and consistently demonstrated a high level of criticism and dissatisfaction with current provision... It is clear that the physical, psychological and therapeutic environment of care must all be attended to.

In addition to an extra £30 million to improve the physical environment of acute wards, the guidance calls for local Acute Care Fora to agree and regularly review operation and co-ordination of the full range of acute services. Additional recommendations are made about a range of different areas of acute care, from admission to ward arrangements, from leadership to staffing and from training to the ward environment. At the same time, a range of research studies have been commissioned on the organisation and delivery of inpatient mental health services, including studies on staff morale, services for young people and inpatient alternatives to traditional inpatient care (NHS Service and Delivery Organisation, 2003). Additional guidance has

Figure 5.10	Acute solutions?

- The Northern Centre for Mental Health's collaborative project for acute inpatient care has brought together a series of mental health trusts to identify local concerns and priorities for change and to share learning
- The Centre for Mental Health Services Development has run a good practice network of trusts to improve the quality of acute care
- The Inner Cities Mental Health group has run development programmes for ward managers in acute care

(Sainsbury Centre for Mental Health (2002c) – see also Rooney (2002) for additional good practice examples.)

Figure 5.11	Longstanding problems in acute care

Inquiries into the hospital scandals of the 1960s and 1970s identify a range of contributing factors, including (Martin, 1984):

- The isolated nature of some acute services (including not only geographical isolation, but also staff being left in charge of large numbers of people and lack of visits by medical staff)
- Closed, institutional settings and a tendency to suppress complaints
- A corruption of care – focusing on the maintenance of order and routine rather than on providing care
- Failures of leadership
- Staff shortages and inadequate training

The Commission for Health Improvement (2003a) identified a very similar list of issues, suggesting a considerable lack of progress over time. Examples include:

- The isolated nature of services
- Institutional environments
- Low staffing levels and high use of bank and agency staff
- Closed cultures
- Poor clinical leadership and supervision

also been produced on education, training and continuing professional development (Clarke, 2004).

Despite these grounds for optimism, however, a number of doubts must still remain about what the future holds for acute inpatient care. In particular, the persistent and longstanding nature of many of the issues outlined above suggest that the problems associated with acute inpatient mental health services are extremely complicated and entrenched. As an example, Figure 5.11 compares findings from the hospital scandals of the 1960s and 1970s with a Commission for Health Improvement report on mental health services published in 2003, providing a stark reminder of the relatively low base from which acute care is starting and a traditional lack of progress in hospital services. While it is much to the government's credit that it has acknowledged deficiencies in acute care and sought to put them right, therefore, it is difficult to be optimistic about the likelihood of substantial progress in the near future.

Conclusion

Overall, it seems as if considerably more can and should be done to improve access to acute hospital beds for those who need them, the quality of the hospital stay and the hospital discharge process. However, what is most surprising about the literature on hospital services is the relatively low number of studies which address this topic. This is highlighted by a number of the commentators cited above, who emphasise two key factors:

■ The relative neglect of hospital services is a product of the current emphasis on community care
■ More research needs to be undertaken in order to improve our understanding of the issues at stake in this important area of policy and practice (see Figure 5.12)

Figure 5.12	The neglect of acute care?

In recent years, political and managerial attention has focused predominantly on the consequences of the failure of National Health Service community services to provide effective care to people with severe mental illness in the United Kingdom... However, what happens inside hospitals has received less scrutiny. Not since the reports and inquiries of the 1960s and early 1970s into the poor standards of nursing care provided in some long-stay psychiatric hospitals has hospital care been under the spotlight.

(Higgins *et al.*, 1999, p. 52)

The combination of increasingly pressured acute wards and high levels of casual staffing cannot be good for the care of patients. These problems are most severe in London, where patients have more severe problems... The policy, managerial, and training focus has been on developing community services. This has resulted in a relative neglect of inpatient settings. [This study] has shown that attention must be given to inpatient wards, which are an essential and major element of mental health care.

(Ford *et al.*, 1998, p. 1823)

There is scant evidence about the effectiveness and quality of care of acute wards in dealing with people with psychiatric problems. Relatively little is known about exactly who are the people who stay on acute psychiatric wards and what happens to them while they are there. There is a sense that hospital care is a black box, with people entering and leaving, and we have high but vague expectations about what happens in between. The issue about quality and effectiveness of care is crucial, however, not least because acute inpatient treatment is the most intensive and expensive form of mental healthcare – but also because patients on acute wards have to sacrifice both privacy and freedom during their stay. Moreover, they are unpopular with many of these patients. It is crucial, therefore, that hospital stays are used to best advantage, treating the patients who need and benefit most from this regime and for the shortest necessary time.

(Sainsbury Centre for Mental Health, 1998b, p. 11)

In seeking to respond to the many issues raised above, it seems clear that they are few 'easy answers' and that the way forward may lie in taking a whole systems approach that considers the full range of mental health services (see, for example, Lee and Bradley, 2000; Minghella and Ford, 1997; Shepherd *et al.*, 1997). Many of the problems of over–occupancy, poor quality acute care and delayed discharges cannot be resolved in isolation, but require concerted action across the full range of available services (see Figure 5.13). Ultimately, as Higgins *et al.* (1999, p. 61) observe:

> Without close examination of what is happening in hospitals... and without suitable remedial action, it is conceivable that hospital care might once again be subject to the scrutiny and criticism that cast a shadow over psychiatric services in the 1960s and 1970s. Nurses and other mental health professionals need to work together to prevent such circumstances arising and to develop the full spectrum of services required in each locality.

Against this background, there are some recent grounds for optimism, but it very much remains to be seen whether the recent rediscovery of acute care and the many shortcomings that exist in inpatient services will be sufficient to tackle the scale and complexity of the problem.

Figure 5.13	The need for a whole-systems approach

In the short term, better bed management at every stage – at admission, throughout the patient's stay and at discharge – can relieve some of the pressures [on hospital services]. To solve the problems of over-occupancy and costly delayed discharges in the longer term, a range of care options, with several... alternatives for different levels of need and different kinds of problems, must be considered. Acute inpatient care should be viewed as one component of such a spectrum, operating a specific, well-defined function – that is to provide intensive 24-hour care for those patients whose needs are for intensive assessment, immediate treatment and stabilisation of symptoms.

(Moore and Wolf, 1999, p. 22)

More important than beds is the total range and quality of services. Inpatient services and community services must be provided together to meet people's needs. The quality of clinical decision-making helps people access appropriate services. We may need more beds, especially in the hardest-pressed inner city areas. But we also need more community mental health services, and to invest in a comprehensive range of inpatient and community services that work together in flexible and integrated ways.

(Lee and Bradley, 2000, p. 31)

Reflection exercises

1.Hospital services
Exercise for all workers

Imagine you are going into an acute hospital after some sort of medical emergency:

- How would you and your family be feeling at the point of admission?
- How would you like to be treated by staff?
- What aspects of hospital provision would you value the most – access to high quality care? The attitude of staff? The cleanliness of wards? The food? The comfort of your stay?
- How might all these impact on your health and your confidence?
- When the time came to go home, how would you feel about leaving hospital?
- What sort of support might you want to be available for you in the community?

Now, imagine you are being admitted to an acute psychiatric hospital and consider the same questions.

2. Hospital services
Exercise for hospital staff

- What would it feel like being a person with a mental health problem being admitted to your hospital?
- Would you be happy for you or a family member to be a patient in your hospital?
- What is good about the service you currently offer?
- What would you like to change about your hospital to make things better for users and carers?
- What would you like to change to make things better for staff?

3. Hospital services
Exercise for community staff

- How much contact do you have with local acute services?
- Do you know the staff there and what the hospital is like for patients?
- What do former patients on your caseload say about local hospital services?
- How would you feel if it were you being admitted to hospital?
- If you know relatively little about acute care, would it be possible to visit and shadow a member of hospital staff?
- What could you do as an individual to improve things for users and carers?

Suggestions for further reading

1. Information about the Sainsbury Centre for Mental Health's *Acute Solutions* Project is available via www.scmh.org.uk and via a series of project publications (Sainsbury Centre for Mental Health, 1998b, 2002b–d).
2. Watson's (2001) inspection of compulsory mental health admissions for the Social Services Inspectorate sets out a series of standards around responsive services, assessment and admissions, care planning and care management, inter-agency collaboration, anti-discriminatory practice, staff development and training, and organisation and management. The final report is also accompanied by a short leaflet outlining key themes from the inspection and providing good practice guidance.
3. The Commission for Health Improvement's (2003a) report on *What CHI has found in mental health trusts* summarises key findings from recent inspections with particular emphasis on capacity, staffing, information, partnership working, safety and user perspectives.
4. The Department of Health's *Mental health policy implementation guide: acute adult inpatient care provision* reviews current problems with acute care and makes a series of recommendations about future policy and practice (Rooney, 2002). An additional guide focuses on education, training and continuing professional development (Clarke, 2004).
5. Above all, however, the user-centred accounts of hospital services cited in this chapter give a clear indication of users' priorities for change and provide very powerful and graphic descriptions of people's experiences as inpatients (see, for example, Sainsbury Centre for Mental Health, 1998b; Baker, 2000; Goodwin *et al.*, 1999).

6 Forensic Mental Health Services

Mental health and risk

There is a common misconception among many members of the public, often reinforced by the media, that mental health is equated with dangerousness and with crime. A good example of this process is the 'not in my back yard' approach, whereby many people recognise the need to move away from institutional forms of care, but resist attempts to locate new hospital or community services near to where they live (see also Chapter 5). More recently, we have also witnessed an enormous public outcry about the presence of people with personality disorders, who have typically been portrayed as 'fiends' and 'perverts' (Markham, 2000, p. 28). That such fears are not always well founded on fact and an accurate assessment of risk is demonstrated by events in South Wales, where a children's doctor was hounded out of her home because neighbours confused 'paediatrician' with 'paedophile' (Hall, 2001).

At its most extreme, a key image is of the 'axe-wielding maniac' or the 'crazed madman' waiting on street corners to assault or murder the unsuspecting passer-by (see Figure 6.1). Research suggests that two-thirds of all British press and television coverage of mental health includes a link with violence, while around 40 per cent of daily tabloids and nearly half of the Sunday tabloids contained derogatory references like 'nutter' and 'loony' (ODPM, 2004, p. 26). In the UK, moreover, media stereotypes have been fuelled by some very high profile and brutal murders, for example of Jonathan Zito and Megan and Lin Russell. While such human tragedies are terrible events they are not representative cases (as evidenced by the substantial media coverage

Figure 6.1	Violence, mental health and the media

Violence is firmly linked to mental illness in media coverage in both the US and UK, and also in New Zealand where, for example, journalists reported a 1996 mass murder in Tasmania in terms of the probable psychiatric disorder of the perpetrator. The fact, when it emerged, that he had no mental illness did not receive a similar degree of media attention (Mental Health Commission, 1997). Different specific 'panics' have emerged in different countries, states and cities, often attaching the fear of madness to other potent concerns of the moment: violence in the workplace – almost none of which is in fact perpetrated by people with mental health problems – an American panic fuelled by one heavily publicised case of a 'crazed' Post Office employee who turned a gun on colleagues; infanticide – a Chicago panic, stemming from the killing of a child by a woman with mental health problems, which exacerbated concerns about the safety of public agencies' decision making; and random street violence, a British panic, fuelled by the emblematic, but highly atypical, British case of Christopher Clunis, a man with mental health problems who killed a total stranger in a London Underground station.

In different localities, 'stories' emerge and succeed each other in varying patterns, not in line with actual trends in crime or other social phenomena but according to subtler cultural shifts. Some countries have a stronger record in including positive 'stories': in Italy, the push for 'democratic psychiatry' enabled users to appear somewhat heroic, of interest for their successes in getting out of institutions rather than for more 'demonic' qualities (Ramon, 1996). British and American experiences are not, however, unique, and globalisation of the media is likely to make 'stories' increasingly international, as framed by more influential nations. This could mean a spread of moral panics – rather as movie watchers internationally are influenced by American films, which make frequent links between madness and violence.

(Wahl, 1995, in Sayce, 2000, p. 7)

which they received). They do, however, raise pertinent and important questions about the nature of risk and the role of risk assessment.

Despite public concerns, there is substantial evidence to suggest that the association between violence and mental health is weak:

1. Very few people with mental health problems commit homicides (perhaps 40 or 50 instances each year) (see Taylor and Gunn, 1999 for all statistics in this paragraph). While this is clearly 40 or 50 cases too many, it should be compared to other risks (for example, some 600 to 700 people are murdered each year, there are an additional 300 deaths from dangerous driving and some 3500 to 4000 deaths per year in road accidents). As Taylor and Gunn (1999, p. 13) suggest:

   On average, every week someone in the UK wins the jackpot on the National Lottery. About 54,999,999 people do not. On average, rather less than one person a week loses their life to a person with mental illness, generally his/her mother, father, sibling, spouse, child or other close contact; 54,999,999 remain safe from this threat.

2. Most homicides carried out by people with mental health problems are committed against family members or people they already know. According to the National Confidential Inquiry into Suicide and Homicide (Department of Health, 2001a, pp. 6, 97), around one-third of the 1579 homicides between 1996 and 1999 were of family members or spouses/partners and another third of acquaintances. However, mentally ill perpetrators were less likely to kill a stranger than those without mental illness.
3. While mental health is a factor in a small number of deaths, others factors such as substance misuse may be much more significant (Swanson *et al.*, 1990; Steadman *et al.*, 1998; Walsh *et al.*, 2002; Walsh and Fahy, 2002). This is often referred to as dual diagnosis (see *further reading* at the end of this chapter for more information) and is frequently a key factor in mental health homicide inquiries.
4. About 95 per cent of violent crime is committed by people without mental health problems (Sayce, 2000, p. 33).
5. People with mental health problems are more likely to be the victims rather than the perpetrators of crime (Jewesbury, 1998; McCabe and Ford, 2001; ODPM, 2004; Sayce, 1997, 1999).
6. Between 1957 and 1995, there has been little fluctuation in the number of people with mental health problems committing homicide, but their contribution to the overall homicide rate has been falling by three per cent annually (Taylor and Gunn, 1999). Thus, as more and more people were being discharged from long-stay hospitals, the homicide rate for people with mental health problems actually fell.

In addition, we know from the wider literature that people with mental health problems in the UK face considerable discrimination, financial poverty and social exclusion (see Chapters 4 and 9), factors which are known to contribute to criminal activity in the wider population. Moreover, some people with mental health problems probably commit some crimes knowing that what they are doing is illegal – in such situations, the criminal activity may be little different from crimes committed by people without mental health problems and should be punished through the criminal justice system. According to Sayce (2000, p. 226), therefore, there are a number of key messages which we need to test out on the public and the media:

■ Most crime is committed by people without mental health problems
■ People with mental health problems often commit crimes for the same reasons as everyone else (poverty, drink and drugs, family/relationship frustrations)
■ It is extremely rare for people with mental health problems to attack someone they don't know

- People with mental health problems are more often victims than perpetrators of crime
- People with mental health problems can usually be held responsible for their crimes

A final consideration with regard to mental health and risk is the difficulty (if not the impossibility) of predicting risk. Whilst violence is rare and while services may try their best to take into account issues of risk when assessing patients, it is difficult to predict risk with any degree of accuracy. A key finding from a range of mental health enquiries has been that many violent incidents committed by people with mental health problems have been hard to predict. As Peck (quoted in Chamberlain, 1998, p. 2) observes:

> The assessment of risk and dangerousness is an art not a science and a difficult art which requires practitioners to balance past and present behaviour with predictions of interventions and the civil liberties of the patient.

Further details about risk assessment and different predictive tools are pro-vided by Blumenthal and Lavender (2000) in their review of violence and mental disorder.

The 'mad' v 'bad' debate

When someone commits a crime that the public finds particularly hard to understand, an immediate response is often to question if the person concerned is either 'mad' or 'bad': did they behave as they did because they are 'evil', or are they experiencing some form of mental health problem? Whereas many would see the need to punish the 'bad', they may often feel that someone with a mental health problem may not have been 'in their right mind' and hence not responsible for their action. As a result, such a person should receive treatment and care in the health service, rather than punishment in prison.

In practice, such distinctions are sometimes hard to make. This is particu-larly the case when the crime is horrific and difficult to comprehend. Examples include infamous figures such as Ian Brady and Myra Hindley, Harold Shipman and Ian Huntley. However, such crimes are so hard to imagine that it is difficult to know with any certainty what caused the person to do what they did (i.e. 'evil' or mental illness). In the case of Ian Huntley, convicted of murdering the schoolgirls Holly Wells and Jessica Chapman, it was suggested that Huntley may have a mental health problem. As a result, he was sectioned under the Mental Health Act and underwent assessment at a high security hospital (Press Association, 2003). At the end of this process, Huntley was assessed as not having a mental health problem, was sent to prison to await trial (Hall, 2002) and convicted of murder.

In Huntley's case, there was a suggestion in the media, either explicit or implicit, that this was deliberate behaviour (that Huntley was 'putting it on' to avoid prison) and that the mental health system 'found him out' (by assessing him as capable of standing trial). Clearly, this was an extreme case, but it does illustrate the profound importance of the mental health assessment, as someone with a mental health problem assessed as not responsible for their actions will 'escape' prison and be treated in a health rather than a penal setting. Of course, whether entering the mental health system in such circumstances is an 'escape' is a moot point. Arguably, the stigma of using forensic mental health services is so significant that many would consider it worse than the stigma of having been in prison (for example, it would be talked about by the neighbours or may lead to discrimination in the workplace in just the same way as a previous criminal conviction, if not more so). However, the fact remains that the initial assessment is crucial to establish why someone acted as they did, whether or not they were responsible for their actions and what should happen to them next.

Forensic mental health services

While the association between mental health problems and violent crime is vastly overstated in the public imagination, there is a small minority of people with serious mental health problems who do pose a risk to the public and who do commit crimes, sometimes very serious ones. Although high quality primary care, community and hospital services will be sufficient to meet the needs of many people with mental health problems, there may always be a small group of people who require even greater levels of support and supervision than is possible in these settings. These people fall under the remit of forensic mental health services. As McFadyen (1999, pp. 1436–7) explains:

> Forensic mental health services deal with those mentally ill people whose presentation has been assessed as requiring a more focused level of expertise and/or increased levels of physical security. Some of these people will have exhibited behaviours which present major challenges, with or without associated violent conduct, beyond the capabilities of general psychiatric services. Others will be mentally disordered offenders who have broken the law or who are deemed to have the propensity to do so. Some patients will have been identified at the level of general NHS psychiatric services and some via the criminal justice system. Of the latter, some will be on remand... Others, however, will be convicted prisoners... who are subsequently transferred from prison during the course of their penal sentence.

From this initial quote, a number of key issues are immediately apparent that are explored in more detail later in this chapter:

- Forensic mental health services are extremely complex, with many different routes in and a wide range of service users
- Forensic services potentially involve a large number of agencies (such as health care, social care, probation and the prison service)
- By definition, forensic services will be working with people who may display extremely challenging behaviour and who may have been found to be too difficult to work with in other settings prior to their referral to forensic care

This complexity and difficulty is captured by McCann (1999, p. 65), whose account of forensic mental health services seeks to summarise current developments in the organisation and delivery of care:

> Mentally disordered offenders, the recipients of forensic care, are a diverse group. They span the range of mental health problems and diagnoses, and the spectrum of criminal offences. Often their needs are complex and involve a number of agencies, requiring a co-ordinated and collaborative approach across service and professional boundaries. Invariably there is also an element of political or media interest; depending on the degree of dangerousness or notoriety of the offence, decisions about an individual's care will be made in a climate of intense scrutiny. This pressure on services to make the 'right' decisions, often with inadequate information, places professionals in a vulnerable position, both clinically and personally. It is understandable therefore that professionals are cautious, treading carefully the narrow path between their roles as therapist and custodian. Generally however the needs of mentally disordered offenders are no different to any other individual with mental health problems, and they require access to a similar range of services.

As McCann (1999) continues, forensic mental health services are typically divided into three different categories depending on the level of service users' needs:

1. Low security services tend to be based near general psychiatric wards in NHS hospitals, but often have higher staffing ratios.
2. Medium secure services often operate on a regional basis and usually consist of a number of locked wards with a greater number and a wider range of staff.
3. High security services are provided by the three special hospitals (Ashworth, Broadmoor and Rampton). These are characterised by much greater levels of security and care for people with mental health problems who pose an immediate and serious risk to others.

In addition, a range of new services are slowly being developed to meet the needs of mentally disordered offenders in the community, either with a forensic specialist working with a community mental health team (an *integrated* model) or with forensic specialists working as a separate specialist team (a *parallel* model) (Judge *et al.*, 2004; Mohan *et al.*, 2004).

In recent years, there have been a number of official reviews of forensic mental health care, which have emphasised a range of principles that should underpin forensic services. Despite this, many aspects of current policy are still based on a series of longstanding principles first articulated in the early 1990s as part of Reed Report (Department of Health/Home Office, 1992, p. 7). This states that services should be provided:

- With regard to the quality of care and proper attention to the needs of individuals
- As far as possible, in the community, rather than institutional settings
- Under conditions of no greater security than are justified by the degree of danger they present to themselves or others
- In such a way as to maximise rehabilitation and the chances of sustaining an independent life
- As near as possible to their own homes or families, if they have them

Another key theme within official policy has been the need to divert people with mental health problems away from the criminal justice system towards the NHS so that their needs can be more appropriately met (Home Office, 1990). This can happen at a number of key stages, including on arrest, during interview, after a court appearance or while on remand/bail. Although this has long been a key feature of forensic mental health services and although specialist diversion schemes tend to be well-regarded by the police and other agencies, there is on-going evidence of a failure to identify and refer suspects and prisoners with mental health problems and concerns about the experience of people with mental health problems within the criminal justice system, both as suspects and as witnesses (see, for example, Independent Police Complaints Commission, 2004; Thompson *et al.*, 2004; Watson, 1997).

In many ways, the literature on forensic mental health services is very similar to that reviewed in other chapters of this book. As with hospital services, there is considerable evidence to suggest that many people in forensic mental health services may be inappropriately placed and many of the issues highlighted in Chapter 5 with regard to inpatient care apply equally here. At the same time, delivering effective forensic services requires a high degree of partnership working, a topic discussed in greater detail in Chapter 7. Forensic mental health services may also raise particular issues with regard to gender and ethnicity (topics covered in more depth in Chapter 9). In many ways, indeed, forensic services are at the 'extreme' end of the mental health spectrum, and any findings from general psychiatric services will probably apply to an even greater extent in forensic mental health, where the issues at stake are even more complex and high profile. To supplement this material, the remainder of this chapter explores three key issues in further detail:

- The level of unmet mental health needs in prison
- The level of inappropriate placements in secure services
- The need for greater partnership working

Unmet mental health needs in prison

Despite the official commitment to divert people with mental health problems away from the criminal justice system, there is widespread evidence to suggest that there are a large number of people with unmet mental health needs in prison, both on remand and as sentenced prisoners (see Figure 6.2). According to official figures, around 90 per cent of the 140,000-strong prison population have a diagnosable mental illness, substance abuse problem or, often, both (see, for example, Department of Health/HM Prison Service/National Assembly for Wales, 2001, p. 3). It is thought that the prison service spends around half its £90 million health care budget on mental health services (p. 25). For young people, the numbers are even higher, with 95 per cent of offenders under the age of 21 having a mental health or substance abuse problem (p. 3). According to a Youth Justice Board report (n.d.), moreover, 48 per cent of young offenders surveyed often felt

Figure 6.2	Mental health needs in prison

Although the reasons behind the high level of mental health needs in prison are probably many and varied, it is possible that the current state of affairs is the result, at least in part, of the current commitment to community care. As Polczyk-Przybyla and Gournay (1999, pp. 894–5) explain:

Prison psychiatry in England… has undergone a transformation in the last decade. The introduction of Care in the Community has had the effect of making an acute psychiatric bed more difficult to find and therefore admissions to general psychiatric inpatient care tend to be on an emergency basis. This has resulted… in the numbers of people with serious mental illness in the prison population growing at an increasing rate… The increase in numbers [of people with mental health problems] in the English prison system has meant that there are more inmates needing transfer to secure hospital accommodation…. Prior to these circumstances the main function of psychiatric services in [prison health care centres] was to provide immediate crisis intervention and to facilitate early transfer to an establishment that could deliver the necessary treatment. Although these roles are still necessary, [prison health care centres] now have to engage and treat the seriously mentally ill for longer periods and in some cases meet individuals' treatment requirements indefinitely.

sad or miserable, 24 per cent had problems eating or sleeping, 10 per cent had deliberately hurt themselves and 11 per cent had thought about killing themselves.

Clearly, such findings raise serious questions about the role that prisons may be being asked to play in caring for people with mental health problems and the extent to which prison staff are equipped to fulfil this role. While a detailed consideration of prison health care is beyond the scope of this book, studies such as that carried out by Reed and Lyne (2000) suggest that many health care workers in prisons lack specific mental health training and that the quality of care may be far below standards in the NHS. In addition, it is important to remember that prisons are potentially very different from hospitals (even high security hospitals) and may have very different cultures and values (Gunn, 2000). That this is the case is increasingly recognised by policy makers, who acknowledge that (Department of Health/HM Prison Service/National Assembly for Wales, 2001, p. 9; see also Figure 6.3):

> Developing effective and appropriate mental health services for people in prison is an enormously challenging agenda. The level of need is very high – surveys conducted by the Office for National Statistics in 1997 indicated that nine out of every ten prisoners have at least one of the five disorders considered in the survey (neurosis, psychosis, personality disorder, alcohol abuse or drug dependency). Between 12%–15% of sentenced prisoners have four of the five. We have a duty to provide proper care and treatment for prisoners, but prisons are struggling to do so in a custodial setting that is neither specifically designed nor primarily intended for this purpose. Equally, the Prison Service is not resourced to provide a full mental health service, and is therefore reliant on the NHS to provide the specialist services which are beyond its own capacity.

In response, there have been a number of key policy initiatives developed to improve prison health care. These include (Department of Health, 2004d; Department of Health/HM Prison Service/National Assembly for Wales, 2001, 2002):

■ *Changing the Outlook* (a joint Department of Health/Prison Service programme to improve mental health care in prisons). This includes the need for all prisons and their local NHS partners to carry out a detailed review of mental health needs, identify gaps in provision and develop action plans to fill these gaps. Chapter 3 of this document – *a vision for the service* – sets out government expectations about prison mental health, including the need to promote mental health, provide access to primary care services, commence/continue the CPA for prisoners with mental health problems, provide access to appropriate day care and inpatient services, ensure speedy transfer to NHS facilities when required and prevent suicides

- A mental health in–reach collaborative (to bring together NHS and Prison Service partners to improve mental health provision, share good practice and learn from each other)
- PCTs to be given responsibility for health care in their local prisons, initially in 18 'trailblazers' sites from April 2004, with front line responsibility for prison health in all English prisons to transfer to local PCTs by April 2006

Figure 6.3	Safer prisons

That unmet mental health problems exist in prison is suggested by the National Confidential Inquiry into Suicides and Homicides by People with Mental Illness, which carried out a study into prison suicides (Shaw *et al.*, 2003). Of 172 suicides between 1999 and 2000, 157 were studied:

- Thirty (21 per cent) people were known to have been victims of bullying
- Thirty-two (21 per cent) did not take part in any prison activities
- Fifty-seven (42 per cent) had received no visits prior to death
- Nineteen (18 per cent) had experienced a recent family bereavement or terminal illness in a family member
- One hundred and ten (72 per cent) had at least one psychiatric diagnosis
- Ninety-five (62 per cent) had a history of drug misuse
- Forty-six (31 per cent) had a history of alcohol misuse
- Seventy-eight (53 per cent) had a history of self-harm
- Eighty-nine (57 per cent) had symptoms of psychiatric disturbance on reception to prison
- Forty-six (30 per cent) had a history of contact with NHS mental health services

While many of these people had been referred to a health professional, admitted to the prison health care inpatient unit or placed on medium or high levels of observation, there were a number of concerns. For example:

- It was unusual for information to be requested from a GP or from mental health services
- Fifteen per cent had no further contact with health care staff after reception
- Twenty-two (15 per cent) suicides were seen by health staff as preventable
- There were a range of antecedents, including expressions of suicidal ideas, deliberate self-harm, adverse life events, bullying, bereavement and family/ relationship problems
- In seven cases a transfer to an NHS hospital was awaited
- Between 1996 and 2000, 354 people died within a year following release from prison. Eighty (23 per cent) died within the first month following release, suggesting the need for better follow-up in the community

Altogether, 141 (90 per cent) of the 157 suicides in this study could have been seen as 'at risk' at reception to prison because of a history of previous NHS mental health care, a lifetime history of mental disorder, current symptoms, current treatment, a history of drug misuse, alcohol misuse or self-harm (p. 43).

The level of inappropriate placements in secure services

An additional factor that may contribute to high levels of unmet mental health needs in prison may be an inappropriate use of existing bed capacity in secure services (see Figure 6.4). According to a number of commentators, somewhere between 37 and 75 per cent of patients in maximum security hospitals may not need the services provided there (see, for example, Coid

Figure 6.4	Inappropriate placements in secure services

Acute psychiatric units are serving an increasing number of more severely disturbed patients detained under sections of the Mental Health Act of 1983... Patients whose needs cannot be met within local acute care units often have to wait several weeks before transfer to a more secure environment. Access to appropriate care and treatment may require recourse to expensive and often private out-of-area placements many miles from the patient's home and family. Other patients may become 'stuck' in high security placements that were suitable at the time of referral but have become inappropriate for their current needs. Their move to a less restrictive placement may be delayed, often for a considerable time, due to the scarcity of suitable accommodation at lower levels of security (Badger *et al.*, 1999, p. 1625).

Surveys have suggested that between 37 per cent and 67 per cent of patients do not need maximum-security provision... and that delays largely come about because of inadequate provision of catchment area resources and a reluctance or delay on the part of the Home Office in agreeing to transfer (Coid and Kahtan, 2000, p. 18).

[The inappropriate placement of people in medium secure units is extremely expensive]. However the financial cost is just part of the problem. The cost to individual patients in terms of unnecessary incarceration and all that entails should not be ignored. Absence of appropriate and adequate community facilities means many people are inappropriately detained in medium secure units who could otherwise be enjoying more fulfilled lives in the community. This also has a knock-on effect on others in the chain. People are kept inappropriately in high security hospitals because there are no medium secure beds available, and people in prison with mental health care needs are left untreated because available high security beds are similarly blocked (McIntyre, 1999, p. 382).

Research shows that between 50 and 75 per cent of patients in high secure care do not require that level of security, and remain there because the long-term medium secure care more appropriate to their needs is not currently available. This need for long-term medium secure care has also been identified as a problem for patients in medium secure care, and there is a shortage of medium secure beds generally because of the high rate of admissions from prisons and courts. There are few studies looking at the needs of patients in low secure care, but those that have been carried out indicate a knock-on effect, in that pressures in one part of the system create pressures in others. This acknowledged lack of medium and low secure beds, particularly long-term beds, has resulted in a number of Department of Health initiatives to estimate levels of need in order to address gaps in provision (McCann, 1999, p. 66).

and Kahtan, 2000; McCann, 1999; McKenna *et al.*, 1999; Vaughan, 1999). In North Yorkshire, Dabbs and Isherwood (2000) describe substantial delays in admitting patients to low secure services from medium security or from prison due to a lack of alternative services for long-stay (non-forensic) patients unable to be managed in general psychiatric rehabilitation units. In the North-West, ten per cent of admissions to a psychiatric intensive care unit were due to the lack of appropriate facilities elsewhere (Dolan and Lawson, 2001), while only 45 per cent of patients in a medium secure unit were found to be appropriately placed (McIntyre, 1999). Difficulties discharging patients to lower levels of security can also make it harder to admit patients, and there is evidence to suggest that some secure services are beginning to develop increasingly long waiting lists or to refuse to admit patients requiring long-term support (see, for example, Gunn and Maden, 1998; Melzer *et al.*, 2004).

When capacity problems occur, patients have to wait for long periods of time to access the services most appropriate for their needs and increasing use is made of independent sector provision (Coid *et al.*, 2001; Lelliott *et al.*, 2001; Polczyk-Przybyla and Gournay, 1999), often some distance away from the area in which the individual concerned lives. This is not only expensive, but also contravenes the stated aim of supporting service users in their own homes or under conditions of no greater security than are justified by the degree of danger they present to themselves or others. As McIntyre (1999, p. 382) observes:

> The inappropriate placement of people in … secure services has long been recognised. The need to develop services that more appropriately meet the needs of these people… has similarly long been recognised. However progress is slow… Absence of [alternative service provision] represents a significant drain on precious financial resources; it forces people needlessly and without clinical justification to be required to live in conditions of significant security and curtailment of liberty, potentially in breach of civil rights. It has to be asked how much longer this will continue unchallenged.

The need for greater partnership working

As highlighted at the start of this chapter, the provision of effective mental health services requires a wide range of agencies to work closely together (see also Figure 6.5). While the more general issue of partnership working in health and social care is discussed in detail in Chapter 7, the literature highlights considerable barriers that will need to be overcome if successful partnerships are to be developed and sustained in forensic mental health. A good example is provided by Vaughan *et al.* (2000), whose study of community teams providing support to mentally disordered offenders in Wessex found that this user group had complex

Figuro 6.5	Partnership working in forensic mental health

The system of care for offenders with mental disorders in the United Kingdom has developed piecemeal over the years, and responsibilities have been divided between the criminal justice system, the National Health Service, and ... social services departments. The specialised secure facilities have also evolved in an ad hoc way throughout the country, without standardised models of service delivery (Badger *et al.*, 1999, p. 627).

In this survey, most community services were not organised in a way that facilitates contact with mentally disordered offenders, who tend to shun services. For the most part, teams... operate within their own strict boundaries and there is a general reluctance to work with other client groups. Each group has its own distinctive cohort of mentally disordered offenders but often cannot meet all of their needs due to limitations within each service. Because of the compartmentalised nature of the services, gaining access to a wider range of skills is difficult. Accordingly, many mentally disordered offenders are denied a comprehensive range of interventions and sometimes get only partial help for their problems (Vaughan *et al.*, 2000, p. 583).

and multiple needs which often fell outside the range of skills and services that individual teams could offer. As a result, community mental health teams felt de-skilled, unsupported and frustrated by the reluctance of some support services to accept referrals for this group. Team members also highlighted a lack of inter-agency communication and co-operation, with each agency reluctant to accept ownership of mentally disordered offenders. From the perspective of probation teams, however, mental health services were seen as difficult to access, slow to respond and poor at sharing information. As a result, many individual teams adopted something of a 'siege mentality', with teams reluctant to offer a service to people outside their normal referral criteria and spending a significant amount of time disputing responsibility for 'borderline' cases (pp. 580–1). Neither probation nor the community mental health team had formal links with special hospitals or the local medium secure unit, and the community mental health team had no formal relationship with the prison service. As a result, teams often relied on the discretion of individual workers to make contact with these institutions and there was little continuity of care or sharing of information as individual users moved through services.

Overall, it is clear that there is still a long way to go before forensic mental health services achieve the principles set out at the beginning of this chapter.

In response to findings such as these, a number of health and social care communities are developing new models of service provision (see Figure 6.6). However, core to most responses is a recognition that the issues at stake are so fundamental that only a whole systems approach will suffice (see also Chapters 4, 5 and 7 for similar findings). Thus, for Maguire (1999, p. 21), there is a need for 'a clear pathway from the point of entry into a service, through to the point of discharge, incorporating community and mainstream mental health services'. Future services could then include:

- High and medium secure acute assessment and treatment services
- High and medium secure long-stay provision
- A broad spectrum of inpatient forensic rehabilitation services
- Community based forensic teams
- Community based work facilities
- Support staff to provide services to prisons and local hospitals

A similar argument is put forward by Markham (2000, p. 31), who advocates an integrated approach based on:

- A range of local services appropriate to patient needs
- Services which enable patients to move through the system on rehabilitation pathways, with an absence of artificial blocks and barriers
- Better links between specialist forensic services and comprehensive mental health services
- Easy access to specialist skills and individual care packages
- The potential to build partnerships with the independent sector
- Links to social care and criminal justice systems, built at all levels

For McFadyen (1999, p. 1438), there is a clear need for 'a spectrum of services in order to allow provision of the appropriate response to any given situation at the appropriate time'. Unfortunately, such a 'spectrum' may be a long way from fruition in some areas, with a range of on-going pressures preventing a more holistic approach from being developed. As an example, Coid and Dunn (2004) describe a forensic mental health system in one health and social care community only able to respond reactively to referrals from other agencies, making no sessional commitments to probation services, prisons or court diversion schemes, providing no dedicated aftercare, relying heavily on private sector provision, accumulating growing waiting lists and unable to reduce the number of people detained in maximum security hospitals who no longer require this level of supervision. Overall, therefore, there remains a strong sense of the necessary direction of travel but a recognition that much more remains to be done.

Figuro 6.6	Possible solutions and good practice examples

Cohen *et al.* (1999) describe the role of a mental health worker attached to a probation service in London. This project uncovered significant unmet mental health needs and helped to bridge the gap between the criminal justice and mental health systems. Other schemes that seek to improve joint working between mental health and the criminal justice system are described by Telfer (2000) and Vanderwall (1997).

Geelan *et al.* (2000) have evaluated a specialised approved bail and probation hostel for mentally disordered offenders (Elliott House in Birmingham). Many traditional bail hostels are reluctant to offer support to people with mental health problems, and the authors concluded that Elliott House demonstrates how a close partnership between probation and forensic mental health services can deliver effective care to a previously marginalised group. Another example of partnership working between probation and forensic services is provided by Nadkarni *et al.* (2000), who describe a partnership to provide specialist psychiatric services to a bail hostel in Newcastle.

Lart's (1997) study of an innovative multi-agency project in Winchester prison (the Wessex Project) outlines how workers were able to identify prisoners with mental health problems and develop co-ordinated packages of care on their release using the CPA.

McFadyen (1999) advocates the creation of forensic, liaison, emergency and assessment teams (FLEATs) to carry out assessments on those identified as potentially mentally disordered offenders, recommend appropriate placements and liaise with the mental health and criminal justice systems. In the same article, the author also recommends in-reach and through-care services (IRTCs) to provide NHS psychiatric care to remand and sentenced prisoners.

Weaver *et al.* (1997a, 1997b) report findings from a pilot unit set up to provide rapid assessment of remand prisoners and to increase the speed of their transfer from prison to NHS care where a need is identified.

Whittle and Scally (1998) call for integrated community forensic teams.

Conclusion

Overall, there is clear evidence of a need for reform in forensic mental health services. With the wrong people in the wrong settings at the wrong time, there are considerable unmet mental health needs in prison, inappropriate placements in secure services and insufficient inter-agency collaboration to provide the spectrum of services necessary to resolve this situation. Despite these unequivocal findings, however, our knowledge of forensic mental health services is limited by a number of shortcomings in the literature contained in this chapter:

■ Most material is very descriptive in nature, examining the characteristics of the patient population in various secure settings but failing to

to respond to the *giant* of 'want' by paying social security benefits to people with low incomes, disabled people, the unemployed and older people via the Department of Social Security (now the Department for Work and Pensions).

Of course, the problem with this way of organising services is that it does not necessarily take account of the complexity and the overlapping nature of many social problems (see reflection exercise 1 at the end of this chapter). Thus, many people living in poverty will also live in poor housing in deprived areas and may also experience poor education services, unemployment and ill health. This complexity can be problematic for a number of reasons:

- Some problems are so multi-faceted that services need to work together to make any inroads at all. Thus, no one service is able to tackle crime and disorder, prevent social exclusion, eradicate substance misuse or tackle teenage pregnancy – these are all issues that require a number of agencies to co-operate and pool their respective resources and expertise to provide even a partial solution
- There is scope for considerable duplication of effort and a waste of scarce resources. Thus, one family with a child who has been in trouble with the police, in the local community and at school might receive input from a large number of welfare agencies, including the education system, the police, social services, the housing department, the youth offending team, the local regeneration initiative, child and adolescent mental health, a behaviour support team, special educational needs services, the youth service, and so. With such a large array of services, there is clearly scope for some sort of co-ordination to provide a more appropriate and less labour intensive input to this one family
- At the same time, there is scope for services to fail to meet the needs of particular individuals. There are many instances of this in the UK, but examples would include a high profile child death in which police, education, social services and the NHS failed to work together or to share information (see Figure 7.2), or a frail older person who is considered too sick for social services, but not ill enough to require NHS care

Put simply, people tend not to live their lives according to the categories we create in our welfare services.

In addition, there is a common tendency to conceive of the welfare state solely in terms of the public sector. However, this ignores the fact that we have always had a mixed economy of care in which welfare is provided by a range of different groups and organisations:

- By family, friends and neighbours (the informal sector)
- By voluntary organisations and self-help groups (the voluntary and community sector)
- By private companies (the private sector)
- By the state (the public sector)

Figure 7.2	Failures to work together

In 2003, Lord Laming published the results of an official inquiry into the death of Victoria Climbié, a young girl who had been killed by her great-aunt and her great-aunt's partner (Marie-Therese Kouoa and Karl Manning) in 2001.

In his inquiry, Lord Laming described the horrific treatment which Victoria had received (p. 1):

> At his trial, Manning said that Kouao would strike Victoria on a daily basis with a shoe, a coat hanger and a wooden cooking spoon and would strike her on her toes with a hammer. Victoria's blood was found on Manning's football boots. Manning later admitted that at times he would hit Victoria with a bicycle chain. Chillingly, he said, 'you could beat her and she wouldn't cry... she could take beatings and the pain like anything'.

Whilst a wide range of factors and mistakes contributed to Victoria's tragic death, the inquiry identified a lack of communication and poor inter-agency working between the large number of organisations who knew Victoria as key contributing factors (pp. 4, 6):

> In his opening statement to the Inquiry, Neil Garnham QC listed no fewer than 12 key occasions when the relevant services had the opportunity to successfully intervene in the life of Victoria.

> Not one of the agencies empowered by Parliament to protect children in positions similar to Victoria – funded from the public purse – emerge from this Inquiry with much credit. The suffering and death of Victoria was a gross failure of the system and was inexcusable.

> The single most important change in the future must be the drawing of a clear line of accountability, from top to bottom, without doubt or ambiguity about who is responsible at every level for the well-being of vulnerable children. Time and again it was disappointing to listen to the "buck passing" from those who attempted to justify their positions.

Thus, in the nineteenth century local authorities were responsible for the water supply, sewage and sanitation, while voluntary agencies offered services such as community nursing services, befriending and financial assistance to the poor. GPs at this time were private practitioners who charged a fee for their services, and a lot of support was provided by neighbours and communities. In the twenty-first century, this is little different (although the balance of services has shifted in favour of the state and health care is now free at the point of delivery): in older people's services, for example, the state funds and provides health care, voluntary organisations such as Age Concern provide lunch clubs and meals services, the private sector operates a range of home care services and residential homes and family and friends provide considerable informal support. As a result, when we talk about the need to work in partnership, this often refers not only to public sector agencies, but also to partnerships across the mixed economy of care.

The health and social care divide

In response, successive governments have sought to encourage services to work more effectively together, both across agency boundaries (such as health care, social care and housing) and across sectors (public, private and voluntary). This is true in a range of different services, but is particularly the case in health and social care (which are often seen as two sides of the same coin and inextricably interlinked). Traditionally, the post–war welfare state is based on the assumption that it is possible to distinguish between people who are sick (health needs) and those who are merely frail or disabled (social care needs). This was enshrined in two pieces of 1940s legislation (the *NHS Act* 1946 and the *National Assistance Act* 1948) and continues to form the basis of service provision in the early twenty-first century (Glasby and Littlechild, 2004). As a result, two separate systems have developed, each with different ways of working, different structures and different priorities (see Figure 7.3).

Figure 7.3	The health and social care divide

Key features of social care include:

- Councillors democratically elected at a local level
- Local government is overseen and monitored by the Office of the Deputy Prime Minister (although the Department of Health has a significant role in the oversight and monitoring of social services departments)
- Subject to means-testing and charges
- Based on specific geographical areas
- Traditional focus on social factors contributing to individual situations and on choice/empowerment
- Strong emphasis on social sciences

Key features of NHS care include:

- Non-executive directors appointed by central government
- Overseen and monitored by the Department of Health
- Free at the point of delivery
- Boundaries are based on GP practice registration (at the time of writing)
- Traditional emphasis on the individual and on medical cure
- Strong emphasis on science

(Glasby and Peck, 2003, p. 2)

Of these, perhaps the most significant difference for members of the public is that health care tends to be provided free at the point of delivery, while social care tends to be subject to a means-test and to charges (which are sometimes very significant). Thus, whether something is defined as health or as social care can be extremely significant for the individual concerned and their family.

More recently, this state of affairs has been recognised as problematic for a number of key reasons:

1. The distinction between health and social care can often appear rather abstract and arbitrary. A famous example is the provision of bathing services: if the bath is for a 'health' reason (such as a skin condition or if the person has specialist lifting and handling requirements), they may receive a bath from the NHS free of charge; if it is simply a 'social' bath then this will be provided by social services and the person will have to pay. Arguably this is a distinction which may not seem very meaningful to the service user (who simply wants a bath, irrespective of who provides it) (Glasby and Littlechild, 2004).
2. Different professionals bring different skills and experiences which, if combined, could lead to a much better, more holistic service. This is often encapsulated in the notion that the whole is frequently greater than the sum of its parts.
3. Considerable time and energy can be expended in deciding whether a particular case is the responsibility of health or of social care, when a more efficient use of resources may be to work together to avoid such 'turf wars'.
4. When resources are scarce, there is a tendency for eligibility criteria for services to be restricted. In such a situation, overstretched departments have a vested interest in trying to define individual cases as the responsibility of the other agency (often known as buck-passing or cost shunting). As an example, it is not uncommon for people with learning difficulties and mental health problems to be passed backwards and forwards between mental health and learning difficulty services, with each agency feeling that the other is responsible for the person concerned (see also Chapter 9).

As the Department of Health (1998c, p. 3) suggests:

All too often when people have complex needs spanning both health and social care good quality services are sacrificed for sterile arguments about boundaries. When this happens people, often the most vulnerable in our society... and those who care for them find themselves in the no man's land between health and social services. This is not what people want or need. It places the needs of the organisation above the needs of the people they are there to serve.

It is poor organisation, poor practice, poor use of taxpayers' money
– it is unacceptable.

The policy context

To prevent the dangers of overly compartmentalised service provision,
successive governments have emphasised the importance of partnership
working. In the 1960s and 1970s, for example, this took the form of:

■ Joint Consultative Committees
■ Joint Care Planning teams of senior officers
■ Joint finance to enable social services to receive funding for projects
deemed to be of benefit to the health service

However, with hindsight many of these initiatives were felt to be insufficient
to resolve the issues at stake and were hindered by the relatively small amounts
of money that were involved in such joint activities (see, for example,
Hudson and Henwood, 2002; Nocon, 1994; Wistow and Fuller, 1982).
While such initiatives may have been sufficient to enable some joint working
around specific projects (for example, some of the hospital closures described
in Chapter 2), they were not sufficient to change the way in which mainstream
health and social care agencies went about their core business.

Following the passage of the *NHS and Community Care Act* 1990, there
was a firm commitment from government to achieve more co-ordinated
services through mechanisms such as care management and CPA (see
Chapters 2 and 4). Indeed, one of the key aims of the Act was to improve
co-ordination by clarifying which agency was responsible for what:

> As has been recognised in child care, it is essential that the caring
> services should work effectively together, each recognising and
> respecting the others' contribution and responsibilities. Much of
> this White Paper is about the clarification of those responsibilities.
> Nonetheless, it will continue to be essential for each of the relevant
> services to keep in mind the interests and responsibilities of the other;
> to recognise that particularly at the working interface there is much
> common purpose; to cross-refer cases when appropriate; and to seek
> and share advice and information when relevant. There is no room
> in community care for a narrow view of individuals' needs, nor of
> ways of meeting them (Department of Health, 1989a, para. 2.20).

This was re-iterated in government policy guidance (Department of Health,
1990b, para. 1.7–1.9):

> Effective local collaboration is the key to making a reality of community
> care. All the authorities and agencies which contribute to the care of

vulnerable people in their own community need to be involved in preparing and developing plans and services to meet these local needs. They need to be aware of and respect each other's roles, responsibilities and objectives and to build relationships based on this mutual under-standing and respect. The interface between health and social care is a key area in planning, assessment, care management, commissioning and service delivery... The objective must be to provide a service in which the boundaries between primary health care, secondary health care and social care do not form barriers seen from the perspective of the service user.

Despite this official rhetoric, significant divisions in health and social care remained in practice throughout the rest of the 1990s, with greater consulta-tion and liaison between health and social care, but on-going professional divisions, demarcation disputes and financial difficulties (see, for example, Hudson *et al.*, 1997; Hudson and Henwood, 2002). Since 1997, however, the election of New Labour has led to much greater emphasis on partner-ship working, with a firm commitment to developing 'joined up solutions' to 'joined up problems'. Key initiatives include:

■ The passage of the *Health Act* 1999. This places a statutory duty of part-nership on the NHS and social services and introduced three new powers to enable these partners to work together more creatively and flexibly (often known as 'the Health Act flexibilities') (see Figure 7.4)

Figure 7.4	The *Health Act* flexibilities

1. *Pooled budgets* – where health and social services put a proportion of their funds into a mutually accessible joint budget. Unlike previous joint finance initiatives, contributions lose their health or social care identity and can be used on either health or social care as appropriate. The newly created joint budget is administered by a pool manager, supervised by a committee made up of representatives from each partner agency.
2. *Lead commissioning* – where one authority transfers funds to the other who then takes responsibility for purchasing both health and social care. Services that might benefit from such an approach could be those for people with mental health problems or those with learning difficulties.
3. *Integrated provision* – where one integrated organisation provides both health and social care. This should facilitate the development of more 'one stop shops' (joint premises where users can receive fast and convenient input from a number of agencies) and encourage joint training across service boundaries.

For further information, see Glendinning *et al.* (2002a)

Figure 7.5	Care Trusts

Care Trusts are statutory NHS bodies, redesignated as Care Trusts under Section 45 of the Health and Social Care Act 2001. They build on PCTs [and] NHS Trusts... They deliver integrated (whole systems) services in a single organisation. NHS & [local authority] health related functions are delegated to them, not transferred. They are able to commission and/or provide. They are voluntary – partners can withdraw.

Care Trusts will be established on a voluntary basis and in partnership where there is a joint agreement at a local level that this model will offer the best way to deliver better health and social care services.

Service configuration will ensure the client group to be covered by the Trust will be determined at a local level, although Care Trusts are likely to focus on specialist mental health and older people's services.

Care Trusts will be able to commission, if they are a PCT based Care Trust, healthcare as well as local authority health related functions. They will also be able to deliver those services that the NHS organisation would normally provide, and local authority functions within the context of both models. Functions will be delivered under delegated authority from local authorities.

The introduction of Care Trusts is a real opportunity to deliver improved, integrated health and social care. It could see:

- An improvement in service provision and an integrated approach
- A system which is designed around patient and users' needs
- Better and clearer working arrangements for staff, with more and varied career opportunities
- A single management structure, multi-disciplinary teams managed from one point, co-location of staff, as well as single or streamlined cross disciplinary assessments
- Financial flexibility and efficiency from integration
- A single strategic approach, with a single set of aims and targets
- A stable organisational framework designed to improve quality of service provision through a single agency.

April 2002 starters:

- Bradford (mental health and learning disability services)
- Camden and Islington (mental health and learning disability services)
- Manchester (mental health services)
- Northumberland (commissioning all health and adult social care; providing primary and community and adult social care services [except working age mental health])

October 2002 starters:

- Witham, Braintree and Halstead (all local health care and health/social care for older people)

April 2003 starters:

- Sandwell (mental health services)
- Sheffield (mental health and learning disability services)

Figure 7.5	Care Trusts (*continued*)

October 2003 starters:

- Bexley (provides and commissions all health care for all residents, provides integrated health and social care services for older people and disabled people aged over 18)

Quotations and information adapted from the Department of Health and cited in Glasby and Peck (2003, pp. 3–4)

■ The introduction of Care Trusts under the *Health and Social Care Act* 2001. Care Trusts are NHS bodies, based on either primary care organisations or NHS provider trusts, which provide and/or commission health care and which have social care responsibilities delegated to them (see Figure 7.5). At the time of writing, there are eight Care Trusts in England – five of which were previously mental health provider trusts and which now bring together both health and social care services for people with mental health problems

However, perhaps the most famous example of partnership working under New Labour is the Somerset Partnerships Health and Social Care NHS Trust. Cited as a good practice example in *The NHS Plan* (Department of Health, 2000a, p. 71), the Trust was the first integrated mental health trust in the UK and took the unprecedented step of commissioning a long term and independent evaluation of its work (see Figure 7.6). The final report of this study (Peck *et al.*, 2002a) represents the most in-depth and substantial contribution to our knowledge of health and social care partnerships, and is a crucial document for anyone wishing to explore this topic in more detail. Significantly, this research painted a rather different picture to the positive spin of *The NHS Plan*, suggesting that the positives of integration in Somerset may also have been accompanied by some negatives (see later in this chapter for further discussion).

As a result of these changes, there is a fear amongst some social care staff in particular about a potential loss of identity and the danger of being dominated by a much larger and more powerful NHS. In some ways, this has been true over a period of time – although this book adopts a multi-disciplinary approach, there is sometimes a tendency to equate mental health services with the NHS and with health care practitioners, overlooking the social care contribution. With current mental health partnerships increasingly located within NHS bodies (such as Care Trusts or Partnership Trusts), some social care staff are currently concerned about the future of social care. For these practitioners, we suggest Blinkhorn's (2004) study of the role of the social worker in multi-disciplinary teams and the work of the Social Perspectives Network (www.spn.org.uk) to develop new approaches to mental health practice that reflect the needs and hopes of service users and that build on a more holistic understanding of mental distress. Also helpful will be reflection exercise 2 at the end of this chapter to help social care workers think through and be confident

Figure 7.6	The Somerset innovations

In 1996, Somerset Health Authority and Somerset County Council issued the findings of a review of mental health services which catalogued a series of problems that would have been familiar to most localities around England at that time. However, the response of the Health Authority and County Council to this report was without precedent. They decided to introduce joint commissioning (through the establishment of the Joint Commissioning Board – JCB) and integrated provision (through the creation of the Somerset Partnerships Health and Social Care NHS Trust – the Trust) simultaneously on April 1st 1999. Almost as unusually, the two agencies also commissioned an evaluation of the impact of these innovations during the first thirty months from the Centre for Mental Health Services Development, Kings College London.

The aims of the evaluation were to identify the impact of joint commissioning and combined service provision through:

- Identification of the impact of the changes on service users and carers
- Assessment of the impact of changes on the professional staff involved
- Identification of aspirations and beliefs of the agencies involved for joint commissioning and joint provision of mental health services in Somerset, and how these changed over time

Over time, the research involved regular interviews with service users and carers, a self-administered survey of all staff members involved with adult mental health service provision, exploratory workshops with self-selected members of staff, semi-structured interviews with senior managers of health and social services and non-participant based observation of the Joint Commissioning Board.

Key findings include:

- For staff, the changes initially led to a reduction in morale, role clarity and job satisfaction, although there were some signs of improvement by the end of the evaluation.
- For service users and carers, there was little change: while some felt that services were better co-ordinated, there were fears that therapeutic/support groups would become more limited as buildings changed into offices for co-located teams, concerns about changes in key workers and a perceived reduction in personnel. Crucially, there were also on-going concerns for some users and carers throughout the study about the attitudes of some staff members, the quality of acute care, the lack of user involvement in drawing up care plans and a failure to consider the needs of carers.

Adapted from Peck *et al.* (2002a, 2003, pp. 39–40)

about the contribution they have to make and the value base they bring with them in health and social care partnerships.

Different models of partnership working

As a result of the current emphasis on partnership working, there is a growing literature which seeks to define what we mean by the term *partnership* and identify the factors that may help and hinder inter-agency working. However, a useful definition is offered by Sullivan and Skelcher (2002) who see partnership working in terms of its emphasis on:

1. A shared responsibility for assessing the need for action, determining the type of action to be taken and agreeing the means of implementation.
2. Negotiation between people from different agencies committed to working together over more than the short term.
3. An intention to secure the delivery of benefits or added value which could not have been provided by a single agency acting alone.

Figure 7.7	Partnership working: what helps and what hinders?

Barriers:

- *Structural* (the fragmentation of service responsibilities across and within agency boundaries)
- *Procedural* (differences in planning and budget cycles)
- *Financial* (differences in funding mechanisms and resource flows)
- *Professional* (differences in ideologies, values and professional interests)
- *Perceived threats to status, autonomy and legitimacy*

Principles for strengthening strategic approaches to collaboration:

- *Shared Vision*: Specifying what is to be achieved in terms of user-centred goals, clarifying the purpose of collaboration as a mechanism for achieving such goals, and mobilising commitment around goals, outcomes and mechanisms
- *Clarity of Roles and Responsibilities*: Specifying and agreeing 'who does what', and designing organisational arrangements by which roles and responsibilities are to be fulfilled
- *Appropriate Incentives and Rewards*: Promoting organisational behaviour consistent with agreed goals and responsibilities, and harnessing organisational self-interest to collective goals
- *Accountability for Joint Working*: Monitoring achievements in relation to the stated vision, holding individuals and agencies to account for the fulfilment of pre-determined roles and responsibilities, and providing feedback and review of vision, responsibilities, incentives, and their inter-relationship

(Hudson *et al.*, 1997)

Figure 7.8	The Partnership Readiness Framework

Successful partnerships depend on the nature and history of local services. For example, to what extent do partners have a proven track record when it comes to:

1. Building shared values and principles?
2. Agreeing specific policy shifts?
3. Being prepared to explore new service options?
4. Determining agreed boundaries?
5. Agreeing respective roles with regard to commissioning, purchasing and providing?
6. Identifying agreed resource pools?
7. Ensuring effective leadership?
8. Providing sufficient development capacity?
9. Developing and sustaining good personal relationships?
10. Paying specific attention to mutual trust and attitude?

(Poxton, 2003, p. 17)

Figure 7.9	Different levels of partnership working (Glasby, 2003)

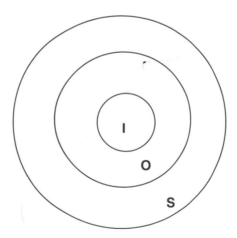

I: the Individual level

O: the Organisational level

S: the Structural level

In terms of barriers to successful partnership working and possible ways forward, common frameworks include those developed by the Nuffield Institute for Health (Hudson *et al.*, 1997) and Poxton's *Partnership Readiness Framework* (see Figures 7.7 to 7.8), both of which seek to identify those factors that can facilitate or hinder effective partnerships.

A further contribution is made by Glasby (2003), who sees partnerships as operating at three interrelated but separate levels of activity: that of the individual practitioner (I), that of local health and social care organisations (O) and that of national policy and the structure of the welfare state (S). These categories have been presented diagrammatically (see Figure 7.9) to illustrate the way in which individual workers can be influenced by the organisations in which they work and the structure of services nationally. At the same time, however, the way services are structured and the way in which local organisations relate to each other depend ultimately on the individuals working on the ground. As a result, Glasby argues that only a multi-faceted approach which seeks to tackle the Individual, the

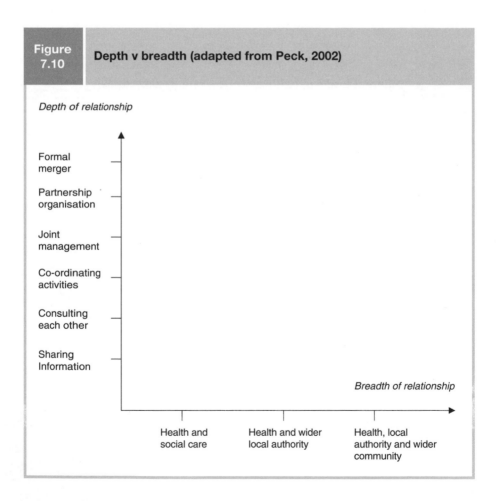

Figure 7.10   **Depth v breadth (adapted from Peck, 2002)**

Organisational and the Structural level all at once can ever hope to achieve more effective partnership working. This model draws on the work of Thompson (2001) with regard to anti-discriminatory practice (see Chapter 9).

A final model is provided by Peck (2002), who suggests that partnerships tend to pursue either depth or breadth. As demonstrated in Figure 7.10, organisations can either pursue a strong relationship between a small number of partners (such as the NHS and social services) or a wider relationship with a larger number of partners (such as the NHS and the wider local authority and voluntary sector). What is currently unclear is the extent to which local partners could seek to achieve both depth and breadth simultaneously.

Why work in partnership in mental health?

Throughout the partnership literature, different commentators are almost unanimous in identifying a multitude of potential benefits associated with partnership working. In North-East England, for example, an evaluation of a Community Mental Health Team found that an integrated team approach improved the transfer of information, encouraged a pooling of expertise, led to enhanced creativity in problem solving and resulted in more responsive services (Cook *et al.*, 2001). In Somerset and Northumberland, service reviews have emphasised the importance of a service with a single point of contact (Gulliver, 1999), while staff in Leeds feel that multi-disciplinary working leads to pooled knowledge and to the opportunities to experience areas of work outside individuals' normal professional roles (Millar, 2000). At the same time, work undertaken by the Sainsbury Centre for Mental Health (2000, pp. 12–14) suggests that partnership working is a 'must do' for mental health services for a range of political, financial and practical reasons:

■ Mental health is complex with a range of different agencies involved (including health care, social care, housing, welfare advice and employment services)
■ Many mental health service users are vulnerable and have limited capacity to negotiate complex bureaucracies. They therefore need services that are well integrated at the point of contact, are easy to negotiate and are focused on their needs
■ Resources are scarce, but the task is broad. It therefore makes sense for agencies to work together to achieve the vision for mental health set out in official policy documents
■ There are strong perverse incentives in mental health, with evidence of, for example, 'bed blocking' due to the lack of community alternatives (see Chapter 5)
■ Integrating the CPA and care management is a high priority and is simpler and more effective when joint working arrangements are sound (see Chapter 4)

■ Partnership working can help to minimise bureaucracy and duplication as well as maximising integration for service users and staff

Above all, partnership working is deemed to be beneficial for service users and their carers, who can often experience fragmented services, a lack of continuity and conflicting information in situations where local agencies fail to collaborate effectively. This has been described by Preston *et al.* (1999) in terms of being 'left in limbo', with users and carers feeling that they are failing to make progress through the mental health system:

> Separate clinics don't talk to each other or ring each other. I find the whole thing incredible the length of time it takes; it's just been horrendous, waiting weeks to see a consultant to be told 'I don't know why you've been referred to me ... It can make you feel very insignificant' (service user, quoted in Preston *et al.*, 1999, p. 19).

Figure 7.11	Engaging 'hard to reach' professional groups

Sometimes, it can be difficult to engage members from particular professions in partnership working:

■ GPs may not necessarily see mental health issues as a priority and most are independent practitioners with very different contractual arrangements to other health and social care services (Cook *et al.*, 2001; Hancock and Villeneau, 1997; Poxton, 1999)

■ Psychiatrists sometimes see themselves as being responsible for the work of the whole multi-disciplinary team and may not support the view that team membership implies equality of status and some form of democratic decision-making. This can lead to high levels of psychological stress, generate conflict amongst team members and inhibit team relationships (Norman and Peck, 1999; Peck and Norman, 1999)

■ Psychologists may sometimes perceive themselves as relatively autonomous, high status practitioners and may be ambivalent about being too closely identified with multi-disciplinary teams (Peck and Norman, 1999)

■ Practice nurses have different employment arrangements to other groups and can feel isolated from other professional colleagues (Nolan *et al.*, 1998)

■ Non-executive board members and local authority councillors are key decision-makers, but are felt by some mental health practitioners to have a poor understanding of mental health issues (Hancock *et al.*, 1997)

In addition to these groups, partnerships may sometimes fail to reach out to services beyond health and social care (such as housing) or to keep other partners (such as services users or voluntary agencies) fully informed of what is happening (Hancock *et al.*, 1997).

Barriers to effective partnerships

As well as the general barriers to partnership working identified above, there are a range of additional factors within mental health services that are also of significance. Thus, Norman and Peck's (1999) study of the views of leading members of professional organisations highlights issues such as a loss of faith by mental health professionals in the system within which they work, strong adherence to uni-professional cultures, the absence of a shared philosophy for community mental health services and mistrust of managerial solutions. For Nolan *et al.* (1998), key obstacles to collaboration include individual practitioners' lack of knowledge of other professionals, a tendency to stereotype other workers, defensive attitudes and a lack of certainty over one's own role. Engaging members of particular professions can also be problematic, as can looking beyond health and social care to include a wider range of partners (see Figure 7.11). For others, moreover, government policy may inadvertently serve to hinder attempts to work in partnership. Examples may include the introduction of separate performance reporting requirements for health and social services (Hayward, 2000; see end of chapter for further discussion), low staff morale and financial difficulties. The latter may be particularly relevant in situations where internal pressures can lead to more restrictive eligibility criteria and an increasing gulf between local organisations rather than a coming together to provide more comprehensive services. Also significant may be on-going tensions between care and control within mental health services, which may deprive staff and their organisations of the shared vision of the way forward so necessary for effective partnerships (see Figure 7.7 above).

Possible ways forward

In order to overcome these barriers, researchers and policy analysts propose a wide range of possible solutions (see Figure 7.12). Sometimes, the existence of a key power broker (often a consultant psychiatrist) can facilitate greater collaboration in a local area, although the resultant partnership is very vulnerable if this person leaves (Norman and Peck, 1999). Personal and leadership styles can also be important, with partnerships dependent on the attitude of senior managers and a willingness to pioneer new approaches (Sainsbury Centre for Mental Health, 2000). In contrast to this emphasis on key individuals or on personal characteristics, other commentators emphasise the need for more formal approaches to partnership working such as interprofessional education (Roberts and Priest, 1997) or inter-agency agreements about how to prioritise and allocate referrals (Maunder *et al.*, 2001; McDermott and Reid, 1999). For Gulliver (1999), the focus should be on more strategic issues such as securing senior management commitment, developing a shared vision, investing time in staff, owning each other's difficulties and recognising that partnerships are a means to an end rather than an end in themselves. Elsewhere,

Figure 7.12	Improving partnership working

Work undertaken by the Sainsbury Centre for Mental Health (2000, pp. 6–9) suggests that successful partnerships may depend upon:

- Avoiding organisationally defensive routines
- Taking into account the user movement
- Understanding changing organisational cultures
- Understanding the key components of effective dialogue
- Taking account of well understood success factors such as having a clear strategic purpose for the partnership
- Creating alliances which form part of the everyday functioning of organisations
- Developing a supportive internal infrastructure
- Looking at external factors when planning and acting
- Taking specific account of key issues such as governance arrangements, performance management, information systems, workforce issues, charging policies, complaints procedures and user involvement

For Norman and Peck (1999, p. 224), the way forward is to:

- Draw upon users' aspirations as an explicit philosophy for guiding the development of the partnership
- Clarify accountability and responsibility of staff
- Clarify staff roles
- Develop a framework to explore the relationships between multi-disciplinary groups
- Draw upon existing theories for understanding team effectiveness

progress towards more effective partnerships seems to have been made by adopting a more developmental approach which seeks to explore the perceptions which different practitioners have of colleagues from other disciplines and working through these preconceptions in multi-agency settings (see, for example, Nolan et al., 1998; Peck and Norman, 1999; see reflection exercise 2 for practical suggestions as to how practitioners can engage in such an activity).

For others, one way forward may lie in structural change and service redesign. Examples of this may include shared offices (Cook et al., 2001), multi-disciplinary records (Yates and Deakes, 1998), integrated service provision (McMillan, 2000) or integrated IT systems (Hayward, 2000). Despite this, a cautionary note is sounded by Peck et al. (2002a), whose research in Somerset suggests that the integration of health and social care led some workers to patrol their professional boundaries more than previously as means of protecting their identity in a time of significant change (Gulliver et al., 2002). There was also a lack of organisational development interventions, with an apparent assumption that simply creating a new organisation would automatically help to change behaviour and attitudes.

Finally, the Somerset study also found evidence of a lack of clarity about what is meant by culture. Although local managers expressed their aspirations for the future in terms of creating a 'shared culture', they could often mean different things by this (Peck and Crawford, 2002). In particular, the researchers identified two different models: a desire to create an entirely new culture comprising elements from existing health and social care professions ('the melting pot' approach) or a desire to enhance existing cultures by improving mutual understanding and respect (the 'orange juice with added vitamin C' approach). Structural solutions, in short, may not necessarily provide a panacea to the thorny issue of partnership working.

Conclusion

Overall, the diverse range of solutions offered above would seem to support an assertion by the Sainsbury Centre for Mental Health (2000, p. 27) that 'there are no "quick fixes", and no magic solutions to complex health and social problems'. Ultimately, therefore, it seems as though the way forward may lie in an incremental approach, whereby individual partners make use of whatever avenue they think may be beneficial and locally appropriate to travel closer to the overall goal of more effective partnership working.

However, as front-line workers and local services try to develop more effective relationships, our knowledge of partnership working is limited by a series of gaps in the current literature. These include:

■ A tendency to focus on the needs and perspectives of policy makers, managers and front-line workers without adequately exploring the views and experiences of service users and their carers. Given that much of the available literature seeks to justify partnership working in terms of more responsive services for users, this failure to include a significant user/carer perspective must be seen as a major oversight
■ A tendency to focus on good practice examples from areas with a strong history of joint working. As a result, we still know very little about how to promote partnership working in areas which have a poor history of collaboration or where local partners are hostile to each other
■ A tendency to focus on the benefits of partnership working rather than on some of the potentially negative consequence (for example, the initial increase in professional defensiveness in Somerset)
■ A tendency to focus on essentially journalistic accounts of apparently successful schemes, emphasising the virtues of partnership working without necessarily citing evidence for the claims made

In addition, the last point is very much a criticism which some may wish to level at national policy, as the evidence base for some of the measures currently being implemented sometimes lacks clarity. Thus, the use of the

Health Act flexibilities was being actively promoted by the government prior to the completion of the national evaluation of this initiative, while legislation has given the Secretary of State powers to impose the flexibilities on organisations in certain situations without any indication that 'forced' partnerships can be effective. At the same time, the concept of the Care Trust is a particular leap of faith, and was introduced in a single page of a much larger 144-page document (Department of Health, 2000a, p. 73). Not only was no evidence cited for the benefits of this new model, but the announcement came at a time when the success of previous developments in health care (such as PCTs) had been insufficiently researched. Since the advent of Care Trusts, moreover, there have been concerns raised about the extent to which forming a Care Trust is a positive step forward for local services or a distraction from the real task of improving local services (Commission for Health Improvement, 2003b; Giles, 2003; Hudson, 2003). As a result, the government has laid itself open to criticism that it was introducing a new model of care when there was very little evidence about the effectiveness or otherwise of the current way of working. As Hudson (2002, p. 82) observes:

> [In the case of Care Trusts], there remains a strong political commitment to an untried model. In the light of the emphasis normally placed by the Department of Health on evidence based approaches to policy and practice, this is perhaps a surprising turn of events.

Of course, this is not to dismiss the concept of the *Health Act* flexibilities or Care Trusts – in time, these policies may well prove to be an effective means of promoting greater partnership working. However, the key issue is that both initiatives appear to be based more on faith than on a firm evidence base and we simply do not know what impact they are likely to have.

Overall, therefore, there is a growing consensus that more must be done to encourage effective partnerships between health and social care (and other relevant agencies). While considerable progress has been made in a range of areas, a number of obstacles still remain before we can finally achieve the 'joined-up solutions to joined-up problems' at the heart of so much recent government policy.

Reflection exercises

1. The structure of the welfare state
Exercise for all workers

Imagine you are part of a group of people about to settle on a new space colony on the Planet Zog!

- What sort of welfare services would you like to have on your utopian colony?
- How will these services be organised? – draw the structure of your new welfare state on a piece of blank paper.
- How does this design compare to the current structure of the welfare state?
- Will this structure have any key gaps or boundaries between different services and, if so, how will you overcome these?

2. Professional roles and identity
Exercise for all workers

- What is it that distinguishes your profession from other disciplines and what do you value about this?
- What do you admire about other professions and what bemuses you (i.e. confuses you, angers you, frustrates you)?

Consider this question with regard to psychiatrists, psychologists, nurses, social workers, general practitioners, local councillors and NHS non-executive board members. If possible, ask professional colleagues from different backgrounds to complete the same exercise and share your answers:

- What does this teach you about how others view your profession?
- Do you agree with others' views about you and do they agree about your views of them?
- If you do not understand something about another profession, can they explain it to you?
- Are there any key contributions that each of the professions make that you can all agree on?
- How can you build on the strengths of each profession and minimise any perceived limitations?

Suggestions for further reading

1. Introductory textbooks on partnership working include:

- Glendinning *et al.* (2002b) *Partnerships, New Labour and the governance of welfare.* Bristol, Policy Press
- Balloch, S. and Taylor, M. (2001) *Partnership working: policy and practice.* Bristol, Policy Press
- Sullivan, H. and Skelcher, C. (2002) *Working across boundaries.* Basingstoke, Palgrave
- 6, P., Leat, D., Seltzer, K. and Stoker, G. (2002) *Towards holistic governance: the new reform agenda.* Basingstoke, Palgrave
- Glasby, J. and Peck, E. (eds) (2003) *Care trusts: partnership working in action.* Abingdon, Radcliffe Medical Press

   For a discussion of the role of the social worker in multi-disciplinary teams and in services which are increasingly based in the NHS, see Blinkhorn (2004).

2. Peck, E., Gulliver, P. and Towell, D. (2002a) *Modernising partnerships: an evaluation of Somerset's innovations in the commissioning and organisation of mental health services – final report.* London, Institute of Applied Health and Social Policy, King's College

   This two-and-a-half year study of joint working in Somerset is a seminal document and one of the most comprehensive studies there has been of partnership working over time and of organisational and professional culture.

3. The Integrated Care Network (www.integratedcarenetwork.gov.uk) produces a large number of publications and other resources designed to promote more effective partnership working. This includes work on Care Trusts, governance arrangements and the practicalities of integration.

4. The Centre for the Advancement of Interprofessional Education (CAIPE) promotes interprofessional learning and has a range of information, publications, case studies and links available on its website (www.caipe.org.uk).

8 User Involvement

What is meant by the term 'mental health service user'?

The language used to describe service users is perhaps more varied in mental health than in any other sector of health and social care. User, survivor, patient, customer, citizen, consumer: all imply different notions of the roles and responsibilities of people with mental health problems and the relationship between services and users. Pilgrim and Rogers (1999) have described a useful four-part typology of users as consumers, survivors, providers or, perhaps most commonly, as patients.

'Consumerism' is a relatively new ideology within the public sector, linked, as we discussed in Chapter 2, to the rise of general management principles in the NHS in the 1980s and the development of a market economy through the introduction of an internal market. It is also linked to the growing acknowledgement of the importance of customer satisfaction, with users of health and social care as customers who can exercise an informed choice about the services they receive and, if not satisfied, take their 'business' elsewhere. However, as Rogers and Pilgrim point out:

many psychiatric patients do not ask for what they get – it is imposed on them. Various sections of the 1983 *Mental Health Act*, like its legal predecessors, are utilised to lawfully impose restraints and treatments on resentful and reluctant recipients. In such circumstances, mental patients could be construed to be consumers if being dragged off the street and force-fed was a feature of being a customer in a restaurant (Rogers and Pilgrim, 2001, p. 169).

Poverty can also limit choice, with private sector mental health services out of bounds, while, at times of crisis, the ability and motivation to obtain information about a range of service and select between them can be difficult (Lester *et al.*, 2004). Choice also implies a possibility of exit from the system, a notion that is difficult to sustain in a society whose courts recognise the validity of advanced directives only when they prospectively authorise treatment, not when they are used to reject the possibility of treatment (Szasz, 2003). Choice, then, as a central part of consumerism, appears to be a relative concept if you are a mental health service user.

In contrast, the user as 'survivor' is linked to the growth in the early 1970s of collective activities of mental health service users initially in the Netherlands and the USA. Recognising the wisdom of the dominant Trade Union philosophy of the time that 'Unity is Strength', organisations such as the Campaign Against Psychiatric Oppression and the British Network for Alternatives to Psychiatry were formed. The image and term 'survivor' is very particularly chosen by groups such as Survivors Speak Out, the UK Advocacy Network (UKAN) and the Hearing Voices Network to portray a positive image of people in distress as those who had the strength to survive the mental health system. 'Survivor' also implies a notion of rejecting forms of professionally-led and produced information.

Linked to this, the conceptualisation of users as 'providers' is reflected in the development of user-led services that are found in the voluntary and statutory sector across the UK. The range of user-led activities includes a spectrum of involvement from patients being mutually supported in professionally-led services to projects that are managed and staffed by users themselves. The latter include safe houses and drop-in day centres and often reflect the user movement priorities of voluntary relationships, alternatives to hospital admissions and personal support.

However, Pilgrim and Rogers suggest that the main way in which users have been portrayed is as 'patients' — as 'objects of the clinical gaze of mental health professionals' (1999, p. 193). With this representation, users are seen in terms of their illness, perceived as irrational and therefore as incapable of having a valid view. Patients and relatives are assumed to share the same perspective and where they do not, relatives' views often take precedence.

A further way of thinking about the meaning of the word 'user' is as a citizen. This is a fluid concept that incorporates a cluster of meanings including defined legal and social status; a means of signifying political identity; a focus of loyalty; a requirement to perform duties; expectations of rights; and a yardstick of behaviour (Heater, 1990). Marshall's (1950) classic

Figure 8.1	Elements of citizenship

Marshall (1950) defined citizenship rights as comprising:

■ Legal or civil rights which enable the individual to participate freely in the life of the community. These rights include property and contractual rights, and rights to freedom of thought, freedom of speech, religious practice, assembly and association
■ Political rights which entitle the citizen to participate in the government of the community: the right to vote and to hold political office
■ Social and economic rights to the circumstances which enable the individual to participate in the general well-being of the community. They include rights to health care, education and welfare

(From Barnes and Bowl, 2001, p. 14)

influential analysis of the development of the meaning of citizenship over time is summarised in Figure 8.1.

A recent shift in the meaning of citizenship is that it entails not only rights but also a moral duty to 'to take part in constructing and maintaining the community' (Meehan, 1993, p. 177). Barnes and Walker (1996) also suggest that citizenship is closely allied to the concept of empowerment rather than consumerism, and includes the right to interactive participation and to share power with health and social care professionals.

However, with respect to mental health service users, we would argue that citizenship rights are eroded in a number of different ways. The potential for compulsory detention, proposed community treatment orders and medical treatment administered without consent are all constraints on legal and civil rights. In practice, people who have spent long periods in psychiatric hospitals have been denied the opportunity to vote. Above all, aspects of the social exclusion experienced by many people with mental illness severely impact on their social and economic rights (Sayce, 2001). See also Chapter 4.

The history of user involvement in mental health services

Although user involvement is largely a twentieth century phenomenon, protest and dissent have been a feature of the relationship between madness and medicine throughout the ages. Campbell (1996), for example, cites 'The Petition of the Poor Distracted People in the House of Beldam' in 1620 as an early example of collective protest. The Alleged Lunatics' Friends Society, a lobbying and campaigning organisation, was formed by 'ex-patients' in 1845 and is credited with extricating the poet John Clare from a Victorian

Figure 8.2	Early user voices

In 1838, John Perceval published 'A narrative of the treatment experienced by a gentleman during a state of mental derangement: Designed to explain the causes and the nature of insanity and to expose the injudicious conduct pursued towards many unfortunate sufferers under that calamity'.

He described how, as a patient in Brislington House, 'men acted as though my body, soul and spirit were fairly given up to their control, to work their mischief and folly upon… I mean that I was never told such and such things we are going to do: we think it advisable to administer such and such medicine in this or that manner. I was never asked, Do you want anything? Do you wish for, prefer anything?'

(Perceval, 1838 quoted in Porter, 1999, p. 182)

asylum, possibly one of the first examples of peer advocacy. Occasionally, users' voices have also been heard in terms of individual experiences and treatment in early asylums (see Figure 8.2).

It is interesting, if disheartening, to note that despite the passage of nearly two hundred years, hopes and desires for treatment remain essentially unchanged.

During the early part of the twentieth century, individual descriptions of life in asylums continued to emerge, often in the context of the treatment of Shell Shock during and after the First World War. However, most were again individual accounts and there was little sense of a collective user voice. It was not until the 1960s and early 1970s that the convergence of a number of different related influences from both within the UK and internationally led to a slow but progressive change in the way in which users perceived themselves, and were perceived by society. For example, social movements such as the women's movement started to develop powerful critiques of the assumptions underpinning social policy. Academic analysis of the nature and impact of the institution (Goffman, 1961) also created an impetus to think differently about patients and their environment. Parallel developments, particularly a series of reports on hospital scandals, similarly focused on the poor care and inadequate living conditions of institutionalised patients (see Chapter 2). The 1960s also saw the rise of the anti-psychiatry movement, a largely professionally-led movement that opposed the traditional medical model of thinking about mental illness and suggested that the symptoms of mental distress reflected an individual's life experiences. The anti-psychiatry movement proposed that the focus should move from symptoms, to the meaning behind them, and that this could only be achieved by listening to the voice of the people experiencing the distress. In the 1970s, a growing concern about individual freedom and the civil rights of the individual, with the National Campaign for Civil Liberties taking a leading role in this respect in the UK, also helped to shape the form and function of the mental health services users' movement.

By the mid-1980s, user-based organisations including the Nottingham Advocacy Group, Survivors Speak Out and the UK Advocacy Network were established, while more traditional voluntary organisations also began to include a greater number of user representatives in their work. Patient councils and user groups became increasingly widespread within mental health services themselves as service providers sought feedback directly from users.

The recent policy context of user involvement

The last twenty years have been characterised by a rapid growth in a range of different user involvement activities, underpinned by a plethora of policy directives. Since the establishment of Community Health Councils in 1973, the rhetoric of user involvement has become a central component of UK health and social policy. In 1990, the *NHS and Community Care Act* was the first piece of UK legislation to establish a formal requirement for user involvement in service planning. Subsequent key policies in the early 1990s included *The Patient's Charter* (Department of Health, 1991) and *Local Voices* (NHS Management Executive, 1992) which aimed to make services more responsible to patients' needs, but stressed consumerism rather than partnership or participation.

Encouragement for user involvement in the context of mental health at that time was provided in documents such as *The Health of the Nation* (Department of Health, 1992), the Mental Health Nursing Review, *Working in Partnership* (Department of Health, 1994) and *Building Bridges* (Department of Health, 1995). Indeed, *Working in Partnership* declared: 'The work of mental health nurses rests upon the relationship they have with people who use services. Our recommendations for future action start and finish with this relationship' (Department of Health, 1994, p. 5).

Since 1997, 'patient and public involvement' in health care has become one of the central tenets of New Labour's NHS and social care reforms. This emphasis has been driven by a number of different agendas (see Figure 8.3).

Figure 8.3	Current drivers for greater user involvement

- Democratic right as tax paying citizens
- Consumerist principles and the patient choice agenda
- The desire to increase accountability within the NHS
- The cross policy partnership agenda

The justification for user involvement can be made on the basic democratic principle that, since 1948, the NHS has been paid for by the taxpayer, so they should have a choice in what is funded and how services are delivered. However, as noted earlier in this chapter, the principle of consumerism has also been a strong justification for user involvement for at least two decades, with users as consumers enabled to exercise choice to ensure their needs are met.

More recently, the patient choice agenda fuelled by the wider availability of information, more treatment options, a growing private sector as well as consumerism (Appleby *et al.*, 2003) has become a particularly strong political imperative. It has generated heated debate, a Patient Tsar and a Command Paper, *Building on the Best* (Department of Health, 2003g), which sets out a series of measures to extend patient choice across primary, secondary and community care (although mental health is mentioned only briefly).

The desire to increase the accountability of the NHS and the professionals who work within it is a further strong driver for increased user involvement. Medical practitioners who fail in their duty of care to patients are perhaps best represented, in the collective public consciousness, by Harold Shipman, the GP found guilty of murdering over 200 of his patients in 2000, and by the Bristol Royal Infirmary cardiac surgeons. While it is tempting to argue that Shipman at least has little to do with the reality of health care in the UK, the 198 recommendations in the Bristol Royal Infirmary Inquiry (2001) and other cases have come to symbolise the unchecked autonomy of the medical profession, and, allied to a growing momentum within the medical profession itself to increase accountability, helped create the patient and public involvement aspect of the broader clinical governance agenda.

The notion of partnership is a further strong driver and is a concept that has cut across a range of New Labour policy areas including local government, health care, education and crime and disorder. This is discussed in more detail in Chapter 7, but examples of New Labour's commitment to 'joined up solutions to joined up problems' include the duty of partnership between health and social care, joint planning frameworks, new intermediate care services to prevent unnecessary hospital admissions and Health Action Zones to improve the health of local communities in areas of high social exclusion (see Poxton, 2003 for a summary). Crucially, ensuring effective partnerships includes engaging users and other local people in ways that make sense to them and that have an impact on resources and decision-making.

Under New Labour, the user involvement agenda has been formalised in policy terms through *The NHS Plan* (Department of Health, 2000a), which emphasised the government's commitment to creating a patient-centred NHS with users' needs central to service design and delivery (see also Figure 8.4):

Figure 8.4	Policies to encourage patient and public involvement in the NHS

- New statutory duties placed on NHS organisations by the *Health and Social Care Act* 2001 now ensure that patients and the public are consulted at an early stage about the planning and organisation of services (Department of Health, 2003h)
- Patient Advisory and Liaison Services (PALS) have been set up in every NHS trust to provide information and on-site help for patients
- A new national network of Independent Complaints Advocacy Services provided locally but operating to national standards has been set up to support people when they want to complain about the NHS
- Since December 2003, Patient and Public Involvement Forums have been in place in every NHS Trust and PCT to influence the day to day operation of the health service and monitor the effectiveness of PALS in their area. Forums are able to elect a member to sit on the trust board as a non-executive director
- Local authority overview and scrutiny committees, made up of elected councillors, now have powers to scrutinise the NHS. The committees can review any aspect of NHS care locally and call NHS managers to account for their actions. They have the power to refer significant changes in service provision to the Secretary of State for Health for a final decision
- The public will be able to become involved in the running of NHS foundation trusts by becoming members, eligible to vote for board members (Department of Health, 2002h)
- In 2006, a new Patient and Public Involvement Resource Centre will be set up to support the delivery of patient and public involvement in health services

Patients are the most important people in the health service. It doesn't always appear that way. Too many patients feel talked at, rather than listened to. This has to change. NHS care has to be shaped around the convenience and concerns of patients. To bring this about, patients must have more say in their own treatment and more influence over the way the NHS works (Department of Health, 2000a, p. 88).

However, despite the new raft of policies, the current legislation is piece-meal and disparate. There is also evidence to suggest that the often very good intentions of policy makers can sometimes fail to move beyond rhetoric into reality, particularly for mental health service users. Thus, user representatives on a national group convened by the Department of Health in 1998 to develop the *National Service Framework for Mental Health* resigned when it became clear that the government was going to insist that com-pulsory treatment orders were non-negotiable (Donnelly, 1998). The final document (Department of Health, 1999a) stated that specific arrangements should be in place to ensure service user and carer involvement, but there are few other references to users throughout the NSF (even though carers' interests are recognised in their own standard). Similarly, while improving choice has enormous popular and political appeal, the entire agenda raises a number of issues and creates particular tensions for people with mental health problems who, as we have already discussed, are rarely seen or treated as consumers of services.

Mental health service user involvement in theory and practice

User involvement, like the concept of user itself, encapsulates a range of different ideas (Braye, 2000) from active participation at the micro level of individual decision making, to more macro level involvement in service planning and evaluation and, increasingly, in training and research. A range of different models to describe and conceptualise user involvement have been proposed. Hoggett (1992, p. 9 quoted in Means and Smith, 1998, p. 89) for example, tries to distinguish between the degree of

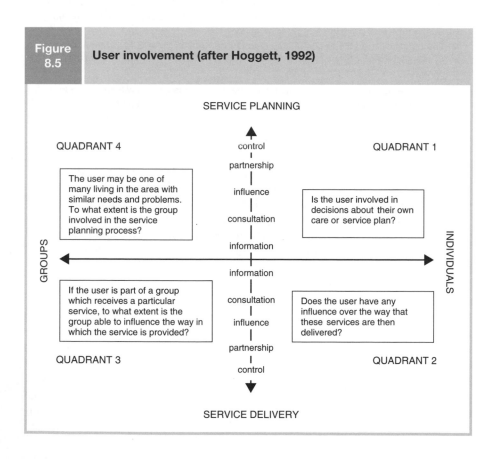

Figure 8.5 User involvement (after Hoggett, 1992)

participation/control available to the individual and whether they are involved as an individual or through collective action (see Figure 8.5).

The four way Pilgrim and Rogers formulation discussed at the beginning of the chapter reflects, in part, Arnstein's classification of citizens' participation (1969) along an eight point ladder of participation from being informed (patient) through consultation and negotiation (consumer) to transfer of power (user–led services). Pilgrim and Roger's categories also correlate with Hirschman's (1970) broader conception of relationships between individuals and organisations involving the three categories of Loyalty, Voice and Exit. Loyalty involves using a service and hoping to exert an influence peripherally. If the organisation has some expectation that it should seek and respond to the views of the individual, then the individual can exercise Voice, perhaps through individual advocacy, campaigning or lobbying. If the individual has authority over the way in which the organisation behaves and the right to reject that behaviour and seek support elsewhere, they demonstrate the ability to Exit.

Figure 8.6	**Examples of user involvement**		
Levels of interaction	**Conceptions of user involvement**		
	Recipient of communication	**Subject of consultation**	**Agent in control**
Interaction between service users	Newsletters Periodicals	Advocacy schemes	Hearing voices Newsletters Periodicals
Interaction between users and professionals	Receiving care plans	Agreeing care plans	Direct Payments
Management of local services	Receiving information about services	Patient Councils User surveys User-focused monitoring	User-run crisis houses Social firms
Planning of overall services	Community care plans	Mental health taskforce membership Stakeholder conferences Users on local implementation teams	

Source: Peck *et al.* (2002b).

In addition, Peck *et al.* (2002b) have constructed a schema using Hirschman, Arnstein and Pilgrim and Roger's formulations that has three distinct conceptions of user involvement as recipients, subjects of consultation or agents in control. At the same time, they suggest user involvement within mental health services operates at four levels:

1. In the interaction between service users and the form of self-help.
2. In the interaction between individual users and professionals working with them.
3. In the management of local services.
4. In the planning of overall services.

Peck *et al.* argue that if these two frameworks are combined, it is possible to construct a matrix for user involvement with the conceptions of user involvement forming one access and the level of user involvement forming the other (see Figure 8.6).

For Peck *et al.* (2002b), the matrix illustrates the sheer diversity of mental health service user involvement activities in the UK currently. However, it is also significant that many initiatives are clustered in the consultation category with the 'user control of the overall service' planning section empty.

Although 'user involvement' is the current 'buzz word' and appears regularly in policy documents, in mission statements and in the academic literature, it may be less meaningful in practice. This view is supported by Wallcraft and Bryant's (2003) survey of the mental health service user movement in England which identified 318 user groups and found that 'local service user groups play a very important role in mutual support, combating stigma, helping people to recover and stay out of services and participating in local service planning and development' (p. 1). However, most groups were small, recently formed, poorly funded and non-representative of black and minority ethnic communities, all of which limited their capacity to achieve change. There also appeared to be tensions between centrally determined agendas that failed to acknowledge local needs and choices, perhaps reflecting a wider debate between the need for local responsiveness within a system of considerable central government control.

Webb *et al.*'s (2000, p. 281) survey of 503 patients across five NHS Trusts, also found a failure to respond to several prominent and longstanding criticisms from the user movement:

> On the face of it… the results of this study point to the old chestnuts that mental health user campaign groups have raised again and again in the past two decades, and that previous studies have reported on: a lack of information, communication and consultation. It would seem that the National Health Service still has some way to go in meeting these basic principles of good quality care.

Figure 8.7	The benefits of user involvement

1. Users are experts about their own illness and need for care.
2. Users may have different but equally important perspectives about their illness and care.
3. User involvement may increase the existing limited understanding of mental distress.
4. Users are able to develop alternative approaches to mental health and illness.
5. User involvement may of itself be therapeutic.
6. User involvement may encourage greater social inclusion.

So, whilst it is true that there are many more user groups than there used to be, it appears that their influence may be limited, with an emphasis on information sharing rather than on partnership or user-led services.

Why is user involvement important?

There are a number of often interrelated reasons for believing that mental health service user involvement is more than a politically mandated 'good thing' but is a worthwhile activity with a range of practical and ethical benefits (see Figure 8.7).

First, there is widespread recognition that service users are experts, with an in-depth knowledge of mental health services and of living with a mental health problem. By definition, no one else, no matter how well trained or qualified, can possibly have had the same experience of the onset of mental illness, the same initial contact with services or the same journey through the mental health system. These experiences are an important resource that can help to improve individual packages of care as well as services more generally. Borrill (2000), for example, emphasises the way in which users can predict when they are about to become unwell and formulate appropriate responses at an early stage. If mental health professionals can tap into this expertise, they make their own jobs much easier and more productive by focusing on users' considerable strengths.

In addition, service users and mental health professionals often have different perspectives. Lindow (1999, p. 154), for example, highlights the way in which users and service providers may have very different priorities:

> Our discussion are seldom about new styles of management, or changes in service organisations: I have heard little interest [among users] in the idea of a GP-led National Health Service. There is, rather, much discussion of poverty, employment, housing; about services that control and rob our experiences of meaning and about dangerous treatment.

Involving users can therefore provide insights that prompt practitioners to re-evaluate their work, challenge traditional assumptions and highlight key priorities that users would like to see addressed. May (2001) suggests that the inclusion of users' experiences and knowledge through service user involvement will elaborate the existing limited understanding of mental distress. User involvement in this sense may also lead to a new way of thinking about the nature of evidence itself, with what was sometimes seen as anecdotal experience given new validity through viewing it as 'human testimony'.

At the same time, users have been able to develop alternative approaches to mental health that can complement existing services. The Strategies for Living group, for example, have highlighted the importance of alternative and complementary therapies (Faulkner and Layzell, 2000; Mental Health Foundation, 2003) while The Hearing Voices Network encourages positive working practices with people who hear voices and works to promote greater tolerance and understanding of voice hearing (http://www.hearing-voices.org). For some people, moreover, user involvement can be therapeutic. Helping to shape services, particularly when users work together collectively, can help users increase their confidence, raise self-esteem and develop new skills (Clark *et al.*, 2004; Mental Health Foundation, 2003).

Finally, user involvement may encourage greater social inclusion (Sayce and Morris, 1999). As discussed in Chapter 4, on almost any indicator, people with mental health problems are among the most excluded within society, particularly in terms of employment opportunities. Some users are excluded geographically from their community by 'nimbyism' and from communities of identity through negative stereotypes of irrationality and violence. Wilkinson (1996) has suggested that it is relative rather than absolute poverty within societies that creates health inequalities through mediating factors such as powerlessness and social stress. Encouraging greater user involvement, including paid activity, can be empowering and address issues of poverty and therefore may act as one mechanism to encourage greater social inclusion.

Figure 8.8	**Barriers to user involvement in mental health services**

1. Lack of information.
2. Financial and time costs.
3. Concerns over representativeness.
4. Resistance to the idea of users as experts.
5. Differences in the balance of power between users and professionals.

The barriers to user involvement in mental health services

Despite the benefits of user involvement and the significant political encouragement in recent years, levels of user involvement in mental health services remain patchy, with an emphasis on consultation rather than influence, partnership or control. There are a number of different though often interlinked barriers to greater user involvement (see Figure 8.8).

First and foremost, accessible information is an essential prerequisite for meaningful involvement, yet there is evidence of a widespread lack of information for service users, including a lack of information about the nature of mental health problems, the side effects of medication, alternative forms of treatment and mental health law (Carpenter and Sbaraini, 1997; Hogman and Sandamas, 2001; Morrissey, 1998; Webb *et al.*, 2000). As an example, the User's Voice project, which included interviews with over 500 users in seven geographical areas across England, found very low levels of involvement in individual care planning and in the planning and delivery of services more generally, and suggested this was often related to a lack of information. As Rose (2001, p. 6) observed:

> Mental health service users need information to make informed choices about their care. Around 50% of users interviewed for this work felt they were not getting enough information on a range of issues and therefore felt themselves to be recipients of rather than involved in their mental health care.

However, user involvement, if done properly, can be expensive and time consuming for the organisation and service users themselves (at least in the short term). A good example is provided by Carpenter and Sbaraini (1997, p. 27), whose account of user involvement in the care management process identified time constraints as a major barrier:

> The main disadvantage [of user involvement] perceived by staff was that the process took more time than previously. The assessment and planning meetings themselves took between 45 minutes and one-and-a-half hours, depending on the amount of preparatory work which had been done, the complexity of the user's needs and their ability to contribute to the discussion. In some cases this was longer than the participants and care manager had allowed. To this must be added the time involved explaining the purpose and procedures to the user, liasing with carers and other professionals, and in setting up the meetings themselves. Following the meetings, the forms had to be written out clearly for typing, typed, checked with the user and distributed. In the event that the user's condition had deteriorated severely, or for some reason the care programme had proved difficult to implement, all the preceding work could sometimes be seen by the care manager as time wasted.

In addition, the results of a survey of policy and practice in payments to mental health service users and carers involved in service development in 46 secondary mental health services organisations in England found that only 12 (26 per cent) made transport available to users and 14 (30 per cent) to carers, while only 15 (33 per cent) paid service users and 12 (26 per cent) paid carers for their time. The authors concluded:

> There is considerable desire to develop practice in this area and the issue of payments is viewed as important in addressing user and carer participation. Significantly, many organisations employed unwritten policies based on custom and practice and were most likely to relate to basic expenses and payments rather than payments for time given (Ryan and Bamber, 2002, p. 635).

They also noted that some respondents felt that having written policies on financial resources might further reduce future user and carer participation because of the cost implications for organisations.

At the same time, professionals wishing to promote user involvement have frequently expressed concerns about the 'representativeness' of individual service users, sometimes suggesting that particular users may be 'too well', 'too articulate' or 'too vocal' to represent the views of users more generally. However, Lindow suggests that the concept of 'representativeness' may be used as a subconscious method of resisting user involvement (see Figure 8.9).

Figure 8.9	User involvement and representation

When workers find what we [users] are saying challenging, the most usual strategy to discredit user voices is to suggest we are not to be listened to because we are too articulate, and not representative. Workers seem to be looking for someone, the 'typical' patient, who is so passive and/or drugged that they comply with their plans. We are developing our own strategies to respond to these challenges in an attempt to reveal to such workers their double standards:

- We ask how representative are they, and the others on the committee? We point out that as they are selected for their expertise and experience, so are we. Indeed, we are more likely to have been selected by a group than they are
- We ask, would workers send their least articulate colleague to represent their views, or the least confident nurse to negotiate for a change in conditions?
- We ask, if a person's criticisms are valid, what relevance has representativeness?
- We point out that it is very rude to suggest that someone is not a 'proper' service user (that is, so disempowered and/or medicated that they cannot speak). We could ask, but do not, that the challenger produce his or her credentials, their certificates of qualification

(Lindow 1999, p. 166)

Figure 8.10	Power differences in user/professional relationships

Where they did come into contact with staff...a worrying feature... was the extent of the feelings of powerlessness and fear that emerged. The anxieties expressed, and the need for reassurance that speaking up would not put them personally at risk, was too common to be put down merely to individual paranoia. People who have experienced compulsory admission to hospital, ECT and having to take medication that they have neither chosen nor understand, know what it is like to be subject to the power of the system and of another person...The way that some of those in authority had managed this, and the legacy of fear this had left, was disturbing to us.

(Morgan, 1998, p. 184)

This also seems to create something of a 'catch 22' situation, with users either 'too well' to be 'representative' or 'too ill' to be involved.

Allied to this is Peck *et al.'s* interesting distinction between tokenism and symbolism (2002a). Their evaluation of the integrated mental health trust in Somerset found that the Joint Commissioning Board (see Chapter 7) was felt by the researchers and by a number of Board members to have a predominantly symbolic function – emphasising the importance of mental health and inter-agency working. Although some Board members recognised and were happy with this, others (mainly GP, service user and carer representatives) felt frustrated by the Board's seeming inability to 'do something'. However, Peck *et al.* suggest that the presence of users and carers was not tokenistic but symbolic, emphasising the importance of user and carer involvement at all levels of the organisation by making a very clear statement about involvement through the composition of the Board.

Finally, some professionals may find it difficult to view service users as experts and resist moves towards greater user involvement. Although there is some evidence to suggest that professionals are generally supportive of user involvement, there are also dissonances between expressed support and actual practice (Campbell, 2001). This could reflect professionals genuinely

Figure 8.11	Examples of positive practice

1. Involvement in prioritising and conducting research.
2. Involvement in staff selection.
3. Employment as paid mental health workers.
4. Involvement in planning and redesign of mental health services.
5. Involvement in education and training.
6. Involvement on Governing Boards.

perceiving themselves to be more supportive than users do (Peck *et al.*, 2002b), resistance to the notion of sharing and transferring power to users, or a clash of professional 'scientific' and users' more 'social' ways of thinking and working (Summers, 2003). At the same time, however, involvement may be difficult from users' perspectives because of differences in perceived and actual power between users and professionals. As an example, Morgan's work on user involvement in three London boroughs revealed a number of worrying findings in this regard, particularly around the difficulty of feeling empowered (see Figure 8.10).

Examples of positive practice in user involvement

Despite the rhetoric/reality gap and barriers to user involvement, there are emerging examples of positive practice in many areas of user involvement in health and social care (see Figure 8.11).

Although mental health professionals are perhaps less familiar with the concept of service users as active participants in the research process than those working in the disability field or engaged in emancipatory research (research with the aim of empowerment at its core), user involvement in research is important for a number of different reasons. Service users' priorities for research are often different from those of academics, health and social care professionals or funding bodies. A consultation exercise organised by the South London and Maudsley NHS Trust with service users, for example, found that highly ranked research topics included discrimination and abuse, social welfare issues and arts as therapies (Thornicroft *et al.*, 2002). Unfortunately, user-led research projects are still relatively rare but key contributions in this area include the recent Strategies for Living projects (Faulkner and Layzell, 2000; Mental Health Foundation, 2003) and Rose's (2001) work on users' experiences of mental health services. These projects highlight the importance of training service users to undertake the research and the added value as participants 'visibly relaxed and opened up once they realised the inter-viewer had "been through the system" and understood their own situa-tion' (Rose, 2001, p. 4). More recently, the Mental Health Research Network has established a service user-led research hub (SURGE) to co-ordinate service user-led research in mental health and collaborative initiatives (Telford and Faulkner, 2004). This may well help to raise the profile and more importantly the active participation of users in all aspects of the research process.

Second, some mental health service users are being involved in recruiting staff. This is not only a symbolic statement about the importance of user involvement, but can also improve the appointment process. Newnes *et al.* (2001, p. 12) describe an attempt to involve service users in recruiting a clinical psychologist. An evaluation suggested that some participants felt that questions from the service user were 'wise and thought-provoking'.

In particular, the user was seen as being able to offer a human perspective that was well respected: 'she came up with questions none of us professionals would ever have thought of and got a much stronger sense of what the candidate was like as a person'.

Third, proposals for the new mental health workforce include the development of Support Time and Recovery (STR) workers (Department of Health, 2003e). STR workers will come from different walks of life with different backgrounds including volunteers and existing and former services users who have the ability to listen to people without judging them. They will work as part of a team that provides mental health services and focus directly on the needs of service users, working across boundaries, providing support, giving time and promoting their recovery. They can be employed by any agency in the NHS or social care field including the private and voluntary sector. It is envisaged that up to 3000 STR workers will be trained and working by 2005.

Fourth, involving users in the planning and delivery of health services has grown considerably over the last decade, with a systematic review (Crawford et al., 2002) identifying 337 relevant studies including a number in the field of mental health. As an example, Collaboratives, part of the governments' modernisation agenda as outlined in *The NHS Plan* (Department of Health, 2000a) use as approach based on the principles of continuous quality improvement and service redesign. They involve a network of organisations working together for a fixed time period on a specific clinical area. The government sees Collaboratives as a method of redesigning services so they are responsive to the needs of patients rather than the organisation. Within mental health, 37 organisations across the former Northern and Yorkshire and Trent NHS regions participated in the Mental Health Collaborative on inpatient care from October 2000 to November 2001. An evaluation of the user involvement in the Collaborative (Robert et al., 2003) found a strong involvement ethos across services and evidence of the positive effects of user involvement. Users were invited to join project teams as members, to attend learning sessions and to be closely involved in all aspects of the work. Improvements made through service user involvement included changes to process issues such as improved documentation. Some of the improvements suggested by service users were not the changes that staff themselves might have prioritised but were perceived as valuable. Many staff also felt that user involvement had challenged their own assumptions and led to new insights about patient care. However, the evaluation also noted scope for future improvements and the need to increase the level of user involvement.

Fifth, there has been recent policy support for greater involvement of both mental health service users and carers throughout the whole education and training process (Department of Health, 2001f). Involving users in training certainly has the potential to challenge some of the myths around mental illness, enabling those responsible for delivering mental health services to gain an insight into what it is like to be on the receiving end of such services.

Finally, there are growing numbers of service users represented on the governing boards of local and national organisations. As an example, a report published by the SCIE on the roles and responsibilities of a small number of services users in senior governance positions on governing boards of the bodies set up to regulate service, workforce, education and training standards in social care, found that the experience of user members on national boards was overwhelmingly positive. Users reported that 'every effort was made to include them' (SCIE, 2003, p. 6) and interviews with other stakeholders found that 'users were felt to contribute a vital perspective to the work' (SCIE, 2003, p. 7). Overall, organisations were perceived to be listening to and learning from the users on their boards. However, a personal account from a mental health service user on the board of an integrated mental health trust shows how isolating and difficult it can be to be the only service user on a governing board and suggests the need for much more planning and forethought about the need for training, support and clarity of role (Brodie, 2003).

The importance of organisational culture and personal attributes

Meaningful user involvement requires organisations to think about their own cultural environment. Service cultures that encourage involvement share a number of common characteristics including a commitment to genuine partnerships between users and professionals and to the development of shared objectives. As the National Schizophrenia Fellowship (1997, p. 10) observes:

> Everyone involved in the delivery of care, including service users and carers, should be treated as equal partners. Occasionally, some professionals may initially feel threatened by the involvement of service users and carers and if this is the case, then it is important that this issue is addressed so that all of the parties involved can work well together. It is essential to remember that every care partner brings something different, but equally valuable, to the relationship and that successful delivery of care depends on effective collaboration between the care partners.

The approach and value base of individual practitioners are also crucial. Thus, for service users in a study by Breeze and Repper (1998, p. 1306), individual attributes were a crucial feature:

> All the informants [in our study] were able to identify 'good' relationships that had developed with 'helpful' nurses. A good

nurse–patient relationship included the nurse: treating the patient with respect, essentially as a person, but, more than that, as a valued person (for example, exuding warmth, displaying empathy and holding 'normal' conversations with the patients); enabling the patient to have some meaningful control over their own care, for example, working with the patients to develop an appropriate and realistic care plan directed towards achieving the patient's own goals; and listening to and, especially, believing the patient.

Future directions in user involvement: from patient to citizen?

In late 1997, the Prime Minister, Tony Blair, announced measures aimed at improving life for an estimated five million citizens affected by crime, unemployment, low educational attainment and poor housing: 'we are passionately committed to making Britain one nation, giving every single person a stake in the future and tackling chronic poverty and social division'. (Tony Blair quoted in *The Independent*, 7 December 1997). It is against this political background that mental health service users have increasingly campaigned for more generalised reform on the grounds that every individual is a citizen with a series of political, civil and social rights. As Campbell (1996, p. 224) eloquently suggests: 'Madpersons as empowered customers of services and madpersons as equal citizens are two quite different propositions'.

Campbell also points out (2001, p. 81):

> The great irony about service user action in the past 15 years is that, while the position of service users within services has undoubtedly improved, the position of service users in society has deteriorated. As a result, it is at least arguable that the focus of service user involvement needs adjustment. Service users and service providers should accept that the quality of life of people with a mental illness diagnosis in society, indeed their proper inclusion as citizens, depends on education and campaigning. Although the quality of mental health services will continue to be a dominant issue for service providers, it might no longer have such a place in the agendas of service user organisations. The climate may be changing – the Disability Rights Commission, the Human Rights Act, bioethics etc. We should not expect service user involvement not to change.

This agenda will almost certainly require partnerships with other groups who face similar challenges to their citizenship status, including people with physical impairments within the wider disability movement. The Disability Rights Commission, which started work in 2000, brought over 150 legal actions under the *Disability Discrimination Act* in its first two years, as well as campaigning for strengthening of the Act to make it harder for employers to justify discrimination and to improve access to business premises and transport. This legislation has provided mental health service users with opportunities to pursue their rights. The first legal case backed by the new Disability Rights Commission was that of Pravin Kapadia, a man with severe depression who had been compulsory retired by his employers. The ruling that Kapadia was disabled under the terms of the *Disability Discrimination Act* enabled him to bring a case under the Act for discrimination and unfair dismissal (Valios, 2000) (see Chapter 9 for further discussion of discrimination issues and links between mental health and a social model of disability).

Conclusion

Meaningful user involvement should not be a one-off intervention or a discrete programme of work, but a much broader and more empowering way of working which affects every aspect of mental health provision. As Hutchinson (2000, p. 26) explains:

> If users are to regain some control over their lives there needs to be a shift in the balance of power between themselves and mental health professionals... The key element to achieving this shift is to involve service users at all levels of the mental health system: in the planning of their own support; in the design and running of statutory and independent services; in the recruitment of staff; in the training of mental health professionals; in monitoring the effectiveness of services; in researching and evaluating services, and finally, in the establishment of user-run or user-led services.

However, at the start of the new millennium, despite a plethora of policy reforms and pockets of good practice, it appears that a fundamental shift in the balance of power between users and professionals still remains to be achieved.

Reflection exercises

1. User involvement within your own organisation
Exercise for all workers

Your organisation has decided to hold a series of meetings to plan their user involvement strategy for the next two years. You have argued strongly that this meeting should include users of mental health services and have now been tasked with organising this aspect of the meetings:

■ How are you going to decide which users should be invited to attend?
■ What are the most appropriate locations for such meetings?
■ What issues will need to be thought through to ensure that the meetings are structured, paced and chaired in an appropriate manner?
■ What issues are raised by offering/not offering payments for attendance?

2. Ethical issues and patient choice
Exercise for all workers

A number of ethical issues may be raised by asking mental health service users to exercise choice and voice, for example when prioritising services.

As a group, imagine your local commissioning manager has convened a group made up of local mental health service users to help him/her decide whether to fund a new Early Intervention Team for young people with first episode psychosis, or redevelop a run down inpatient forensic ward within their geographical boundary.

■ What ethical issues do you think are raised from the users' perspectives in being asked to help make this decision?
■ What are the implications of convening such a group from the commissioner's perspective?
■ What implications do you think greater patient choice has for wider society? (Remember, choice emphasises the value of the individual, yet in practice, within a cash-limited NHS free at the point of use, can we prioritise one patient's treatment if this means denying someone else treatment?)

Suggestions for further reading

1. The Mental Health Foundation (2003) *Surviving user-led research: reflections on supporting user-led research projects*. London, The Mental Health Foundation

   Based on the experiences of the Strategies for Living project, this practical workbook describes the positives, practicalities and the pitfalls of user-led research from the perspective of the research team.

2. Barnes, M. and Bowl, R. (2001) *Taking over the asylum: empowerment and mental health*. Basingstoke, Palgrave Macmillan

   This book discusses action amongst users/survivors of mental health services, and initiatives from within the mental health system to 'involve' users with a particular emphasis on social care. Drawing on international research and writings of activists, Barnes and Bowl, both distinguished writers in this area, consider evidence of the effectiveness of collective action amongst service users, and the place of user/survivor movements within the broader social change strategies of new social movements.

3. Read, J. and Reynolds, J. (eds) (2000) *Speaking our minds: an anthology*. Basingstoke, Palgrave

   This uplifting, thoughtful, funny and demanding book contains over 50 testimonies from mental health service users on the experience of treatment, life as an inpatient and in the community and a particularly challenging final section on 'working for change'.

4. Sayce, L. (2000) *From psychiatric patient to citizen: overcoming discrimination and social exclusion*. Basingstoke, Palgrave

   This book proposes new theoretical models and practical strategies for tackling the widespread social exclusion faced by people with mental illness. Based on research in the US and UK, it analyses evidence of discrimination and the effectiveness of different responses including disability discrimination law, work to reframe media and cultural images, grassroots inclusion programmes, and challenges to the 'nimby' factor. The book also includes an introduction to the ideas of the social model of disability (explored in more detail in Chapter 9).

9 Anti-Discriminatory Practice

In this chapter we discuss:

- The concept of discrimination and anti-discriminatory practice
- The current policy context and relevant legislation
- Discrimination in mental health services
- The experience of various marginalised groups
- Policy responses and prospects for the future

Discrimination and anti-discriminatory practice

Traditionally, the British welfare state has ignored issues of discrimination, seeing its role as providing a range of standard services to those in need, irrespective of who these recipients are (Dominelli, 1988). For minority ethnic communities, for example, this is sometimes described as a welfare state which is 'colour blind', failing to recognise the different needs of different groups of people due to a commitment to treating everyone the same. In many ways, this is particularly true of the NHS, which has prided itself on offering health care to everyone on the basis of clinical need alone. Unfortunately, however, we know from the wider sociological literature that different groups of people do not always start from a level playing field. By treating everyone in the same way, therefore, there is a danger that we perpetuate existing inequalities and fail to challenge the divided and unequal society in which we live and work. If, on the other hand, we acknowledge that we all start from a different level within society, then it is possible for us to do things differently for different people to help us all achieve the same outcomes and quality of life. By treating people differently, therefore, we could argue that we are providing more support for those who need it most in order to pursue true equality.

However, current UK society is a long way away from achieving this aim. While our welfare services aspire to treating everyone the same, we nevertheless live in a society that likes to categorise people according to a range of social divisions: whether or not they are male or female, what colour their skin is, how old they are, their sexuality, whether or not they are disabled. How we categorise people can then help to shape how we respond to them, treating some groups more or less favourably than others. As Payne explains (2000, p. 1):

> It is impossible even to begin to think about people without imme-
> diately encountering 'social divisions'. We automatically perceive
> other human beings as being male or female, black or white, older
> or younger, richer or poorer, sick or well, or friend or foe. In
> forming a perception of them, we place them in pigeon-holes,
> adapting our behaviour and attitude to them in terms of the slots
> into which we have placed them.

As a result, it is naïve to assume that we can respond in the same way to all people:

- As a result of our tendency to make assumptions about people based on their gender, ethnicity, age and other characteristics, we will often find ourselves treating different groups of people very differently (either consciously or subconsciously)
- The services which the welfare state provides have often been designed from the point of view of dominant groups of people within society (typ-ically white males). As an example, many day centres for older people have served very traditional English meals and have produced all their information in English, without recognising that people from particular minority ethnic communities may have particular dietary needs (such as Halal meat for Muslims) and may not necessarily speak English. Thus, a service which was probably designed to meet the needs of all local older people has perhaps inadvertently discriminated against people from certain minority groups
- Discrimination does not only exist in health and social care, but is also widespread throughout society. Thus, an older woman who has been widowed may find herself financially penalised due to discrimination in the workplace and the social security system, while an Asian disabled person may find himself living in poor housing due to discriminatory employment practices and a failure by local housing services to provide accessible information in community languages. As a result, it is not appropriate to provide a standard level of service to everyone as different groups may well have a much greater need for support due to the discrimination they have faced

One of the earliest disciplines to recognise and respond to issues of dis-crimination was social work (see, for example, Dominelli, 1988; Thompson, 2001). Building on the civil rights movement of the 1960s, the school of radical social work has emphasised the importance of politi-cal, economic and social factors in shaping the lives of social care service users. While this analysis often tended to focus on social class, the debate has since expanded to include issues such as race, gender, sexuality and disability (see Thompson, 2001 for a more detailed description). More recently still, issues of discrimination have begun to be taken on board by other disciplines and are now a key feature of a number of government policies (see later in this chapter).

While many textbooks have typically focused on the experiences of different groups of people, there is a danger that each can see itself in isolation and vie for position as the group that is most discriminated against. As a result, this approach is increasingly being replaced by a new way of understanding and responding to discrimination – anti-discriminatory practice. Instead of focusing on one particular aspect of discrimination (such as racism or sexism), it is important to emphasise the concept of 'multiple oppressions' (a recognition that some groups face a range of different forms of discrimination at once and that the target should not only be sexism or racism by themselves, but discrimination itself in whatever form this takes). This has been most forcibly demonstrated by Neil Thompson (2001), whose introduction to *Anti-discriminatory practice* is one of the standard textbooks in this area (see *Further reading* at the end of this chapter). The main advantage of this approach is that it has the potential to unite the activities of different civil rights campaigners, creating a greater momentum for a more equal, inclusive society. In addition, it also helps to acknowledge the way in which different aspects of people's lives and identities interact. Thus, a 'black'[1] woman will have potentially very different experiences to a 'black' man, while a disabled 'black' woman may have different needs again. This is sometimes expressed in terms of 'jeopardy' – the 'single jeopardy' that a member of a disadvantaged group (for example, a 'black' person) faces, the 'double jeopardy' that a 'black' woman may experience and the 'triple jeopardy' (Norman, 1985) that a 'black' older person with a low socio-economic status may face.

For Thompson, discrimination operates at a number of different levels, each reinforcing and being reinforced by other levels (see Figure 9.1). Thus, discrimination can exist at the personal (P) level (of individual thoughts, actions, feelings and attitudes). However, this aspect of discrimination takes place within a cultural context (the C level of common values and shared ways of seeing, thinking and doing). This in turn is embedded in a structural (S) level (the established social order and accepted social divisions). As a result, action is needed at all three levels if discrimination is to be tackled – focusing on the individual alone will not be enough (see Dalrymple and Burke, 1995; Dominelli, 1997 for further discussion and models).

---

1   We use this term to describe the common experiences of those who encounter racism as a result of the colour of their skin. While this term is useful in emphasising the shared experience of racism, it should not distract from the fact that 'black people' are an extremely diverse group and should not overlook the fact that many white minority ethnic groups may also experience racism (such as Irish people).

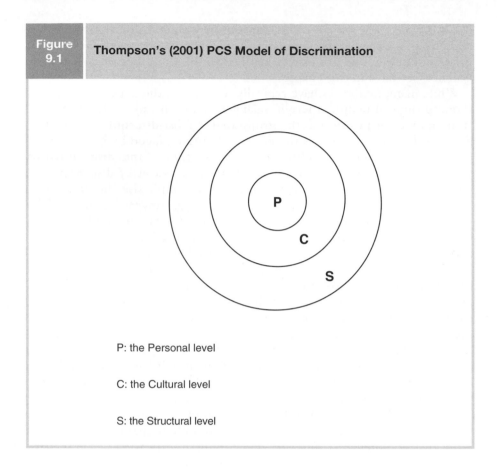

Figure 9.1 **Thompson's (2001) PCS Model of Discrimination**

P: the Personal level

C: the Cultural level

S: the Structural level

The policy context

In recognition of the discriminatory society in which we live, there have been a number of official policies and pieces of legislation designed to promote greater equality (see Figure 9.2).

While all these statutes and regulations have traditionally been overseen by separate bodies (such as the Equal Opportunities Commission, the Disability Rights Commission and the Commission for Racial Equality), there is now a commitment to bringing together these various organisations into a single commission for equalities and human rights (Department of Trade and Industry, 2004). While this helps to link the struggles of different marginalised groups and emphasises the cross-cutting nature of discrimination, it also runs the risk of diluting existing campaigns with regard to race, gender, disability and other social divisions, and opinion is divided on the best way forward.

Figure 9.2	Anti-discrimination legislation and policy

- The *Race Relations Act* 1976 makes it unlawful to discriminate on the grounds of race, colour, nationality or ethnic or national origin
- The *Equal Pay Act* 1970 eliminates discrimination with regard to pay and other terms and conditions between men and women doing equal work
- The *Sex Discrimination Act* 1975 makes it unlawful to discriminate on the grounds of sex (in employment, education, housing and the provision of goods, facilities or services)
- The *Disability Discrimination Act* 1995 ends discrimination in employment, education, the provision of goods, facilities and services, and, to a limited extent, public transport
- The *Human Rights Act* 1998 incorporates the European Convention on Human rights into UK law and gives a clear statement of people's basic rights and freedoms
- The *Race Relations (Amendment) Act* 2000 imposes duties on many public authorities to promote race equality and good race relations
- The Employment Equality (Sexual Orientation) regulations 2003 ban discrimination on the grounds of sexual orientation in employment
- The Employment Equality (Religion or Belief) regulations 2003 ban discrimination on the grounds of religion or belief in employment
- Under the European Union Employment Directive on Equal Treatment, all EU member states are required to introduce legislation prohibiting discrimination on the grounds of age, sexual orientation, religion and belief, and disability by 2006

(Department of Trade and Industry, 2004)

Discrimination in mental health services

If discrimination exists in health and social care and in wider society more generally, it should come as no surprise to find that similar issues also exist in mental health services. In particular, there is a significant literature on the experience of people from lower social classes and the impact of poverty, with poorer people more likely to receive biological rather than psycho-logical treatments and more likely to receive coercive rather than voluntary forms of treatments than richer people (see Pilgrim and Rogers, 1999 and Figure 9.3). There have been a range of explanations put forward for this, including social stresses that may contribute to mental ill health (such as poverty, poor housing and unemployment) and the 'cultural gap' that may exist between some mental health workers and their service users (who may sometimes come from very different class backgrounds). However, while still acknowledging this longstanding link between class and mental health (see, for example, Ferguson, 2000), more recent research has criticised this emphasis on class because of its association with traditional Marxist politics (which were felt to have focused on class at the expense of other

Figure 9.3	Class and health

Generally, in health care there is an 'inverse care law', that is, access to health care increases with increasing class status. However, the reverse appears to be the case in mental health care systems. Psychiatric services are dominated by patients from low social class backgrounds. Superficially this might suggest that those with the greatest need are being responded to... However, there is a problem with this logic. While most health care interventions are voluntary and ameliorative in intent in their response to the needs of sick people, in psychiatric services, involuntary detention and treatment are never far away... In light of these peculiar features about psychiatry, it might be more accurate to conceptualise mental health work as part of a wider state apparatus which controls the social problems associated with poverty... Once conceived in this way, it lowers our expectations that service contact should necessarily be about aiming for, or achieving, a gain in the mental health status of service recipients, given that the latent, and sometimes the explicit, function of psychiatry is that of successful coercive social control. The latter entails mental health services serving the interests of parties (such as relatives and strangers in the street) other than the patients they contain and treat.

...It is clear that whatever conceptual problems exist about understanding mental illness in the same way as physical illness, the social impact of low social class (especially its associated poverty) is similar for each. Basically, poorer people are significantly less healthy, both physically and mentally, then richer people.

(Pilgrim and Rogers, 1999, pp. 32 and 39)

social divisions such as race or gender) (Day, 1992; Thompson, 2001). As a result, there is now greater recognition of the needs of other groups, such as women, people from minority ethnic communities, people with physical impairments, people with learning difficulties, older people, and gay men, lesbians and bisexuals. The remainder of this chapter focuses on each of these groups in turn, before exploring the overall track record of mental health services in tackling discrimination and possible ways forward.

Women

Many commentators suggest that some women are likely to have extremely negative experiences of various aspects of mental health care (see Figure 9.4). Above all, a recurring theme in the literature is the risk of abuse or harassment while staying on mixed psychiatric wards. A substantial proportion of women using mental health services are thought to have experienced physical or sexual abuse as children and/or as adults (see, for example, Fleischmann, 2000; Killaspy et al., 2000b; Payne, 1998; Warner and Ford, 1998) and there is a clear danger that such abuse may be replicated in hospital after women have been admitted to mixed wards. This has been a crucial issue for some time – in the late 1980s, one commentator claimed that acts of sexual harassment, rape and abduction were an 'everyday occurrence' on some wards (Feinnman, 1988, p. 16) and accusa-tions of sexual assault have continued to emerge (see, for example, Cohen, 1992; Copperman and Burrows, 1992).

That sexual harassment is a key concern is demonstrated by the 1996 national visit of 118 mental health trusts carried out by the Mental Health Act Commission and the Sainsbury Centre for Mental Health (Warner and Ford, 1998). Here, the researchers found that 162 out of 291 mixed wards (56 per cent) reported problems of sexual harassment of women patients, ranging from sexual assault in a small number of cases to exploitation, inap-propriate touching, exposure and sexually disinhibited behaviour (see Figures 9.5 and 9.6). While ward staff identified a range of policies and prac-tices designed to protect women, only 34 wards had written procedures and only 26 of these were able to supply a copy to the researchers. Some policies were out of date and others were not always enforced due to pressures on hospital wards. Thus, there was sometimes insufficient female staff to have a female worker on duty each shift, male patients who had persistently harassed women patients could not always be transferred to another ward

Figure 9.4	Women's experiences of mental health services

Two-thirds of the users of mental health services are women. The majority of service planners and managers are men. This immediately raises key questions, such as how can male managers know what women want? And are mental health services meeting the needs of the majority of users? (Black and Shillitoe, 1997, p. 27).

Studies in the UK and US show that at least 50 per cent of women using mental health services have been sexually or physically abused as children and/or as adults.

On psychiatric wards they have to mix with men, who have good opportunities for getting away with harassment and assault. Both female and male mental health service users are in acute stages of distress when they are admitted to hospital. Women's vulnerability to assault is increased when they have reached a crisis point in their lives. During stays in hospital most people are disoriented and have very low self-esteem. The side effects of medication also play a role as they can cause drowsiness, apathy, confusion and physical debilitation. In these circumstances women might not be able to fend off unwanted sexual advances. Having a mental health problem makes it more likely that women will not be believed if they make a complaint about sexual harassment or abuse. Sometimes an accusation is thought to be part of a woman's illness. Therefore many women stay quiet about what happens to them in hospital (Fleischmann, 2000, p. 20).

There has been recent recognition that women in acute mental distress may be poorly served by existing mental health facilities where there is a lack of privacy, assaults are common and the atmosphere highly aroused. Female patients' vulnerability to sexual harassment and assault has been highlighted by [a number of commentators]... Many women admitted to psychiatric wards have experienced childhood sexual abuse or domestic violence and their vulnerability on the ward is especially worrying (Killaspy *et al.*, 2000b, p. 102).

Figure 9.5	Sexual harassment of women patients in mixed-sex wards (n = 162)

Type of problem	Number of wards reporting
Sexual assault	6 (4%)
Exploitation of vulnerable women	60 (37%)
Touching female patients	12 (7%)
Exposure/nudity of male patients	21 (13%)
Watching or following female patients	31 (19%)
Verbal harassment	43 (26%)
Disinhibited behaviour and remarks	67 (43%)

Source: Warner and Ford (1998), p. 226.

Figure 9.6	Policies or practices concerning women's safety (n = 212)

Policy/Practice	Number of wards reporting
Staff-related policies or practices:	
■ Choice of female keyworker	90 (42%)
■ Use of chaperones with male staff	27 (13%)
■ Female staff to provide intimate care	24 (11%)
■ Female staff on each shift	22 (10%)
■ Observation by female staff	11 (5%)
Practice-related policies or practice:	
■ Policy for vulnerable women	22 (10%)
■ Transfer of harassing male patients	20 (9%)
■ Policy on harassment	10 (5%)
Organisational/structural policies or practices:	
■ Women-only areas	42 (20%)
■ Security measures	20 (9%)

Source: Warner and Ford (1998), p. 226.

and male patients were placed in women-only areas if no beds were available elsewhere. Also of concern was the layout of some wards, which made it difficult to observe patients at all times and which did not always allow sufficient space to defuse potential tensions.

While much of the literature has tended to focus on the issue of single versus mixed-sex hospital wards, it is clear that there are other equally significant issues at stake concerning the way in which mental health services respond to the needs of women. As Payne (1998) demonstrates in her summary of women's experiences of mental health services:

- Women are more likely than men to be treated for a mental health problem and to be admitted to hospital at some point in their lives (particularly for depression and anxiety). Until recently, women were more likely than men to be compulsorily admitted to hospital and are still more likely to receive certain forms of treatment (such as ECT), while men are more likely to be referred by their GP to specialist services
- Women may be more heavily represented in the mental health statistics because particular pressures in their lives put them at greater risk of mental health problems, but also because of discriminatory attitudes and practice within health and social care. As an example, there is evidence to suggest that members of the medical profession may, in the past, have held stereotypical views about women and that women who behave in approved, female ways (e.g. paying attention to their hair/appearance and helping to clean the ward) may be more likely to be discharged from hospital (Chesler, 1974)

At the same time, other commentators emphasise a range of additional issues:

- Some mental health workers may lack awareness of gender issues, with Black and Shillitoe (1997) citing examples of male workers entering women's rooms unannounced
- Women with children admitted to hospital may need to make alternative child care arrangements, often at short notice and sometimes involving the placement of their children in the care of the local authority (Killaspy *et al.*, 2000b)
- The needs of men with mental health problems may take precedence over those of women as men are believed to engage in more problematic behaviours (such as failing to comply with medication or becoming violent) (Mallon, 2001)
- Women often feel that they have insufficient privacy in hospital. During the two national visits carried out by the Mental Health Act Commission and the Sainsbury Centre for Mental Health, for example, only three per cent of wards were women-only and many women did not have access to self-contained facilities for washing, sleeping or going to the toilet (Ford *et al.*, 1998; Warner and Ford, 1998)
- Where women complain of sexual harassment, there may be insufficient attempts to prevent it happening again. This was a key finding to emerge from a survey of hospital patients conducted by Mind, which found that

almost one in six patients had experienced sexual harassment, but that 72 per cent of those who complained felt that no action was taken (Baker, 2000)

In response to issues such as these, commentators propose a number of possible solutions. Most prominent of all is the call for more women-only spaces within mental health services, for segregated accommodation in hospital and for specialist women-only services (see Figure 9.7 for a good practice example). Certainly, this is the direction of current policy, with a pledge to eliminate mixed-sex accommodation (Department of Health, 1999a, p. 2002). However, whether or not this is a sufficient response is open to question in a number of key areas:

■ The debate about the relative merits of single- and mixed-sex provision has existed for some years and thinking has changed over time. Traditionally, hospital services were strictly segregated, with mixed wards only developing in the 1970s in response to suggestions that this might promote a more normal atmosphere which is a more accurate reflection of life outside hospital (Fleischmann, 2000; McMillan, 1997a; Warner and Ford, 1998). Now, the emphasis is on developing segregated services once more. Throughout, the rationale behind such changes has rarely been clearly articulated and there has been insufficient research into the outcomes of different types of service provision for men and women (Kohen, 1999). In particular, there appears little recognition that the 'normal' nature of mixed-sex settings is based on a white UK view of the world and may not apply to some minority ethnic communities

Figure 9.7	Specialist services for women: Drayton Park

Drayton Park in London is cited as a good practice example by a range of commentators (see, for example, Killaspy *et al.*, 2000b; McMillan, 1997b; Payne, 1998). According to a Camden and Islington Mental Health NHS Trust (2001) leaflet:

Drayton Park is an alternative to hospital admission for women.... It has been open since December 1995. The service recognises the need for women to have a safe place in which they can recover from crises and it focuses on issues that cause mental health problems for women. It was inspired and supported nationally by government recommendations and work such as the [1994 Mind] Stress on Women campaign. In 1999, it became a Beacon Service as part of the NHS Learning Network... A management advisory group consisting of women who have used services and women who work in mental health organisations within Camden and Islington guided [Drayton Park] in its first few years. This group maintained an alternative focus and supported the project in its development stages. In 1999, users of the service, in partnership with staff developed a Women's User Forum. This group has taken over some aspects of the advisory group along with other responsibilities.

■ Some people (male and female) may prefer mixed provision and are hostile to the idea of single-sex services (Batcup, 1997; Black and Shillitoe, 1997)

Above all, however, it seems that the difficulties women experience when accessing and using mental health services are much more fundamental than simply introducing women-only areas. While the debate about single- versus mixed-sex services will continue, it seems likely that the issues at stake are so significant and so ingrained that they will require much concerted action (see later in chapter for further discussion).

People from minority ethnic communities

There is overwhelming evidence to suggest that 'black' people experience mental health services in a very different way to white people. In particular, 'black' people are over-represented in mental health services, tend to receive more coercive forms of treatment (such as compulsory hospital admissions and admission via contact with the police and forensic services) and suggest that existing services are too culturally insensitive to meet their needs (see Figure 9.8 for a summary of the key issues). This may be the result of a number of different factors, and it can be difficult to isolate individual causal explanations (see Figure 9.9 for a summary of some of the key contributing factors emphasised in the literature).

As a result of the experiences set out in Figures 9.8–9.9, there have been a number of attempts to promote more culturally sensitive mental health services (see, for example, Department of Health, 1999a). As the Mental Health Act Code of Practice suggests (Department of Health/Welsh Office, 1999, p. 3):

> [People should] be given respect for their... diverse backgrounds as individuals and be assured that account will be taken of their age, gender, sexual orientation, social, ethnic, cultural and religious background, but that general assumptions will not be made on the basis of any one of these characteristics.

While the needs of 'black' service users have received greater attention in recent policy documents, there is widespread evidence to suggest that many 'black' people continue to have very negative experiences of mental health services. A national visit conducted by the Mental Health Act Commission and the Sainsbury Centre for Mental Health in 1999 found that many patients from minority ethnic communities were not receiving care sensitive to their cultural backgrounds (Warner et al., 2000b). Despite several examples of good practice, three-quarters of the 119 wards had no policy on dealing with racial harassment, two-thirds had no policy on race equality training and a similar number had used patients' relatives or friends to interpret for them. While half the units had a policy on the provision and use of interpreters, only three-quarters used interpreters who were trained

Figure 9.8	'Black' people's experiences of mental health services

Bahl (1999, pp. 10–11) identifies the following key issues:

African-Caribbean population:

- African-Caribbean people in Britain have higher admission rates to psychiatric hospitals and are diagnosed as having schizophrenia 3–6 times more often than the white population
- The incidence of schizophrenia in British-born Caribbean people is proportionately higher than the incidence reported for Jamaica and Trinidad
- Rates of schizophrenia in second-generation British-born black people may be greater than the rates in the first generation
- Black people are over-represented among patients compulsorily detained in psychiatric hospitals under the Mental Health Act, and also through police admissions
- African-Caribbean people receive differential and stronger forms of treatment, although differences in clinical management can partly be explained by differences in diagnosis...

Asian population:

- Some studies show higher hospital admission rates among Asian people than those for the British-born population
- The balance of evidence... suggests that Asian people have rates of psychiatric morbidity similar to or lower than the indigenous population... It is not known whether these patterns reflect genuinely lower psychiatric morbidity or differences in detection rates, reluctance of Asian people to present themselves as having mental health problems, or differences in the manner of presentation
- Linguistic and/or communication problems make it harder for GPs to recognise [mental health] problems when they arise...
- Suicide rates are low in some subgroups born on the Indian subcontinent, whereas women born in India or east Africa show a significant excess
- The rate of suicides among first-generation Asian women is greatest among the young. The rate in girls aged 15–24 years who were born on the Indian subcontinent is more than double the national average and at ages 25–34 years is 60 per cent higher in those who were born in India
- Young Asian women also have high rates of attempted suicide and are clearly a high-risk group...

Other key issues include (Bahl, 1999; Commander *et al.*, 1999; Parkman *et al.*, 1997):

- Excessive use of drug therapy for African-Caribbean people
- 'Black' people are less likely to have voluntary contact with services (that is, they are less likely to see a GP prior to contact with psychiatric services, have fewer voluntary admissions to hospital, have more absences without leave from hospital and are more likely to discharge themselves against medical advice)
- On discharge, 'black' patients may be less likely to remain in contact with services or to be seen by senior clinicians
- Independent of diagnosis, 'black' people are more likely to have contact with the police and with forensic services, and are more likely to be treated in intensive care facilities if detained under the Mental Health Act 1983

Figure 9.9	'Black' people and schizophrenia

Sharply *et al.*'s (2001) review of the literature on the increased rate of schizophrenia among African-Caribbean people in England highlights a wide range of potential hypotheses:

- African-Caribbean people may be misdiagnosed as having schizophrenia
- Biological factors such as genetic predisposition, prenatal and perinatal complications, certain risk factors in childhood and use of cannabis may play a role
- Social factors such as social disadvantage, concentration in inner-city areas, a reluctance to seek GP support, patients' and relatives' opinions and the experience of racism may all be significant
- Psychological factors such as the experience of adverse life events or low self-esteem brought about by racism, unemployment and deprivation may also be a contributing factor

in interpreting and some unit managers did not know if the interpreters they worked with were trained or not. Although the vast majority of units recorded the ethnicity of patients, this information was seldom put to great use.

The National Schizophrenia Fellowship (2000) has carried out a survey of 450 people with mental health problems from a range of different ethnic backgrounds. This found that people from minority ethnic communities, particularly African–Caribbean people, had more negative experiences of mental health services than other groups. In particular, 'black' service users were more dissatisfied with the care they received than white respondents, were more likely to feel that their cultural needs had not been met, were more likely to disagree with the diagnosis they had been given, experienced far more detentions under the Mental Health Act and had been forcibly restrained more often. As one participant observed (National Schizophrenia Fellowship, 2000, p. 1), 'I am treated unfairly because of the colour of my skin, although I was born in London. This is not fair'.

Wilson and Francis' (1997, p. 33) survey of 100 African and African-Caribbean users across England and Wales found that 'a significant proportion of [respondents] feel they are largely misunderstood within the mental health system – either because they are feared, stereotyped or ignored. The stereotypes interact in complex ways and appear to have a powerful impact, as people are seen as black, as mad, as dangerous, as inadequate. This can reduce people's trust in the services on offer, and potentially damage their sense of identity and thus their mental health'. A more in-depth qualitative study conducted by Pierre (1999) paints a similar picture of disputed diagnoses, lack of consultation and information, physical and verbal abuse from hospital staff and a failure by staff to challenge racism from other patients.

In addition to these studies, other key issues have been found to include:

- Discriminatory attitudes among mental health workers. As Webbe (1998, p. 12) observes, many practitioners have preconceptions of 'black' people as 'big, black and dangerous'. Whereas mental illness is often equated with 'danger', 'black' mental illness is equated with 'danger x 2' (see also Browne, 1997)
- A frequent complaint from 'black' service users is the lack of accessible information about the services available, the nature of their mental health problem and their legal rights (see, for example, Arshad and Johal, 1999; Grant-Pearce and Deane, 1999; Li et al., 1999)
- The importance of primary care as an arena in which mental health problems can be identified at an early stage before a crisis has occurred. Unfortunately, this opportunity is often lost as a result of the failure of some GPs to diagnose mental health problems in some of their 'black' patients and to over-diagnose in the case of other 'black' groups (see, for example, Bahl, 1999; Browne, 1997; Koffman et al., 1997; Thornicroft et al., 1999)
- A failure to appreciate the importance of religious beliefs in shaping people's attitudes to mental health and their willingness to seek help from western services (Copsey, 1997a, 1997b)
- A lack of understanding of or knowledge about mental health issues in particular minority ethnic communities (see, for example, Li et al., 1999; Tabassum et al., 2000)
- A lack of 'black' staff in mental health services (Pierre, 1999). Often, the small numbers of 'black' staff that do exist can experience just as much discrimination as 'black' service users (Webbe, 1998)
- Often, ethnicity can interact with gender. Thus, Asian women may have different needs than white women and than Asian men (see, for example, Arshad and Johal, 1999; Tabassum et al., 2000)

Above all, however, there is evidence to suggest that all of these factors combine to create a 'vicious circle' (Parkman et al., 1997, p. 264), whereby 'black' people have negative experiences of mental health services and are therefore less inclined to seek help at early stage in the future or to comply with medication. This can then lead to relapse and readmission to hospital, where existing negative expectations are reinforced. This has been described by the Sainsbury Centre for Mental Health (2002e) in terms of a downward spiral or a 'circle of fear' (see Figure 9.10).

In many ways, issues such as these reached a head in late 2003 with the publication of the Independent Inquiry into the death of David Bennett (Norfolk, Suffolk and Cambridgeshire Strategic Health Authority, 2003). A 38-year-old African-Caribbean man, David Bennett died in a medium secure unit in 1998 after being forcibly restrained by staff face down on the floor for some 25 minutes. According to some commentators, Bennett may have been one of at least 27 'black' people since 1980 to die while in

Figure 9.10	Circles of fear

Stereotypical views of Black people, racism, cultural ignorance, and the stigma and anxiety associated with mental illness often combine to undermine the way in which mental health services assess and respond to the needs of Black and African-Caribbean communities. When prejudice and the fear of violence influence risk assessments and decisions on treatment, responses are likely to be dominated by a heavy reliance on medication and restriction.

Service users and carers become reluctant to ask for help or to comply with treatment, increasing the likelihood of a personal crisis, leading in some cases to self-harm or harm to others. In turn, prejudices are reinforced and provoke even more coercive responses, resulting in a downward spiral, which we call 'circles of fear', in which staff see service users as potentially dangerous and service users perceive services as harmful.

Black people see using mental health services as a degrading and alienating experience: the last resort. They perceive that the way services respond to them mirror some of the controlling and oppressive dimensions of other institutions in their lives, e.g. exclusion from schools, contact with police and criminal justice system. There is a perception that mental health services replicate the experiences of racism and discrimination of Black people in wider society, particularly instances where individuals have experienced more controlling and restricting aspects of treatment...

Coming to mental health services was like the last straw... you come to services disempowered already, they strip you of your dignity... you become the dregs of society (Service User).

(Sainsbury Centre for Mental Health, 2002e, pp. 8 and 24)

psychiatric services and this case is 'typical of the poor care' received by 'black' people (Leason, 2003a, 2003b, p. 12). As part of the subsequent Inquiry, evidence was taken from a range of national experts with regard to mental health and ethnicity, and one of the key recommendations of the final report was for 'Ministerial acknowledgement of the presence of institutional racism in the mental health services and a commitment to eliminate it' (p. 67). This concept is particularly associated with the 1999 Macpherson inquiry into the murder of a 'black' young man, Stephen Lawrence. Macpherson's definition of institutional racism was directly quoted by the Bennett Inquiry (see Figure 9.11), which also included a statement from the then Chief Executive of the National Institute for Mental Health in England, Antony Sheehan, that the NHS is racist in parts and that 'institutional racism was a true accusation that should be levelled at the NHS who should have no tolerance of it' (p. 43).

In seeking to respond to issues such as these, there is a range of possible ways forward. For some commentators, this may require a dual approach – working *inside* mental health services to make them more appropriate for people from minority ethnic communities, while at the same time working *outside* mental health to build capacity within black and minority ethnic

Figure 9.11	Institutional racism

Institutional racism is the collective failure of an organisation to provide an appropriate and professional service to people because of their colour, culture, or ethnic origin. It can be seen or detected in processes, attitudes and behaviour which amount to discrimination through unwitting prejudice, ignorance, thoughtlessness and racist stereotyping, which disadvantage minority ethnic people.

(Norfolk, Suffolk and Cambridgeshire Strategic Health Authority, 2003, p. 43)

communities and the voluntary sector for dealing with mental ill health. This has been usefully summarised in a NIMHE (2003a) report which highlights these concepts in its title: *Inside, Outside*.

At a very basic level, however, the provision of effective interpretation services with workers trained in mental health issues could help to make services more accessible (Tabassum *et al.*, 2000; Warner *et al.*, 2000a). In addition, a key contribution has been made by the voluntary sector, which has traditionally been able to provide more flexible, responsive and culturally sensitive services (La Grenade, 1999; Sashidharan, 1999). Smaller and more informal than the state, voluntary agencies have often been able to provide a more personal approach, may have a better knowledge of local community needs and can sometimes employ a more diverse workforce (Bhui *et al.*, 2000). However, developing specialist culturally sensitive services is only part of the solution, and several commentators emphasise the mixed messages that this can create. Rather than promoting the needs of 'black' service users, there is a danger that specialist services can marginalise people from minority ethnic communities even further, suggesting to workers that ethnicity is a fringe rather than a mainstream issue. Often, moreover, there is a tendency for workers to assume that ethnicity will be addressed by 'black' staff – an approach which many 'black' workers feel can de-skill them and fails to recognise the importance of ethnicity for all workers irrespective of their own skin colour (La Grenade, 1999).

To ensure that culturally sensitive services become a mainstream feature of mental health services rather than an 'optional extra', the majority of commentators emphasise the central importance of training. For some commentators, this would enable staff to explore their own attitudes to people from minority ethnic communities, understand the health beliefs and lifestyles of different communities and provide more culturally sensitive services (see, for example, Bahl, 1999; Koffman *et al.*, 1997; Webbe, 1998). Another key issue is the need for meaningful two-way communication between service providers and minority ethnic communities to ensure that minority ethnic users are involved in the planning and provision of services (Pierre, 1999).

Other potential methods of improving the experiences of 'black' users is the focus team approach advocated by Bhui and Bhugra (1999) – whereby each team is responsible for familiarising itself with a particular community and allowing the community to access their skills and knowledge (see also Copsey, 1997a, 1997b). Above all, however, a number of commentators emphasise that good quality, responsive mental health services will benefit all service users, irrespective of their ethnicity. Thus, for Bhui and Bhugra (1999, p. 231) 'all services need to be local, accessible, comprehensive, flexible and consumer-orientated, empowering those using the services'. For La Grenade (1999, p. 188), moreover, good services should be 'available, affordable, accessible, adaptable and acceptable' – principles that may well apply to 'black' people and white people alike.

Unfortunately, our knowledge of 'black' people's experiences of mental health – although extremely well documented – is limited by two key short-comings in the current literature. First, the majority of documents focus on the African-Caribbean community, with much fewer attempts to consider groups such as south-east Asian people. With a few notable exceptions (see, for example, Li *et al.*, 1999), moreover, the needs of refugees and asylum seekers, Irish people and smaller minority ethnic communities such as Chinese or Vietnamese people have often been overlooked (Bahl, 1999; Bhui *et al.*, 2000). Second, and even more fundamentally, is the tendency for the majority of documents focusing on ethnicity and mental health to *describe* ethnic differences in service provision. Often, these studies are written by research or health professionals without necessarily considering the experiences and views of service users from different minority ethnic communities. As Thornicroft *et al.* (1999, p. 163) explain:

> Substantial differences have been demonstrated in the pattern of con-
> tacts with psychiatric services of patients from different ethnic groups,
> especially between those who are White and Black Caribbean. These
> differences spread across most aspects of specialist mental health service
> provision. So far, these are largely expert-reported differences, or are
> aggregated data from inpatient service contacts. It is striking that
> information is largely absent in the psychiatric literature from the
> perspective of the patients themselves, of whatever ethnic group. Since
> types of contact with services vary so much, it is reasonable to hypo-
> thesise that service users' views of services prior to, during and after
> such contact may also differ substantially by ethnic group. These views
> may then affect how such people use services in the future. In this way
> the experiences that patients accumulate from using services progress in
> ways which reflect their expectations, satisfaction, perception of illness
> and 'harder' aspects such as the number of admissions, particularly
> those which are compulsory. The ways in which such psychiatric
> 'careers' develop in relation to ethnic group, and their implications for
> how services can be sensitised to ethnic issues, are yet to be properly
> understood.

People with physical impairments, people with learning diffioultioe and older people

In contrast to the extensive body of literature on women and people from minority ethnic communities, the experiences of people with physical impairments, people with learning difficulties and older people have often been neglected in relation to mental health servies. Despite this, more recent research and campaigning has suggested that each of these user groups may face particular difficulties when seeking to access mental health services:

1. While some *people with physical impairments* may also develop mental health problems, attention has tended to focus primarily on sensory impairments. For example, the mental health charity, Mind (2003a), has drawn attention to the emotional and mental health problems which can develop as a result of difficulties coming to terms with loss of sight and feelings of anxiety, depression, isolation and uncertainty. Also significant are the barriers faced by many deaf people who have mental health problems, including the failure of staff to communicate effectively with deaf people, a subsequent risk of misdiagnosis and a lack of specialist service provision (Clark, 2003; Evans, 2003; Mind, 2003b; Sign, n.d.). In addition, Morris' (2004a) study of twenty-five people with physical impairments and mental health problems reveals a range of difficulties with physical access and with workers not recognising the 'whole person', with both physical and mental health needs (see Figure 9.12).
2. *People with learning difficulties* have more mental health problems than the general population (NHS Executive, 1998), yet may experience difficulties accessing services. This may be to do with communication barriers and a lack of accessible information produced by mental health services. However, also significant is a lack of clarity about who should take the lead in meeting the needs of people with mental health problems and learning difficulties. In the past, some mental health services have been reluctant to work with people with learning difficulties, while learning disability services sometimes lack the expertise to work with mental health problems in their service users (personal communications, frontline workers and people with learning difficulties). In response, the government's learning disability White Paper, *Valuing People*, argues that people with learning difficulties should have full access to general psychiatric services like everyone else in society, but that specialist learning disability workers could help to facilitate and support this process (Department of Health, 2001h). This may require substantial changes before mainstream mental health services are able to work as effectively with people with learning difficulties as they do with members of the general population.
3. *Older people* (often defined as people aged 65 and over) with mental health problems are sometimes considered to be the 'Cinderella' of mental health and often nobody's priority at all (see Figure 9.13). This is despite

| Figure 9.12 | People with physical impairments and mental health problems |

- The majority of respondents said they had difficulty accessing mental health services because of their physical impairments. The majority also had difficulty using physical disability services because of inadequate recognition of mental health needs and negative attitudes amongst staff towards mental health issues
- In-patient experiences were often characterised by inaccessible physical environments and a lack of assistance for even simple things...
- Medication required for a physical condition was commonly withdrawn on admission to a psychiatric ward and was not always available when needed...
- Community mental health... staff were often unfamiliar with needs relating to physical impairment and this could be associated with unhelpful attitudes
- There was commonly poor or no communication between mental health and physical disability services...
- Medication given for mental health needs often had an impact on physical impairment, but most people said they had not been warned about these potential effects
- 'Talking treatments' received the highest rating of any service, but it was often difficult to find an accessible and, within the private sector, affordable therapist or counsellor
- When people were asked about what they wanted from services, they said they wanted to be seen as 'a whole person', with attention paid to both mental health needs and those relating to physical impairment. They wanted services and professionals to communicate and work together, and easy access to flexible services which could address individual needs. Above all, they wanted to be listened to and treated with respect.

(Morris, 2004b, p. 1)

the fact that older people with mental health problems form a significant user group (and that current numbers are set to rise dramatically as a result of demographic changes). According to one commentator (Barnes, 1997):

- In the 1990s, around 600,000 people in Great Britain had dementia, and this number is predicted to increase to 900,000 by 2021
- At any one time, between two and four per cent of older people have a major depressive episode and ten to 20 per cent have less severe forms of depression
- Older people accounted for 19 per cent of all suicides in England and Wales, often linked to depression, pain and feeling unwell. Deliberate self-harm is usually a failed suicide attempt in older people and is associated with serious depression
- Schizophrenia develops in one to two per cent of people over 65
- About three to four per cent of older people have an alcohol problem

Figure 9.13	**Older people with mental health problems – nobody's priority?**

The care of older people with a mental health problem... is a major cause for concern and presents a significant challenge for community care.... Social trends show that the number of very elderly people in Britain is increasing, older people are more likely to live alone, and the prevalence of mental ill health rises markedly with age. Therefore, the size of this group is growing and yet it is often forgotten. It is an easy group to ignore. Older mentally ill [people] are reluctant to speak out, are rarely dangerous and are often sad, poor and confused. They may have no family to speak for them. In community care terms, they fall between traditional mental health and older people's services. Their care confronts different professional value systems as a balance is sought between protection and treatment, independence and risk. It requires typically a multi-agency and multi-professional response. Even so, older people with mental health problems are often nobody's priority.

(Barnes, 1997, p. 1)

Responding to the needs of older people with mental health problems can be particularly difficult, as social services department tend to include this user group as part of their generic older people's services, while NHS provision tends to include this group as part of its mental health services, making inter-agency working all the more complex (Glasby and Littlechild, 2004).

Uniting all these groups is the concept of a social model of disability (see also Chapter 2). In contrast to traditional medical approaches (which see disability in terms of individual physiological and biological conditions), the social model acknowledges that disabled people have *impairments*. However, rather than focus on individual medical factors, many disabled people define disability in terms of the discrimination and exclusion they face as a result of the way in which society in organised. As UPIAS (1976) has argued (quoted in Oliver and Sapey, 1999, p. 22):

In our view, it is society which disables physically impaired people. Disability is something imposed on top of our impairments by the way we are unnecessarily isolated and excluded from full participation in society. To understand this it is necessary to grasp the distinction between the physical impairment and the social situation, called 'disability', of people with such an impairment. Thus we define impairment as lacking part or all of a limb, or having a defective limb, organism or mechanism of the body; and disability as the disadvantage or restriction of activity caused by a contemporary social organisation which takes no account of people who have physical impairments and thus excludes them from the mainstream of social activities. Physical disability is therefore a particular form of social oppression.

Using this 'strong' model approach, the emphasis shifts from medical inter-vention and cure for the individual to tackling the way society discriminates against disabled people. As an example, a person who uses a wheelchair may be unable to use public transport – however, depending on the model of dis-ability we adopt, we could attribute this to the person's impairment (they need to use a wheelchair) or to social causes (buses are not always designed for people in wheelchairs). With the current state of medical technology, intervening at a social level can be more effective – thus, it would probably be easier to raise the curb of a bus stop so that a wheelchair user can get on than it would be to intervene individually (working with the individual to try to 'heal' their impairment). Such an approach is also more cost-efficient – by altering the bus stop, planners and policy makers could make the bus accessible for all wheelchair users.

In theory, a social model also has the potential to develop a common cause between people with mental health problems, people with physical impair-ments, older people, people with learning difficulties and others. While the disability movement has not always been as inclusive of some of these groups as it perhaps could have been, a social model emphasises the way in which all these people are disabled not by their impairment, frailty, learning difficulty or mental distress, but by the way in which society responds to such people and the exclusion and discrimination they face as a result of their impairment. While much more work is required to develop these links, there is at least scope for a much broader and potentially very powerful coalition of groups whose focus is not on individual impairments, but on the way society is organised and the way in which discrimination operates.

Gay men, lesbians and bisexuals

Prohibited since legislation in 1885, homosexuality was only legalised in 1967 when men over 21 were permitted to have sexual relationships with each other (although some parts of the UK did not follow suit until 1992 when the Isle of Man came into line with the rest of the country). In con-trast, lesbianism has never been included in legislation and has therefore never been illegal (see Mind, 1996 for all dates quoted in this paragraph). Despite this, homosexuality has traditionally been seen as a form of mental illness, and was not declassified as such by the American Psychiatric Association until 1973 and, by the World Health Organisation, until 1992. Even as late as 1989, the Oxford Textbook of Psychiatry included homosex-uality under 'problems of sexuality and gender' and discussed ways of 'curing' homosexual people. While such overt discrimination no longer exist, much of the misunderstanding and prejudice behind these statutes and practices remain. As Mind (1996) emphasises:

> Although blatant examples of bigoted, misinformed theory are no longer common in psychiatric writing, evidence shows that homosexuality continues to be referred to as a mental disorder in some psychiatric texts, and anecdotal evidence shows that homosexuality continues to be

Figure 9.14	The experiences of lesbian, gay and bisexual service users

Golding's (1997) interviews with 55 gay, lesbian and bisexual service users identified some positive experiences of mental health care, but also found that 73 per cent said they had experienced some sort of prejudice or discrimination in connection with their sexuality:

- 88 per cent of people experiencing discrimination felt unable to challenge it, largely because of feelings of fear or vulnerability
- 22 per cent said they had experienced direct victimisation in connection with their sexuality in the form of violence (including instances of rape or sexual assault)
- 38 per cent experienced additional discrimination due to their religious beliefs, race, physical ability or age
- 16 per cent had partners at the time when they were using mental health services. Two-thirds of these people felt that their partners had not been treated on an equal par with the partners of heterosexual service users
- 51 per cent said that their sexuality had been inappropriately used to explain the cause of their mental distress
- Seven per cent of participants said that they felt they were forced to have a blood test for HIV

Price's (1997) literature review and in-depth interviews emphasise:

- The prevalence of suicide and self-harm within the gay/lesbian community
- The discriminatory nature of the 'nearest' relative regulations, which discriminate against gay or lesbian partners
- The distress caused by homophobia and harassment
- Professionals seeking to blame or cure people's sexuality
- The value which gay/lesbian users place on 'out' workers
- The tendency for gay or lesbian workers to be seen as 'the gay expert'
- Workers ignoring or responding inappropriately to people's sexuality

McFarlane's (1998) research with 35 service users and 35 mental health workers concluded that (p. 117):

Lesbian, gay and bisexual mental health services users are discriminated against and oppressed, not only by the attitudes and behaviour of society at large, but also from within mental health services. Judgement is made on the basis of their sexual identity and their identity as service users. Not only that, they are also discriminated against from within lesbian, gay and bisexual communities, again on the basis of their use of mental health services.

King et al. (2003) conclude that gay men, lesbians and bisexual people are more likely than heterosexuals to:

- Experience psychological distress
- Harm themselves
- Experience harassment or bullying because of their sexuality
- Have contact with the mental health system
- Experience negative reactions from professionals when being open about their sexuality

thought of as a mental illness per se by society in general and by some mental health professionals.

That gay men, lesbians and bisexual people continue to have negative experiences of mental health services is demonstrated by a small number of key research studies (see Figure 9.14).

Policy responses

Over time, the research findings set out above point to a poor track record with regard to tackling discrimination in mental health services. However, in the early twenty-first century, there are signs that issues of discrimination and equality are beginning to become more of a mainstream feature of the policy agenda, with as series of key policy documents and initiatives. Examples include:

- Official guidance on women's mental health (Department of Health, 2002i, 2003i)
- Official policy documents on the experience of minority ethnic communities and on race equality in mental health (Department of Health, 2003j, 2005b, 2005c; NIMHE, 2003a, 2003b, 2004a)
- The development of an older person's work programme at NIMHE
- A strategic plan (2004–09) to tackle stigma and discrimination (NIMHE, 2004b)
- The creation of a new Commission for Equalities and Human Rights (Department of Trade and Industry, 2004)

While these policies all place a welcome focus on tackling discrimination, many of the themes and issues highlighted in this chapter are longstanding and complex. Moreover, some media accounts appear to cast doubt on the extent of official commitment to the radical action required to promote anti-discriminatory practice. For example, the social work press has criticised the government for apparently rejecting some of the Bennett Inquiry recommendations, refusing to acknowledge the existence of institutional racism (Community Care, 2004; Gillen, 2005). In addition, there have been claims that the Department of Health watered down a critical report into mental health services for people from minority ethnic communities. According to the report author (quoted in Leason, 2003c, p. 8):

> They [the Department of Health] tried to dilute it as much as they could. We had to fight all the way... The experience of working with the DoH around this document, and subsequently, has reinforced my view that this is an example of institutionally racist attitudes and behaviours on its part.

As a result, it may well be that discrimination in mental health services persists and that the negative experiences of some of the groups set out above continue.

Conclusion

Overall, the particular forms of discrimination addressed in this chapter have a number of themes and issues in common. For example, individual forms of discrimination can interact. Thus, 'black' women may have very different experiences to white women, while gay, lesbian or bisexual service users may face additional discrimination due to their age, physical ability, religion or ethnicity. While specialist services that are sensitive to the needs of a particular marginalised group of people may be welcome, this may actually hinder change in more mainstream services. There is also an additional danger that staff from a particular group may be perceived as the 'expert' on a particular issue (e.g. 'black' staff members as 'experts' on ethnicity and gay staff as 'the gay expert'). This not only de-skills and exploits these staff members, but also takes the responsibility away from other workers for making services more responsive to the needs of service users from particular backgrounds.

Above all, however, many of the negative experiences cited above are longstanding issues which policy makers and practitioners have known about, but have so far been unable to resolve. This suggests either a lack of political will or that the issues concerned are so complex and deep-seated that they are extremely difficult to put right (or both). As we discussed at the beginning of this chapter, discrimination does not only exist within mental health services, but in health and social care as a whole and in wider society. Also, discrimination cannot be tackled simply by changing the way individuals behave. Instead, attempts to root out discrimination in mental health services need to be accompanied by efforts to root out discrimination in wider society at a personal, cultural and structural level. Discrimination, in short, is pervasive and multi-faceted, and only an equally multi-faceted response will suffice. Of course, this is not to deny that mental health services can do a range of things to tackle discrimination. However, it may mean that changes within mental health should take place alongside more widespread and fundamental action to ensure that services and wider society function in a non-discriminatory manner.

Reflection exercises

1. Experiencing discrimination in mental health services
Exercise for all workers

Thinking about the mental health service where you work/train, what would it feel like to be using your service as:

- A woman?
- A person from a minority ethnic community?
- A person with a physical impairment?
- A person with a learning difficulty?
- An older person?
- A gay man, lesbian or bisexual person?

Do you have policies and procedures for working with these different groups of people? Do you know where these policies are and what they say? Are they implemented in day-to-day practice?

Have you had any training on any of these issues and does such training exist in your organisation?

Have service users had an input in developing your policies and procedures?

Share these answers with colleagues from different professional backgrounds – do they agree with you?

2. Tackling discrimination
Exercise for all workers

Think of different ways you, your profession and your organisation could begin to tackle discrimination. List your answers according to the three categories set out by Thompson (2001) above – personal, cultural and structural. Share these with colleagues – are there any of these actions you or your team could implement now to try to make an immediate impact?

Suggestions for further reading: mental health services

For an overview of the issues presented in this chapter, Pilgrim and Rogers' (1999) A *Sociology of Mental Health and Illness* is an essential starting point. However, more detailed reading is listed below for specific topics:

1. Women
   In addition to official policy documents on mental health and gender (Department of Health, 2002i, 2003i), the national visit carried out by the Sainsbury Centre for Mental Health and the Mental Health Act Commission provides an accessible overview (Warner and Ford, 1998), as do Payne (1998), Busfield (1996) and Pilgrim and Rogers (1999, Chapter 3).
2. People from minority ethnic communities
   Key introductions to the experiences of people from minority ethnic communities include the Sainsbury Centre for Mental Health's (2002e) *Circles of Fear*, the inquiry into the death of David Bennett (Norfolk, Suffolk and Cambridgeshire Strategic Health Authority, 2003) and NIMHE's (2003a) *Inside Outside*. In addition, national voluntary agencies such as Mind (Wilson and Francis, 1997) and the National Schizophrenia Fellowship (2000) also report extremely powerful findings from the views and experiences of 'black' service users. Mind also publish a number of factsheets on mental health and the African-Caribbean, Chinese and Vietnamese, Irish and South Asian communities (www.mind.org.uk/Information/Factsheets/Diversity).
3. People with physical impairments, people with learning difficulties and older people
   Key sources for people with physical impairments and mental health problems include factsheets by Mind (www.mind.org.uk) on visual impairments and deafness, and research by Sign (n.d.) into mental health services for deaf people (see also www.signcharity.org.uk). The Disability Rights Commission has also established a Mental Health Action group (see www.drc-gb.org) to explore links between mental health service users and the disability rights agenda. A member of this group, Peter Beresford, is lead author of a journal article exploring this issue in more detail (Beresford *et al.*, 2002). Morris' (2004a) study into the experiences of people who have physical impairments and mental health problems is also an important and interesting study.
   For older people, the Audit Commission (2000a, 2000b, 2002b) has produced a number of key reports, while the *National Service Framework for Older People* includes a specific standard about older people with mental health problems (Department of Health, 2001i).
   The government's learning disability strategy, *Valuing People*, summarises official policy and introduces the concept of health facilitation

to support people with learning difficulties to access mainstream community services (Department of Health, 2001h). *Signposts for Success* provides a good practice guide to commissioning and providing health services (including mental health services) for people with learning difficulties (NHS Executive, 1998). A toolkit for improving mental health services for people with learning difficulties is also available from the Valuing People Support Team (2004).

Additional information about the social model of disability is available from introductory disability studies textbooks such as those by Oliver (1990; Oliver and Sapey, 1999) and Swain *et al.* (2004).

4. Sexuality

In addition to the studies cited in the main body of the chapter, good practice guidance in working with lesbians, gay men and bisexuals in mental health services is available via the website of PACE, a London-based counselling and mental health project working to promote lesbian and gay health and well-being (www.pacehealth.org.uk).

Suggestions for further reading: wider policy and practice

1. Thompson, N. (2001) *Anti-discriminatory practice* (3rd edn.). Basingstoke, Palgrave

    Outside mental health services, Thompson's introduction is a key text and a good starting point for those who wish to move beyond individual manifestations of discrimination (sexism, racism etc.) to understand and tackle discrimination as a whole.
2. Department of Trade and Industry (2004) *Fairness for all: a new Commission for Equality and Human Rights.* London, TSO

    Also helpful is the Department of Trade and Industry's (2004) White Paper on creating a new Commission for Equality and Human Rights (CEHR), which summarises existing policies and future changes.
3. Prior to the creation of the CEHR, existing equality bodies include:

- The Commission for Racial Equality (www.cre.gov.uk)
- The Equal Opportunities Commission (www.eoc.org.uk)
- The Disability Rights Commission (www.drc-gb.org)

Additional information is available from the Equalities Coalition (www.equalities.org), which is a network of organisations with an interest in equalities and non-discrimination issues.

In this chapter we discuss:

- The importance of carers
- Definitions of 'the carer'
- The policy context
- The neglect of carers of people with mental health problems
- Marginalised groups
- The needs of carers

The importance of carers

When working in health and social care, it is tempting to assume that the people workers meet are somehow representative of society as a whole. When all you see on a daily basis are people facing considerable difficulties or changes in their lives, and who need input from formal services, it is easy to get a distorted view of the world. In fact, most people make little or no use of formal health or social care, and manage by themselves or with help from friends and family. As an example, around 60 per cent of adults with a learning difficulty live with their families, and up to 25 per cent of people with a learning difficulty do not become known to formal services until their parents become too frail to continue caring for them (Department of Health, 2001j, pp. 56–7).

Even when they do need help from statutory welfare services, most people do not rely solely on this form of provision. On the contrary, the vast majority of care is (and always has been) provided by carers: family members, friends and neighbours who support someone else as a result of a personal relationship with that person, not as a paid job or as part of a statutory service. In the UK, it has been estimated that there are 5.2 million carers, providing support worth around £57 billion per annum (Carers UK quoted in Sims, 2004, p. 25). Without this support – often unseen and unheard – statutory services would be unable to function. As Prime Minister, Tony Blair, has stated (Department of Health, 2000c, p. 3):

> When I talk about the importance to Britain of strong communities
> and of people having responsibilities towards each other, I'm not

speaking of abstract ideas, but of real people and real events: the things many people do to make things better for those around them. The extraordinary work which carers do may well be the best example of what I mean. Extraordinary not in ways which make headlines, but in ways which really matter and which really make a difference to those they are caring for. Carers devote large parts of their own lives to the lives of others – not as part of a job, but voluntarily… For the sick, the frail, the vulnerable and the elderly, carers provide help and support in ways which might otherwise not be available. By their effort, their patience, their knowledge, their understanding, their companionship, their determination and their compassion, carers very often transform the lives of the people they're caring for… Carers are among the unsung heroes of British life.

In many respects, therefore, this chapter is in the wrong place in this book – it should not be last after primary, community and hospital services, but should come first, because carers provide the bulk of support. However, as explained below, it is only in the last twenty years or so that we have come to recognise the needs and contribution of carers, and, until relatively recently, this has often been a neglected area. As an example from mental health, when the *Cases for Change* (Glasby *et al.*, 2003) report on which this book draws was published in 2003, we were only able to identify 11 studies (out of 653 documents), many of which were essentially journalistic accounts of new services in practitioner magazines rather than detailed research into the needs of carers and the best way of responding. A similar finding had previously emerged from an official review of NHS-funded research as part of the development of the *National Service Framework for Mental Health* (Wright *et al.*, 2000). Since then, there have been a number of new and important contributions to the debate, and this material is included throughout the remainder of this chapter. However, despite all this, the needs of carers remain an under-researched and undervalued area.

Definitions of 'the carer'

Part of the difficulty in discussing the needs of carers revolves around terminological and conceptual problems. This is true in four main areas:

1. There is a tendency within health and social care to refer to 'informal carers'. This term is usually adopted to distinguish between paid carers in statutory services and those family members and friends who provide care on a non-statutory, voluntary basis. However, many carers suggest that they find this phrase highly patronising and demeaning, implying that they are not 'proper' carers – they are merely 'informal' with the 'real' care provided by professionals. As we have already seen, exactly the opposite is often true and we have adopted the term 'carer' in this book to reflect the central importance of carers within health and social services.

2. Much of the generic literature on carers portrays the caring task in a negative light and as 'a burden'. While there are many difficulties associated with caring (see below), it can also be very hard for the person being cared for, who may feel frustrated and angry as a result of their perceived dependence on someone else. In addition, caring can be a very positive experience. At its best, caring *for* someone arises out of caring *about* someone, and the word itself implies warm and loving relationships. Of course, as noted below, carers can be spouses, parents, children or siblings, and caring has the potential to cement relationships and bring people closer together. At the same time, service users can contribute positively to the lives of carers. As an example, an American study by Greenberg *et al.* (1994) highlighted the contribution made by people with mental health problems in terms of providing family members with companionship, helping with meal preparation and household chores, listening to problems and providing advice, helping with shopping and providing care for others during periods of illness.

3. For some people, the term 'service user' and 'carer' are artificial constructs which do not reflect the reality of people's lives and relationships. For example, an older married couple may both have needs that the other can help meet, while a child or young person can be a carer for a parent with a learning difficulty or a mental health problem. In many ways, this is true of all of us: in practice, no one is completely independent of family or friends and we all rely on other people to meet some of our needs, whether it be practical or financial support from parents to young people, emotional support, neighbours babysitting or communities getting together to tackle a particular issue locally. While it is true that some people have greater support needs than others as a result of a physical impairment, mental health problem or learning difficulty, we are all interdependent.

4. There is an on-going debate about the usefulness of the term 'carer'. While it is helpful to distinguish users' family and social networks, many people do not see themselves as 'carers' and do not respond to official policies or sources of support badged in this way. As Sayce (2000, p. 11) observes:

> A further personal dimension was added when I became involved with a partner who has a diagnosis of manic depression. I do not, however, think that this makes me a 'carer', because this is a mutual relationship, not one in which 'care' goes one way, and not one involving 'burden' (an offensive term that should be dropped).

This may be particularly true for young carers, older people, people from minority ethnic communities and the carers of people with mental health problems (Department of Health/Social Services Inspectorate 1997, 1998a, 1998b; Heron, 1998; Rogers, 2000), who may see themselves as children, spouses and family members rather than as 'carers'. This is a significant issue and one which defies an easy answer. Our own personal preference is to adopt a generic term such as 'carer' as a useful shorthand for a group of people who offer support to someone close to them; however, we are equally aware that others would argue that if a term does not make sense to carers themselves then it has little meaning.

The policy context

In the late twentieth century, the needs of carers slowly began to acquire increasing recognition and significance. Much of this began in the 1980s, with a series of research studies, often influenced by feminism and the gendered nature of caring, which began to highlight the substantial caring tasks which family members and friends (often women) were undertaking on behalf of older people, people with physical impairments, people with learning difficulties and others (see, for example, Baldwin and Twigg, 1990; Finch and Groves, 1983; Ungerson, 1987). In 1989, the *Caring for People* White Paper provided one of the first official acknowledgements of the substantial role played by carers, and made support for carers a key priority (Department of Health, 1989a, p. 4):

> The government acknowledges that the great bulk of community care
> is provided by friends, family and neighbours. The decision to take on
> a caring role is never an easy one. However, many people make that
> choice and it is right that they should be able to play their part in
> looking after those close to them. But it must be recognised that carers
> need help and support if they are to continue to carry out their role.

While this commitment to meeting the needs of carers was an important statement of government intent, the White Paper and 1990 Act did little to deliver substantial change for carers. The disputed and shifting nature of the concept of community was simply ignored and huge assumptions were made therefore about the ability, desire and capacity of the community to care.

In 1995, the *Carers (Recognition and Services Act)* gave people providing care on a regular basis to someone eligible for community care services the right to an assessment of their needs, but with a number of limitations (Mandelstam, 1998, p. 45; see also Department of Health, 1996b):

- Entitlement to an assessment depended on the carer either providing or intending to provide a substantial amount of care on a regular basis
- Entitlement depended on the carer requesting an assessment
- Carers' assessments could only take place if the person being cared for was themselves being assessed under the *Community Care Act* – carers had no independent right to an assessment
- Any services provided would be offered to the 'service user', and carers were not entitled to any services to meet their own assessed needs
- Social services were not given any additional funding to implement the Act

As a result, the *Carers (Recognition and Services) Act* 1995 attracted a degree of criticism from the field – while it certainly focused on *carers*, it offered little *recognition* and very little by way of *services* (personal communications, front-line workers). In addition, while the emphasis on assessing carers' needs may, in time, help to raise them up the policy agenda of health and social care, it also suggests that carers carry problems that need to be assessed and managed. Viewed in this way, it may be difficult for carers to develop equal and constructive relationships with services, or to be treated, along with the service user, as experts in their own right.

In recognition of some of these previous shortcomings, the 1998 *National Carers' Strategy* underlined the government's commitment to improving information, support and care for carers (Department of Health, 2000c). This was followed in 1999 by the *National Service Framework for Mental Health*, which included a specific standard about the needs of carers (see Figure 10.1). In 2000, *The Carers and Disabled Children Act* 2000 strengthened the entitlement to an assessment by giving carers aged 16 or over the right to an assessment (even where the person they care for has refused an assessment by social services or has refused services following an assessment). Policy guidance also emphasised that workers should give carers verbal and written information about their right to an assessment. In addition, local authorities were given the power to supply certain services direct to carers

Figure 10.1	The NSF for Mental Health

Standard Six: Caring about carers

Aim: To ensure health and social services assess the needs of carers who provide regular and substantial care for those with severe mental illness, and provide care to meet their needs.

Standard six – all individuals who provide regular and substantial care for a person on CPA should:

■ Have an assessment of their caring, physical and mental health needs, repeated on at least an annual basis
■ Have their own written care plan which is given to them and implemented in discussion with them

Rationale: Carers play a vital role in helping to look after service users of mental health services, particularly those with severe mental illness. Providing help, advice and services to carers can be one of the best ways of helping people with mental health problems. While caring can be rewarding, the strains and responsibilities of caring can also have an impact on carers' own mental and physical health, and these needs must be addressed by health and social services.

(Department of Health, 1999a, p. 69)

Figure 10.2	The failure to meet the needs of carers

A large body of research demonstrates that carers may be unaware of their rights to an assessment, that they may feel unsupported in their role as carers and that health and social care agencies may not always perceive support for carers as a high priority. For example, Henwood's (1998) survey of 3031 carers found that:

- A large number received little or no practical support from social services
- Many people not receiving NHS support would have found it helpful and there were high levels of unmet need for nursing support
- Over half had sustained an injury (such as back strain) since becoming carers
- Over half had been treated for a stress-related illness since becoming a carer
- 60 per cent had never been told by an NHS member of staff that they were carers or how they could contact an appropriate support organisation

(such as short-term break voucher schemes or direct payments) (Department of Health, 2001j). Finally, in 2004, the Carers (Equal Opportunities) Act seeks to ensure that all carers are informed of their right to an assessment, that councils take account of carers' outside interests (such as wishes to work, undertake education or training and leisure activities), and that the NHS and social services work together more effectively to provide support for carers.

Despite this emphasis on the needs of carers, there is evidence from the wider literature to suggest that such policy measures have not always been translated fully into practice (see Figure 10.2).

The neglect of carers of people with mental health problems

In 2001, the case of James Lawson provided a powerful example of the lack of support which some carers of people with mental health problems receive and the sense of helplessness which they may experience (see Figure 10.3).

Shortly after the Lawson case, the Department of Health and the National Schizophrenia Fellowship launched their *Commitment to Carers* campaign to coincide with *National Carers Week* (Department of Health/National Schizophrenia Fellowship, 2001). Figures published by the National Schizophrenia Fellowship (n.d.) suggest that almost one in four of Britain's 5.7 million carers (22 per cent or 1.26 million people) are caring for someone with a mental health problem, often with only limited support from statutory services. Traditionally, the needs of carers of people with mental health problems have received even less attention than carers of people from other user groups. This was initially highlighted in a groundbreaking study of *Families Caring for People Diagnosed as Mentally Ill* (Perring *et al.*, 1990)

Figure 10.3	The pressures facing carers

The assisted suicide of Sarah Lawson brought the plight of people caring for those with mental health problems sharply into focus. The reality of looking after people with such severe problems means they often live under unimaginable pressures with very little support.

When Sarah Lawson committed suicide in April last year, it was a desperate act by a severely depressed young woman. The fact that her father, James Lawson, assisted in her suicide by placing a bag over her head as she lay dying from an overdose is shocking – even appalling.

But few of the estimated 1.26 million people caring for a friend or relative with some form of mental illness are going to be appalled by the actions of this man – an exhausted, distraught and desperate parent. Caring for someone in these circumstances can be tough, unremitting and lonely. Every year, a few people are inevitably pushed beyond the limit of their endurance (Winchester, 2001).

James Lawson later received a two-year suspended sentence (Community Care, 2001).

funded by the Department of Health and conducted by the Social Policy Research Unit at the University of York. In particular, Perring *et al.* argued that the carers of people with mental health problems had been neglected for two main reasons:

1. The literature on caring tends to focus on physical caring tasks (i.e. of people with physical impairments and frail older people).
2. Mental health services have tended to focus on the person with mental health problems, without necessarily recognising the needs and contributions of the user's family and friends. This may be partly because of the strong medical influence within mental health practice and research which had tended to focus on definitions and theories of mental illness and neglected 'the more general non-medical, societal and familial aspects' of living with a mental health problem (Perring *et al.*, 1990, p. 3). Even where families have been considered, this is often only as an adjunct to helping 'the patient'. On other occasions, families have been seen as 'part of the problem' rather than 'part of the solution' – either contributing to the mental health problem in the first place or exacerbating it (personal communications, mental health workers).

Despite these limitations in the literature, Perring *et al.* were able to identify a number of key issues for the carers of people with mental health problems, including the considerable stresses and strains of the caring role and a lack of support from formal services (see Figure 10.4).

Figure 10.4	The carers of people with mental health problems

Perring *et al.*'s (1990) review of the literature suggests that:

- Carers of people with mental health problems face 'difficult' behaviour, including social withdrawal, uncontrollable restlessness, threatened or actual suicide or hypochondriacal preoccupations. Often carers are uncertain how to respond, wanting to be sympathetic, but feeling baffled and frustrated
- Carers often take on unexpected new roles, from personal care to household and financial responsibilities
- There can be a substantial impact on every aspect of family life (marital and parental relationships, domestic routine, social life, leisure activities, employment and financial circumstances)
- Caring can provoke a range of emotions (including negative feelings such as fear, anger, resentment and a sense of being overloaded, as well as positive emotions such as warmth and love)
- Caring can have a negative effect on health and mental health
- Carers are concerned about the low quality and quantity of their contact with formal services. Key issues include frequent staff changes and a lack of continuity, family concerns being ignored until a crisis is reached, unsympathetic workers and poor communication between workers and families
- There are high levels of unmet need

Overall:

The ability of families to cope against a background of inadequate formal support does not mean that services to families need no improvement. The issues of unreported need, the continuing evidence that care by the family is associated with various indicators of stress, and criticisms that families make of their experience with professional workers all underline the fact that some effective intervention for families with a mentally ill member is essential, for the benefit of the family and identified patient alike (Perring *et al.*, 1990, p. 44).

Many of these themes have since been supported and developed in more recent studies. For example, in 1995 the National Schizophrenia Fellowship published a national survey of carers' needs on behalf of the Department of Health's Mental Health Taskforce (Hogman and Pearson, 1995). For the research authors, the carers of people with mental health problems had become 'silent partners' in community care: so used to the difficulties associated with caring and with lack of support from formal services that they see this way of life as the norm and do not ask for help (see Figure 10.5). As a result, the study began with 'four facts you need to know about carers' (p. 4):

1. Every carer has individual caring responsibilities and individual needs. Carers cannot be classified as one group with a shared set of needs.
2. Carers are experts in severe mental illness.

Figure 10.5	'The silent partners'

71 per cent said that caring had resulted in health problems such as stress, depression, heart trouble, sleep problems and anxiety: 'Don't you know anyone it hasn't affected? You live on a knife edge all the time'.

58 per cent said that caring led to significant extra expense: 'We are doing the government's job for them for free without it being acknowledged'.

42 per cent said that time spent caring had prevented them from working as much as they would have liked: 'As a carer I had to go part-time and also had to have time off... Therefore I did not reach my full potential in work, and therefore could not demand a higher salary, thus affecting my pension on retirement'.

Many carers wanted more services than they were receiving to help them continue in their role: 'We have never yet met a social worker in connection with our son's illness'.

'The problem is that there are not enough facilities within the community, and many people do not know how to gain access to what little there is'.

'I have never been offered help, advice or support from any agency'.

Information is crucial for carers, yet is often neglected: 'I have had to search for all the information regarding services, sections and care management, nothing has been offered'.

Many carers had experienced a crisis and felt that there was insufficient support: 'I found it very frustrating that nothing was being done to help when she was ill'.

Overall, many people found caring without adequate support extremely difficult: 'It has been a nightmare which I wouldn't wish on any living soul. It has broken a part of my heart, which I feel will never heal'.

'The carer is almost as much a victim of the illness as the patient'.

'I know how to care – but I have had enough. I want to be able to live whatever life I have left – my way – and know my daughter is safe and will be helped'.

(Hogman and Pearson, 1995: assorted quotes; sample: 400 carers)

3. Carers do not always want to care.
4. Carers have a low ceiling in terms of demands for services. They are not a group that make unrealistic demands.

Of course, both these studies took place prior to more recent carers' legislation, and considerable progress might have been expected given the policy initiatives set out earlier in this chapter. Despite this, Wright *et al.*'s (2000) thematic review of NHS-funded research suggests that there are significant variations in terms of the amount of support available to carers, with many not receiving the services they need to continue in a caring role or to maintain their own health. This is echoed by a number of other commentators, who suggest that the contribution of carers is often undervalued and their needs unrecognised (see, for example, Allen, 1997, p. 34):

Carers are the invisible corner-stone of community care. For the relatives and friends of someone with a severe and enduring mental health problem, community care represents a 24-hour burden with serious, often unacknowledged consequences.

More recently, the needs of the carers of people with mental health problems have received renewed attention from the national voluntary organisation Rethink (2003b). According to a survey of 1451 users and carers, around half of carers felt that improvements were taking place in mental health services, but that there was still a long way to go, with many people not receiving a proper break from caring, not sufficiently involved with health and social care professionals and concerned about the availability of relevant services (see Figure 10.6). Similar issues have also been raised by monitoring undertaken on behalf of the Department of Health, which emphasises the adverse effect which caring can have on carers' own mental health (Singleton *et al.*, 2002).

However, one of the most substantial contributions to date has been the work of Arskey *et al.* (2002) at the University of York. Commissioned by the NHS Service Delivery and Organisation Research and Development programme, Arskey *et al.*'s review of the literature and consultation with key stakeholders suggests that services should be underpinned by four key principles:

1. Positive and inclusive: mental health professionals should have a positive approach to carers, involve them in decision making and recognise them as partners or 'co-experts'.
2. Flexible and individualised: services should be person-centred, reflecting the diversity of carers.

Figure 10.6	Rethink survey 2003

92 per cent of carers want contact with a professional, but only 49 per cent say they are in regular contact all or most of the time. A key barrier was concerns about 'patient confidentiality', which many carers felt was used by professionals in an unhelpful way to block the sharing of information.

One in four carers said they had been denied access to help during the past three years. For one person, a 'lack of beds and resources locally means my son doesn't get help until a crisis', while for another carer 'no one ever phones back when I make a call requesting help. [It] usually takes seven or eight calls to get hold of anyone'.

Key frustrations for carers include shortage of adequate service provision locally (30 per cent), difficulty accessing crisis services (16 per cent), difficulty getting access to mental health professionals (14 per cent), concerns about the quality of mental health staffing (11 per cent) and a feeling of not being listened to or valued by professionals (ten per cent).

One in four carers feel that they don't have any information to help them.

(Rethink, 2003b)

3. Accessible and responsive: services should be available at all times, including outside 'office hours', and offer a rapid response.
4. Integrated and co-ordinated: services should be 'joined up'; carers' services should be embedded within mainstream mental health services.

Overall (Arskey *et al.*, 2002, p. 40):

> Support for carers of people with mental health problems needs to be offered in the form of a flexible package of services that is tailored to suit the individual carer-care recipient dyad; that is underpinned by key principles of service delivery such as inclusiveness, responsiveness and co-ordination; and that takes account of local contexts. The content of these packages will vary, and will reflect the diversity of carer experience in terms of geography, socioeconomic variables, patient diagnosis and stage of illness, as well as differing delivery methods provided by both the statutory, private and voluntary sectors.
>
> A consensual view emerged... that ... interventions should be tailored to the needs of both individual carers and care recipients; disregarding care recipients can lead to unanticipated outcomes, as well as hindering the full realisation of benefits... On this basis, we feel that it is important to identify and examine what carers, and care recipients, believe is effective in terms of the range of services available and explore how best these can be delivered in order to lead to improved outcomes for both carers and care recipients.

Marginalised groups

A key criticism of some of the existing literature is the implicit assumption that carers are a single category of people, each with similar needs. As the quote from Arskey *et al.* above suggests, this is an oversimplistic view that runs the risk of neglecting the needs of individual carers. In particular, we know relatively little about (Arskey *et al.*, 2002, p. 11):

- 'Black' and minority ethnic community carers
- Carers of people with dual diagnosis
- Carers supporting more than one person
- Less-common caring situations (for instance, caring in gay and lesbian relationships or caring at a distance)

An additional group traditionally neglected in the literature are young carers – children and young people caring for a parent with a mental illness. This issue has been particularly highlighted in recent years as a result of a general growth in our awareness of the needs of young carers (through research and campaigning carried out by academic bodies such as the Young Carers

Research Group at Loughborough University) and by a specific research study into young carers and mental health by Aldridge and Becker (2003). Although estimates vary, there may be some 68,000 young carers in Britain, with anywhere between 6000 and 17,000 young carers looking after mentally ill parents. Overall, (Aldridge and Becker, 2003, p. 137):

> The findings [of this study] suggest that, where professionals engage in effective intervention procedures (recognising children's caring roles, acknowledging needs, making appropriate assessments and referrals), these can be crucial in preventing crises and allowing children (and parents) some degree of choice in undertaking informal care responsibilities. Furthermore, when professionals offer sensitive and non-demeaning assistance, this help is also highly valued by families. However, in most cases it seems that professionals fail to engage in these effective intervention procedures and to offer needs-led assistance.

The needs of carers

Despite this neglect of the needs of carers, it is clear that caring for someone with a mental health problem can have significant implications for almost every aspect of daily life. Whilst some people describe positive aspects of caring (such as increasing self-confidence and putting other issues into per-spective), negative aspects of caring include the potential impact on the carer's family and social life, work and health (see Figure 10.7).

Figure 10.7	The impact of caring

Hill *et al.*'s (1998) survey of 1113 carers of people with manic depression found that many participants saw caring as having a negative effect on their friends and social life, with some also reporting a negative impact on their self-esteem, their family relationships and their work/work prospects.

Huang and Slevin's (1999) review of the literature on carers who live with someone who has schizophrenia suggests that many carers may experience:

- Physical problems (such as sleeping problems, headaches and chest tightness)
- Social difficulties (such as economic problems, stigma, social alienation and loss of leisure time/employment)
- Relationship difficulties (such as the disruption of family life, marriage problems or loss of friends)
- Psychological or emotional difficulties (such as anxiety about the future, grief reactions, mental health problems such as depression, loneliness and loss of motivation)

Figuro 10.7	The Impact of oaring (*continued*)

Leavey *et al.*'s (1998) study of 50 carers in north London found that 56 per cent saw caring as moderately stressful and 36 per cent considered it very stressful. Fifty-six per cent sometimes felt unable to cope with the person being cared for and 20 per cent often felt unable to cope.

In one evaluation of voluntary family support workers, interviews with 62 carers revealed the stressful nature of caring (Weinberg and Huxley, 2000, pp. 500–1). Of the 62 people, 21 had consulted their GP for help with an emotional problem in recent months and a further 20 had received treatment for a potentially stress-related illness (such as high blood pressure, chest pains and palpitations). Carers also reported significant restrictions on their social and leisure activities, hidden expenses, a lack of understanding from family or friends and difficulties engaging in paid employment.

'Black' carers may have particular unmet needs as a result of culturally insensitive services and the difficulty of obtaining information in languages other than English (Arshad and Johal, 1999).

Figure 10.8	Carers' priorities

Top Five Services Desired by Carers	% rating as a high priority	% reporting difficulty accessing service
24-hour professional support 7 days/week	67	67
Information about illness	61	55
Opportunity to learn personal coping strategies	41	70
Regular updates from professionals	35	60
More education about manic depression	31	53

Source: Hill *et al.* (1998)

In response to these issues, carers have expressed a desire for a range of support services to enable them to carry on in their caring role (see Figure 10.8). In Leeds, for example, a carers' support service identified the importance of emotional support, respite, advocacy, 24–hour crisis support and good quality information (Allen, 1997). Also in the north of England, an evaluation of voluntary sector family support workers found that carers valued the workers as a counselling, information, listening and advocacy resource, providing both emotional and practical support (Weinberg and Huxley, 2000).

Similar findings have also emerged from Hill *et al.*'s (1998) study of the carers of people with manic depression. When asked to rate the importance of 17 areas of need and whether they had experienced any difficulties in accessing services in these areas, the carers concerned gave a very clear indication not only of the support they wanted, but also of the significant unmet need which continues to exist (see Figure 10.8). Crucially, many of the priorities expressed by carers are also highly valued by service users – information, being involved by professionals (see Chapter 8) – and it may well be that a good quality service for users is also a good quality service for carers.

Similar issues have also been raised by Huang and Slevin (1999, pp. 91–2) in their review of the literature on the carers of people with schizophrenia. According to this review, carers particularly value:

- Advice and guidance on the use of medication
- Education in the use of cognitive and behavioural strategies
- Education of the total family regarding the need for family support
- Contact information for external support groups
- Family and individual counselling if required
- Education about schizophrenia to improve family knowledge
- Practical advice and guidance, including financial advice
- Education on the use of stress–management techniques
- Access to adequate respite services
- 24-hour access to professionals in emergencies
- Carer and client involvement in care planning
- Access to multi-disciplinary services via a keyworker
- Access to specialist mental health services when required

As with user involvement in Chapter 8 of this book, ensuring that services are responsive to the needs of carers is likely to require an explicit commitment to carer involvement, both in designing individual care packages and in shaping services more generally. As an example of the importance of carer involvement, Allen (1997) describes the development of a carer's service in south Leeds, emphasising the following guiding principles:

- The participation of carers in service provision, service development and service evaluation
- Involvement that gives carers the power to influence policy and practice
- Carer-led rather than service-led provision
- Commitment to a continuing process rather than a one-off activity
- Flexibility in the face of the diverse and potentially conflicting needs of users and carers
- The strategic development of carer involvement in all aspects of the agency's work

Conclusion

Despite much greater official recognition of the needs of carers, much remains to be done if carers generally (and the carers of people with mental health problems in particular) are to receive sufficient support to be able to continue in their role. Caring has a substantial impact on the lives of many people in the UK and, although we have only begun to acknowledge it relatively recently, it is the contribution of carers that makes the work of statutory health and social services possible. While caring can be a positive experience, it can also bring a series of negative consequences (both for the carer and for the person being cared for). As a result, statutory services have a duty to provide much better and more responsive support than they currently do in order to give carers the help they deserve and need. While there has been relatively little research in this area (compared to other chapters in this book), it seems clear that the way forward must lie in providing a range of support (from accessible information and practical advice to specialist and crisis support). However, also significant seems to be the value base and interpersonal skills of individual workers, with a much greater need for human skills such as empathy and the ability to listen, and a much greater willingness to acknowledge the expertise of carers and value them as people with a key contribution to make. Hopefully, if we could achieve this, then the 'silent partners' of Hogman and Pearson's (1995) study could one day become genuine partners – valued, listened to and supported to continue in their role as the key providers of community care.

Reflection exercises

1. The impact of caring
Exercise for all staff

Imagine you are caring for a family member with a mental health problem:

- How would this make you feel?
- How would it feel for the person with a mental health problem?
- Which areas of family life might this impact upon?
- What sort of support would you want from formal services?

2. Services for carers I
Exercise for all staff

Consider the services available in your organisation and local area for the carers of people with mental health problems:

- What services are available?
- If your organisation does not provide any specific support, do other statutory agencies?
- Are there local voluntary organisations that work with carers?
- How easy are local services to access?
- If a carer asked you for help, would you know where to go?
- How do carers access support outside office hours?
- Do you know anything about the quality of such services?
- How effective might they be in meeting the needs of carers (compare this with your own thoughts and experiences after completing exercise 1 above)?

3. Services for carers II
Exercise for individual professional groups

As an individual, what could you do to ensure that the needs of carers are met more effectively in your organisation/area?

If possible, repeat this exercise at a team meeting or away day – what more could your profession/organisation/health and social care community be doing to support carers?

Suggestions for further reading

1. Arskey *et al.*'s (2002) *Services to support carers of people with mental health problems: overview report.* York, Social Policy Research Unit, University of York

    This report summarises a review of the literature (1985–2001) and consultation with national statutory and voluntary agencies, local managers and practitioners and carers. Detailed yet accessible, it offers one of the most up-to-date and informative overviews of the key issues, exploring topics such as the different interventions and services to support carers, effectiveness and cost effectiveness, methodological issues and gaps in the literature. In addition to the overview report, there are additional reports on the literature review, the consultation and a short briefing paper. For further information, visit www.sdo.lshtm.ac.uk.

2. The government's carers website (www.carers.gov.uk) provides a range of facts, figures and definitions with regard to the work of carers, background information on current policy and links to relevant websites.

3. Carers UK is a national voluntary organisation which campaigns for the rights of carers, conducts research, produces policy briefings and develops good practice guides based on the experiences of carers. For further information, visit www.carersonline.org.uk. Additional information is also available from the Princess Royal Trust for Carers, who have worked with the Royal College of Psychiatrists to campaign for the carers of people with mental health problems and people with learning disabilities (see www.partnersincare.co.uk).

4. For young carers, Aldridge and Becker's (2003) *Children caring for parents with mental illness* is the first in-depth study of its kind, drawing on detailed research with 40 families. After exploring prevalence and previous research, the book examines the views of children, their parents and professionals, before making a series of recommendations for future policy and practice. In addition, the book contains an invaluable chronology and guide to policy which has an impact on young carers looking after a parent with a mental illness, stretching from the *National Health Service Act* of 1946 to debates around the review of the *Mental Health Act*.

5. For background reading on carers more generally, the Department of Health's (2000c) *Caring about carers* is a national strategy outlining the government's proposals for improving the support available to carers. Stalker's (2003) *Reconceptualising work with 'carers'* also provides a useful overview, reviewing the carers' literature, exploring the nature and diversity of caring relationships, and examining issues such as the needs of families, assessment, carer involvement, employment, poor care and the legal framework.

11 Conclusion

Overall, this summary of current mental health policy and practice reveals some grounds for optimism, but also a number of longstanding issues and tensions that show little sign of being tackled. On a positive note, mental health is higher up the political agenda and arguably better funded than often in its past. There is growing emphasis on primary care as a key part of the mental health system, new community teams, attempts to raise the standard of acute care and work underway to reform prison health care. At the same time, there are also increasing attempts to promote inter-agency collaboration, to involve service users in decisions about their own care and services more generally, to root out discrimination and to support carers.

Despite this, a chronological approach to understanding mental health services and the large body of research evidence reviewed in this book raise serious questions about the extent to which some of these measures will be successful. Over time, mental health services have struggled to reconcile ongoing tensions between care and control, between community and acute care, and between user involvement and the regulation of potentially dangerous behaviour. Throughout the main body of the book, there have been constant references to the shortcomings of primary and community mental health care, negative service user experiences in mental health hospitals, the deep-seated nature of discrimination (both in services and in wider society), the lack of support perceived by the families and friends of people with mental health problems and significant barriers to more effective partnership working and genuine user involvement. Although we seem to know what the key issues are, we also seem remarkably unable to solve them, as the same themes and concerns keep recurring throughout the history of mental health services.

As a conclusion to this book, it seems difficult to explain this apparent inability to resolve such fundamental problems. In Chapter 2, we briefly reviewed some of the key reasons why policies can fail to be implemented in practice including the problems of organisational culture and of the policy torrent that has descended in a top down manner particularly since 1997. However, the failure to make positive changes illustrated in this book seems so significant that other explanations may be required to supplement these more generic issues about gaps between policy rhetoric and reality.

For us, one possible explanation may lie in the broad range of stakeholders involved in mental health services and the very different views they have about the world and about what constitutes valid evidence. While this is true of all areas of health and social care, it is particularly the case in mental health, where there are well-defined groups of people with seemingly incompatible beliefs about the way forward. Although this is an argument that we develop in more detail elsewhere (Glasby and Beresford, 2006), examples of these stakeholders include:

- The medical establishment, with an emphasis on medical diagnosis and intervention
- The pharmaceutical industry, with a vested interest in developing pharmacological responses to mental distress
- A more social approach which emphasises the role of social factors and the environment in explaining mental distress (typically associated with social work, but also true of a number of other disciplines)
- A survivor movement, highly critical of attempts to medicalise ordinary human distress
- The media, influenced by a desire to generate profit by publishing stories that are likely to catch the public imagination
- Policy makers, seeking to make the best available use of scarce public resources and to balance the competing demands made on them by the different stakeholders

Although these groups are likely to have different perspectives, the key difference lies in the priority that each might give to different forms of evidence and different ways of knowing the world. Thus, whilst psychiatrists might look to formal randomised controlled trials, service users might emphasise the importance of their personal experiences as a source of evidence. While the former would see this as 'anecdotal evidence', the latter would portray it as 'expertise by experience' and 'human testimony'. In the same way, social workers have traditionally had less commitment to the 'evidence-based practice' movement within medicine, and may tend to prioritise their own professional experience (often referred to as 'practice wisdom' or 'tacit knowledge'). In contrast, some sections of the pharmaceutical industry have been accused of presenting evidence about the effectiveness of drugs in a particular way, prioritising large studies with positive clinical outcomes over negative studies and user-reported experiences of side-effects. Similarly, the media is sometimes felt to focus more on stories that seem to confirm popular stereotypes about people with mental health problems, choosing 'evidence' and reporting style to suit what they see as current public opinion. The treatment of the boxer Frank Bruno by the tabloid newspapers and their subsequent change of tone in response to public opinion is a case in point (see Chapter 4).

Underneath a seemingly academic discussion about what constitutes valid evidence, lies a more complex and far-reaching debate about:

- Who is the expert and who knows best what it is like to live with a mental health problem: the 'professional experts' or someone with lived experience of the condition in question?

- Whose voice is heard when debates about mental health policy take place, and are some stakeholders excluded more than others from this process?
- How can different groups work together to make the best of their respective expertise?
- How do policy makers make sense of these different perspectives and steer a middle course through such apparently competing views?

Ultimately, however, something has to change if we are to create the kind of mental health services that we would all like to use, work in and make available for our citizens. Health and social care workers, and increasingly users and carers have spent decades innovatively trying to address complex and difficult mental health issues in the field, but have often been met with the same policy responses. Examples of this might include the on-going programme to develop effective community care (despite an arguable lack of political will to develop properly resourced alternatives to acute care), the repeated reorganisation of the NHS, the apparent belief in structural solutions to the problem of the health and social care divide and the temptation to retreat back into notions of public safety ('control') rather than support and user-focused services ('care') whenever mental health hits the headlines. Whatever the solution, there is an urgent need for more effective policy learning so that future policy does not repeat previous mistakes. Perhaps this is best encapsulated in a quote attributed to Albert Einstein:

> 'Insanity: doing the same thing over and over again, and expecting different results.'

Bibliography

6, P. (2002) Can policy making be evidence based?, *Managing Community Care*, 10(1), 3–8

6, P., Leat, D., Seltzer, K. and Stoker, G. (2002) *Towards holistic governance: the new reform agenda*. Basingstoke, Palgrave

Abel-Smith, B. (1964) *The hospitals 1800–1948: a study in social administration in England and Wales*. London, Heinemann

Aldridge, J. and Becker, S. (2003) *Children caring for parents with mental illness: perspectives of young carers, parents and professionals*. Bristol, Policy Press

Allebeck, P. (1989) Schizophrenia: a life-shortening disease, *Psychiatric Bulletin*, 15(1) 81–9

Allen, C. (1997) Somebody cares, *Health Service Journal*, 107(5558), 34–5

Anthony, W.A. (1993) Recovery from mental illness: the guiding vision of the mental health service system in the 1990s, *Psychological Rehabilitation Journal*, 16, 11–24

Appleby, J., Harrison, A. and Devlin, N. (2003) *What is the real cost of more patient choice?* London, Kings Fund

Armstrong, L. (1997) Do practice nurses want to learn about depression?, *Practice Nursing*, 8, 21–6

Armstrong, E. (2002) *The guide to mental health for nurses in primary care*. Abingdon, Radcliffe Medical Press

Arnstein, S.R. (1969) A ladder of citizen participation, *American Institute of Planning Journal*, July, 216–24

Arshad, J. and Johal, B. (1999) Culture club, *Nursing Times*, 95(9), 66–7

Arskey, H., O'Malley, L., Baldwin, S., Harris, J., Newbronner, E., Hare, P. and Mason, A. (2002) *Services to support carers of people with mental health problems: overview report*. York, Social Policy Research Unit, University of York

Auckland, G., Bontoft, C. and Feaviour, P. (2000) Resource management: making a difference in mental health, *Nursing Standard*, 14(24), 42–6

Audini, B., Duffett, R., Lelliott, P., Pearce, A. and Ayres, C. (1999) Over-occupancy in London's acute psychiatric units: fact or fiction?, *Psychiatric Bulletin*, 23(10), 590–4

Audit Commission (1986) *Making a reality of community care*. London, HMSO

Audit Commission (1997) *The coming of age: improving care services for older people*. London, Audit Commission

Audit Commission (2000a) *The way to go home: rehabilitation and remedial services for older people*. London, Audit Commission

Audit Commission (2000b) *Forget me not: mental health services for older people*. London, Audit Commission

Audit Commission (2002a) *A focus on general practice in England*. London, Audit Commission

Audit Commission (2002b) *Integrated services for older people: building a whole systems approach in England*. London, Audit Commission

Audit Commission (2004) *Transforming primary care*. London, Audit Commission

Badger, D., Vaughan, P., Woodward, M. and Williams, P. (1999) Planning to meet the needs of offenders with mental disorders in the United Kingdom, *Psychiatric Services*, 50(12), 1624–7

Bahl, V. (1999) Mental illness: a national perspective, in D. Bhugra and V. Bahl (eds) *Ethnicity: an agenda for mental health*. London, Gaskell

Baker, S. (2000) *Environmentally friendly? Patients' views of conditions on psychiatric wards*. London, Mind

Baldwin, S. and Twigg, J. (1990) Women and community care: reflections on a debate, in M. Maclean and D. Groves (eds) *Women's issues in social policy*. London, Routledge

Balloch, S. and Taylor, M. (eds) (2001) *Partnership working: policy and practice*. Bristol, Policy Press

Barnes, C. (1998) Review of the rejected body by Susan Wendall, *Disability and Society*, 13(1), 145–6

Barnes, D. (1997) *Older people with mental health problems living alone: anybody's priority?* London, Department of Health

Barnes, M. (1997) *Care, communities and citizens*. London, Longman

Barnes, M. and Bowl, R. (2001) *Taking over the asylum: empowerment and mental health*. Basingstoke, Palgrave

Barnes, M. and Walker, A. (1996) Consumerism versus empowerment: a principled approach to the involvement of older service users, *Policy and Politics*, 24(4), 375–93

Barnes, M., Davis, A. and Tew, J. (2000) Valuing experience: users experiences of compulsion under the Mental Health Act 1983, *Mental Health Review*, 5(3), 11–14

Bartlett, C., Holloway, J., Evans, M. and Harrison, G. (1999) Projection of alternatives to acute psychiatric beds: review of an emerging service assessment method, *Journal of Mental Health*, 8(6), 555–68

Batcup, D. (1997) The problems of researching mixed sex wards, *Journal of Advanced Nursing*, 25, 1018–24

Bean, P. and Mounser, P. (1993) *Discharged from mental hospitals*. Basingstoke, Macmillan

Beck, A., Croudace, T.J., Singh, S. and Harrison, G. (1997) The Nottingham Acute Bed Study: alternatives to acute psychiatric care, *British Journal of Psychiatry*, 170, 247–52

Bentall, R. (2003) *Madness explained: psychosis and human nature*. London, Allen Lane

Beresford, P. (2000) What have madness and psychiatric system survivors got to do with disability studies?, *Disability and Society*, 15(1), 167–72

Beresford, P., Harrison, C. and Wilson, A. (2002) Mental health service users and disability: implications for future strategies, *Policy and Politics*, 30(3), 387–96

Bevan, A. (1948) A message to the medical profession, *British Medical Journal*, ii, 1

Beveridge, W. (1942) *Social insurance and allied services*. London, HMSO

Bhui, K. and Bhugra, D. (1999) Service provision for ethnic minorities, in D. Bhugra and V. Bahl (eds) *Ethnicity: an agenda for mental health*. London, Gaskell

Bhui, K., Bhugra, D. and McKenzie, K. (2000) *Specialist services for minority ethnic groups?* (Maudsley discussion paper no. 8). London, Institute of Psychiatry

Bierer, J. (1951) *The day hospital.* London, H & K Lewis

Bindman, J., Beck, A., Thornicroft, G., Knapp, M. and Szmukler, G. (2000) Psychiatric patients at greatest risk and in greatest need: impact of the supervision register policy, *British Journal of Psychiatry*, 177, 33–7

Birchwood, M., Todd, P. and Jackson, C. (1998) Early intervention in psychosis: the critical period hypothesis, *British Journal of Psychiatry*, Supplementrum, 172, 53–9

Black, K. and Shillitoe, R. (1997) Developing mental health services sensitive to women's needs, *British Journal of Health Care Management*, 3(1), 27–9

Blashfield, R.K. (1996) Predicting DSM V, *Journal of Nervous and Mental Disease*, 184, 4–7

Blinkhorn, M. (2004) *Social worker: leading roles in mental health – adjustment to change, new ways of working and other potential solutions.* Durham, Northern Centre for Mental Health

Bloor, K. and Maynard, A. (1994) An outsider's view of the NHS reforms, *British Medical Journal*, 309, 352–3

Blount, A. (1998) *Integrated primary care: the future of medical and mental health collaboration.* London, Norton and Co.

Blumenthal, S. and Lavender, T. (2000) *Violence and mental disorder: a critical aid to the assessment and management of risk.* London, Jessica Kingsley (published for the Zito Trust)

Boardman, R.E. and Hodgson, A.P. (2000) Community in-patient units and halfway hospitals, *Advances in Psychiatric Treatment*, 6, 120–7

Borrill, J. (2000) *Developments in treatment for people with psychotic experiences* (Updates, volume 2, issue 9). London, Mental Health Foundation

Bower, P. (2002) Primary care mental health workers: models of working and evidence of effectiveness, *British Journal of General Practice*, 11, 926–33

Bower, P. and Sibbald, B. (2003) On-site mental health workers in primary care: effects on professional practice (Cochrane Review), *The Cochrane Library*, 1, Oxford, Update Software

Bradshaw, T. and Everitt, J. (1999) The benefits of training in psychosocial intervention, *Nursing Times*, 95, 48–9

Braye, S. (2000) Participation and involvement in social care: an overview, in H. Kemshall and R. Littlechild (eds) *User involvement and participation in social care: research informing practice.* London, Jessica Kingsley

Breeze, J. and Repper, J. (1998) Struggling for control: the care experiences of 'difficult' patients in mental health services, *Journal of Advanced Nursing*, 28(6), 1301–11

Bristol Royal Infirmary Inquiry (2001) *Learning from Bristol: The report of the public inquiry into children's heart surgery at the Bristol Royal infirmary 1984–1995.* CM5207 (11), London, TSO

British Medical Association (1992) *Priorities for community care.* London, British Medical Association

British Medical Association/NHS Confederation (2003) *Investing in General Practice: the new general medical services contract.* London, British Medical Association

Brodie, D. (2003) Partnership working: a service user perspective, in J. Glasby and E. Peck (eds) *Care trusts: partnership working in action.* Abingdon, Radcliffe Medical Press

Brown, G. (2003) A modern agenda for prosperity and social reform. Speech by Chancellor of the Exchequer, Gordon Brown to the Social Market Foundation at the CASS Business School, London, 3 February, in S. Leatherman and K. Sutherland (eds) *Quest for quality in the NHS: a mid-term evaluation of the tenure/ten year quality agenda*. London, TSO

Brown, G.W. and Harris, T. (1978) *The social origins of depression*. London, Tavistock Press

Browne, D. (1997) *Black people and sectioning: the black experience of detention under the civil sections of the Mental Health Act*. London, Little Rock Publishing

Burchadt, T. (2003) *Employment retention and the onset of sickness or disability: evidence from the Labour Force Survey longitudinal datasets*. Department of Workforce and Pensions in-house report no. 109

Burns, T. (2004) *Community mental health teams: a guide to current practices*. Oxford, Oxford University Press

Busfield, J. (1996) *Men, women and madness: understanding gender and mental disorder*. Basingstoke, Macmillan

Butterfield, W.J.A.H. (1964) *New frontiers in health*. London, Office of Health Economics

Byng, R. and Single, H. (1999) *Developing primary care for patients with long term mental illness: your guide to improving services*. London, King's Fund

Byng, R., Jones, R., Leese, M., Hamilton, B., McCrone, P. and Craig, T. (2004) Exploratory cluster randomised controlled trial of shared care development for long term mental illness, *British Journal of General Practice*, 54, 259–66

Cabinet Office (1999) *Modernising government*. London, TSO

Calnan, M. and Gabe, J. (1991) Recent developments in General Practice: a socio-logical analysis, in J. Gabe, M. Calnan, M, Bury (eds) *Sociology of the health service*. London, Routledge

Camden and Islington Mental Health NHS Trust (2001) *Drayton Park crisis project for women: an alternative to hospital admission for women in mental health crisis*. Unpublished leaflet, London, Camden and Islington Mental Health NHS Trust

Campbell, J. and Oliver, M. (1996) *Disability politics in Britain: understanding our past, changing our future*. London, Routledge

Campbell, P. (1996) The history of the user movement in the United Kingdom, in T. Heller (eds) *Mental health matters*. Basingstoke, Macmillan

Campbell, P. (2001) The role of users in psychiatric services in service development – influence not power, *Psychiatric Bulletin*, 25, 87–8

Carpenter, J. and Sbaraini, S. (1997) *Choice, information and dignity: involving users and carers in care management in mental health*. Bristol, Policy Press

Cawley, S., Praveen, S. and Salib, E. (1997) Brief psychiatric admissions: a review, *Nursing Standard*, 12(10), 34–5

Centre for Mental Health Services (1995) *Additions and resident patients at end of year, state and county resident mental hospitals by age and diagnosis*. Rockville, Maryland (US), Centre for Mental Health Services

Chamberlain, L. (1998) Murdered worker's family win apology from Kingston, *Community Care*, 9–15th July, 2

Chambers R., Boath, E. and Wakley G. (2001) *Mental healthcare matters in primary care*. Abingdon, Radcliffe Medical Press

Chesler, P. (1974) *Women and madness*. London, Allen Lane

Chisholm, A. and Ford, R. (2004) *Transforming mental health care: assertive outreach and crisis resolution in practice*. London, Sainsbury Centre for Mental Health

Clark, M. (2003) First of the few, *Community Care*, 2–8 October, 30–1

Clark, M., Glasby, J. and Lester, H.E. (2004) Cases for change: user involvement in mental health services and research, *Research Policy and Planning*, 22(2), 31–8

Clarke, S. (2004) *Acute inpatient mental health care: education, training and continuing professional development for all*. Leeds, NIMHE

Cohen, A., Bishop, N. and Hegarty, M. (1999) Working in partnership with probation: the first two years of a mental health worker scheme in a probation service in Wandsworth, *Psychiatric Bulletin*, 23(7), 405–8

Cohen, P. (1992) High risk mix, *Social Work Today*, 23(31), 10

Coid, J. (1994) Failure in community care: psychiatry's dilemma, *British Medical Journal*, 308, 965–6

Coid, J. and Dunn, W. (2004) Forensic psychiatry assessments and admissions from East London, 1987–1994, *Journal of Forensic Psychiatry and Psychology*, 15(1), 76–95

Coid, J. and Kahtan, N. (2000) Are special hospitals needed?, *Journal of Forensic Psychiatry*, 11(1), 17–35

Coid, J., Kahtan, N., Gault, S., Cook, A. and Jarman, B. (2001) Medium secure forensic psychiatry services: comparison of seven English health regions, *British Journal of Psychiatry*, 178, 55–61

Commander, M.J., Cochrane, R., Sashidharan, S.P., Akilu, F. and Wildsmith, E. (1999) Mental health care for Asian, black and white patients with non-effective psychoses: pathways to the psychiatric hospital, in-patient and after-care, *Social Psychiatry and Psychiatric Epidemiology*, 34(9), 484–91

Commission for Health Improvement (2003a) *What CHI has found in mental health trusts*. London, Commission for Health Improvement

Commission for Health Improvement (2003b) *Investigation into matters arising from care on Rowan ward, Manchester Mental Health and Social Care Trust*. London, TSO

Community Care (2001) Father given suspended sentence for killing depressed daughter, *Community Care*, 11 June. Available online via www.communitycare.co.uk (accessed 08/04/2004)

Community Care (2004) Government rejects Bennett proposals, *Community Care*, 19 February. Available online via www.communitycare.co.uk (accessed 28/05/2004)

Connolly, M.A. and Ritchie, S. (1997) An audit of in-patients aged 18–65 in acute psychiatric wards who are inappropriately placed three months after admission, *Health Bulletin*, 55(3), 156–61

Cook, G., Gerrish, K. and Clarke, C. (2001) Decision-making in teams: issues arising from two UK evaluations, *Journal of Interprofessional Care*, 15(2), 141–51

Copperman, J. and Burrows, F. (1992) Reducing the risk of assault, *Nursing Times*, 88(26), 64–5

Coppock, V. and Hopton, J. (2000) *Critical perspectives on mental health*. London, Routledge

Copsey, N. (1997a) *Keeping faith: the provision of community mental health services within a multi-faith context*. London, Sainsbury Centre for Mental Health

Copsey, N. (1997b) *Forward in faith: an experiment in building bridges between ethnic communities and mental health services in East London*. London, Sainsbury Centre for Mental Health

Corney, R. (1999) Mental health services in primary care: the overlap in professional roles, *Journal of Mental Health*, 8, 187–94

Craig T.K.J., Garety, P., Power, P., Rahaman, N., Colbert, S., Fornells-Ambrojo, M. and Dunn, G. (2004) The Lambeth Early Onset Community Team: a randomised controlled trial of assertive outreach for psychosis, *British Medical Journal*, 329, 1067–73.

Crawford, M.J., Rutter, D., Manley, C., Weaver, T., Bhui, K., Fulop, N. and Tyrer, P. (2002) Systematic review of involving patients in the planning and development of health care, *British Medical Journal*, 325, 1263–5

Creed, F., Black, D., Antony, P., Osborn, M., Thomas, P. and Tomenson, B. (1990) Randomised controlled trial of day patients versus in-patient psychiatric treatment, *British Medical Journal*, 300, 1033–7

Creed, F., Mbaya, P., Lancashire, S. Tomenson, B., Williams, B. and Holme, S. (1997) Cost effectiveness of day and inpatient psychiatric treatment, *British Medical Journal*, 314, 1381–5

Crosland, A. and Kai, J. (1998) They think they can talk to nurses: practice nurses' views of their roles in caring for mental health problems, *British Journal of General Practice*, 48, 1383–6

Crowther, R., Marshall, M., Bond., G. and Huxley, P. (2001) Helping people with severe mental illness to obtain work: systematic review, *British Medical Journal*, 322, 204–8

Dabbs, H. and Isherwood, J. (2000) Bridging the gap: service developments in forensic psychiatric rehabilitation at district level, *Journal of Forensic Psychiatry*, 11(1), 198–205

Dalrymple, J. and Burke, B. (1995) *Anti-oppressive practice: social care and the law.* Buckingham, Open University Press

Dawson, A. and Tylee, A. (2001) *Depression: social and economic time bomb – strategies for quality care.* London, BMJ Books

Day, L. (1992) Women and oppression: race, class and gender, in M. Langan and L. Day (eds) *Women, oppression and social work: issues in anti-discriminatory practice.* London, Routledge

Deegan, P.E. (1988) Recovery: the lived experience rehabilitation, *Psychiatric Rehabilitation Journal*, 11, 11–19

Department for Work and Pensions (2002) *Incapacity Benefit and Severe Disablement Allowance.* London, DWP

Department of the Environment Employment, Transport and the Regions (1998) *Modernising local government.* London, TSO

Department of Health (1989a) *Caring for People: community care in the next decade and beyond.* London, HMSO

Department of Health (1989b) *Working for Patients.* London, HMSO

Department of Health (1990a) *The care programme approach for people with a mental illness referred to the specialist psychiatric services.* London, Department of Health

Department of Health (1990b) *Community care in the next decade and beyond: policy guidance.* London, HMSO

Department of Health (1991) *The patient's charter.* London, HMSO

Department of Health (1992) *The health of the nation.* London, TSO

Department of Health (1993) *Attitude to mental illness.* London, Taylor Nelson Sofres

Department of Health (1994) *Working in partnership: a collaborative approach to care – report of the mental health nursing review.* London, HMSO

Department of Health (1995) *Building bridges: a guide to the arrangements for interagency working for the care and protection of severely disabled people.* London, Department of Health

Department of Health (1996a) *The National Health Service: a service with ambitions.* London, TSO

Department of Health (1996b) *Carers (Recognition and Services) Act 1995: policy guidance and practice guidance.* London, Department of Health

Department of Health (1997a) *The New NHS: modern, dependable.* London, TSO

Department of Health (1997b) *Omnibus survey of public attitudes to mental illness.* London, Department of Health

Department of Health (1998a) *Modernising mental health services: safe, sound and supportive.* London, Department of Health

Department of Health (1998b) *Frank Dobson outlines third way for mental health.* Press Release 98/311, 29th July, London, Department of Health

Department of Health (1998c) *Partnership in action: new opportunities for joint working between health and social services – a discussion document.* London, Department of Health

Department of Health (1998d) *Modernising social services: promoting independence, improving protection, raising standards.* London, TSO

Department of Health (1999a) *National service framework for mental health: modern standards and service models.* London, Department of Health

Department of Health (1999b) *Effective care co-ordination in mental health services: modernising the care programme approach – a policy booklet.* London, Department of Health

Department of Health (1999c) *Report of the expert committee: review of the Mental Health Act 1983.* London, Department of Health

Department of Health (1999d) *Reform of the Mental Health Act 1983: proposals for consultation.* London, TSO

Department of Health (2000a) *The NHS Plan: a plan for investment, a plan for reform.* London, Department of Health

Department of Health (2000b) *Attitudes to mental illness.* London, Taylor Nelson Sofres

Department of Health (2000c) *Caring about carers: a national strategy for carers* (2nd ed. – first published in 1999). London, Department of Health

Department of Health (2001a) *Safety first: five-year report of the National Confidential Inquiry into Suicide and Homicide by People with Mental Illness.* London, Department of Health

Department of Health (2001b) *The journey to recovery: the government's vision for mental health care.* London, Department of Health

Department of Health (2001c) *Shifting the balance of power within the NHS: securing delivery.* London, Department of Health

Department of Health (2001d) *Reforming the Mental Health Act – part I: the new legal framework.* London, Department of Health

Department of Health (2001e) *Reforming the Mental Health Act – part II: high risk patients.* London, Department of Health

Department of Health (2001f) *Mental health national service framework (and The NHS Plan) workforce planning, education and training underpinning programme: adult mental health services: final report by the Workforce Action Team.* London, Department of Health

Department of Health (2001g) *Mental health policy implementation guidance.* London, Department of Health

Department of Health (2001h) *Valuing people: a new strategy for learning disability for the 21st century.* London, Department of Health

Department of Health (2001i) *National service framework for older people: modern standards and service models.* London, Department of Health

Department of Health (2001j) *Carers and Disabled Children's Act 2000: carers and people with parental responsibility for disabled children – policy guidance.* London, Department of Health

Department of Health (2002a) *Draft mental Health Bill Cm 5538–1.* London, TSO

Department of Health (2002b) *Shifting the balance of power: the next steps.* London, Department of Health

Department of Health (2002c) *Adult acute in-patient care provision.* London, Department of Health

Department of Health (2002d) *National suicide prevention strategy for England.* London, Department of Health

Department of Health (2002e) *Improvement, expansion and reform – the next 3 years: priorities and planning framework, 2003–2006.* London, Department of Health

Department of Health (2002f) *Primary Care Trust revenue resource limits, 2003/4, 2004/5, 2005/6 and exposition tables 2003–6.* London, Department of Health

Department of Health (2002g) *Mental health policy implementation guidance: community mental health teams.* London, Department of Health

Department of Health (2002h) *A guide to NHS foundation trusts.* London, Department of Health

Department of Health (2002i) *Women's mental health: into the mainstream.* London, Department of Health

Department of Health (2003a) *Practitioners with special interests in primary care: implementing a scheme for nurses with special interests in primary care – liberating the talents.* London, Department of Health

Department of Health (2003b) *Fast-forwarding primary care mental health: graduate primary care mental health workers – best practice guidance.* London, Department of Health

Department of Health (2003c) *Guidelines for the appointment of General Practitioners with special interests in the delivery of clinical services: mental health.* London, Department of Health

Department of Health (2003d) *National statistics on adults' attitudes to mental illness in Great Britain.* London, Department of Health

Department of Health (2003e) *Mental health policy implementation guide: support, time and recovery workers.* London, Department of Health

Department of Health (2003f) *Change Agent Team.* Available online via www.doh.gov.uk/changeagentteam/index.htm (accessed 25/04/2003)

Department of Health (2003g) *Building on the best: choice, responsiveness and equity in the NHS.* London, TSO

Department of Health (2003h) *Strengthening accountability: involving patients and the public – policy guidance, Section 11 of the Health and Social Care Act 2001.* London, Department of Health

Department of Health (2003i) *Mainstreaming gender and women's mental health.* London, Department of Health

Department of Health (2003j) *Delivering race equality: a framework for action – mental health services – consultation document.* London, Department of Health

Department of Health (2004a) *The NHS improvement plan.* London, Department of Health

Department of Health (2004b) *The national service framework for mental health – five years on.* London, Department of Health

Department of Health (2004c) *Choosing health: making healthier choices easier.* London, Department of Health

Department of Health (2004d) *Ministers announce prison healthcare trailblazers.* Press release 2004/0111. Available online via www.dh.gov.uk (accessed 23/03/2004)

Department of Health (2005a) *Commissioning a patient-led NHS.* London, Department of Health

Department of Health (2005b) *Community development workers for black and minority ethnic communities.* London, Department of Health

Department of Health (2005c) *Delivering race equality in mental health care: an action plan for reform inside and outside services and the government's response to the independent inquiry into the death of David Bennett.* London, Department of Health

Department of Health and Social Security (1975) *Better Services for the Mentally Ill.* London, HMSO

Department of Health and Social Security (1983) *NHS management inquiry.* London, Department of Health and Social Security

Department of Health/HM Prison Service/National Assembly for Wales (2001) *Changing the outlook: a strategy for developing and modernising mental health services in prisons.* London, Department of Health

Department of Health/HM Prison Service/National Assembly for Wales (2002) *Mental health in-reach collaborative: launch document.* London, Department of Health

Department of Health/Home Office (1992) *Review of services for mentally disordered offenders and others requiring similar services: final summary report* (the Reed Report). London, HMSO

Department of Health/National Schizophrenia Fellowship (2001) *A commitment to carers.* London, National Schizophrenia Fellowship

Department of Health/Social Services Inspectorate (1997) *Young carers: something to think about.* London, Department of Health

Department of Health/Social Services Inspectorate (1998a) *Young carers: making a start.* London, Department of Health

Department of Health/Social Services Inspectorate (1998b) *A matter of chance for carers? Inspection of local authority support for carers.* London, Department of Health

Department of Health/Social Services Inspectorate (1999) *Review of social work services in the high security hospitals.* London, Department of Health

Department of Health/Social Services Inspectorate (2001) *National standards for the provision of social care services in the high security hospitals.* London, Department of Health

Department of Health/Welsh Office (1999) *Mental Health Act 1983: code of practice.* London, TSO

Department of Trade and Industry (2004) *Fairness for all: a new Commission for Equality and Human Rights.* London, TSO

Docherty, J.D. (1997) Barriers to the diagnosis of depression in primary care, *Journal of Clinical Psychology,* 58, 5–10

Dolan, M. and Lawson, A. (2001) Characteristics and outcomes of patients admitted to a psychiatric intensive care unit in a medium secure unit, *Psychiatric Bulletin,* 25(8), 296–9

Dominelli, L. (1988) *Anti-racist social work.* Basingstoke, Macmillan

Dominelli, L. (1997) *Sociology for social work.* Basingstoke, Macmillan

Donnelly, L. (1998) Service user quits mental health group in fury over Hutton speech, *Health Service Journal,* 12 November, 4–5

Durkheim, E. (1897) *Le suicide.* Paris, Alcan

Elder, A. and Holmes J. (2002) *Mental health in primary care*. Oxford, Oxford University Press

Engel, G. (1980) The clinical application of the biospychosocial model, *American Journal of Psychiatry*, 137, 535–44

Enthoven, A. (1985) *Reflections in the management of the NHS*. London, Nuffield Provincial Hospitals Trust

Etzioni, A. (1995) *The spirit of community: rights, responsibilities and the communitarian agenda*. London, Fontana

Evans, P. (2003) Silent fight, *The Guardian*, 20 August. Available online via www.society.guardian.co.uk (accessed 20/08/2003)

Faulkner, A. and Layzell, S. (2000) *Strategies for living: a report of user-led research into people's strategies for living with mental distress*. London, Mental Health Foundation

Faulkner, A. and Morris, B. (2003) *User involvement in forensic mental health research and development*. Liverpool, National R&D Programme on Forensic Mental Health

Feinmann, J. (1988) Corridors of fear, *Nursing Times*, 84(39), 16–17

Ferguson, I. (2000) Identity politics or class struggle? The case of the mental health users' movement, in M. Lavalette and G. Mooney (eds) *Class struggle and social welfare*. London, Routledge

Finch, J. and Groves, D. (eds) (1983) *A labour of love: women, work and caring*. London, Routledge

Fleischman, P. (2000) Separating the sexes, *Nursing Standard*, 14(25), 20–1

Ford, R., Beardsmore, A., Norton, P., Cooke, A. and Repper, J. (1993) Developing case management for the long term mentally ill, *Psychiatric Bulletin*, 17(7) 409–11

Ford, R., Durcan, G., Warner, L., Hardy, P. and Muijen, M. (1998) One day survey by the Mental Health Act Commission of acute adult psychiatric inpatient wards in England and Wales, *British Medical Journal*, 317(168), 1279–83

Foucault, M. (1961) *Madness and civilization: a history of insanity in the age of reason*. New York, Vintage Books

Freeman, G., Weaver, T., Low, J., de Jonge, E. (2002) *Promoting continuity of care for people with severe mental illness whose needs span primary, secondary and social care*. London, SDO

French, S. (1993) Can you see the rainbow, in J. Swain, S. French, C. Barnes and C. Thomas (eds) *Disabling barriers – enabling environments*. London, Sage

Fryers, T., Melzer, D., McWilliams B. and Jenkins, R. (2002) *Social inequalities and the distribution of mental disorders: a systematic literature review*. Unpublished paper commissioned by the Department of Health

Fulop, N., Koffman, J. and Hudson, M. (1992) Challenging bed behaviours: the use of acute psychiatric beds in an inner-London District Health Authority, *Journal of Mental Health*, 1, 335–41

Fulop, N.J., Koffman, J., Carson, S., Robinson, A., Pashley, D. and Coleman, K. (1996) Use of psychiatric beds: a point prevalence study in North and South Thames regions, *Journal of Public Health Medicine*, 18(2), 207–16

Gask, L., Sibbald, B. and Creed, F. (1997) Evaluating models of working between mental health and primary care, *British Journal of Psychiatry*, 70, 6–11

Gask, L., Rogers, A., Oliver, D., May, C., Roland, M. (2003) Qualitative study of patients' perceptions of the quality of care for depression in general practice, *British Journal of General Practice*, 53, 278–83

Gater, R., Goldberg, D., Jackson, G., Jennett, N., Lowson, K., Ratcliffe, J., Saraf, T. and Warner, R. (1997) The care of patients with chronic schizophrenia: a comparison between two services, *Psychological Medicine*, 27(6), 1325–36

Geelan, S., Griffin, N., Briscoe, J. and Haque, M.S. (2000) A bail and probation hostel for mentally disordered defendants, *Journal of Forensic Psychiatry*, 11(1), 93–104

Georgiades, N.J. and Phillimore, L. (1975) *The myth of the hero-innovator and alternative strategies for organisational change*. New York, Associated Scientific

Gerada, C., Wright, N. and Keen, J. (2002) The general practitioners with special interest: new opportunities or the end of the generalist practitioner?, *British Journal of General Practice*, 52, 796–8

Gibbons, J. (1988) Residential care for mentally ill adults, in I. Sinclair (ed.) *Residential care: the research reviewed*. London, HMSO

Giddens, A. (1998) *The third way: the renewal of social democracy*. Cambridge, Policy Press

Giddens, A. (2000) *The third way and its critics*. Cambridge, Policy Press

Giles, S. (2003) Care trusts: a positive option for service improvement, in J. Glasby and E. Peck (eds) *Care trusts: partnership working in action*. Abingdon, Radcliffe Medical Press

Gillen, S. (2005) Campaigners furious as government 'ducks' key Bennett inquiry findings, *Community Care*, 13–19 January, 6

Glasby, J. (2003) *Hospital discharge: integrating health and social care*. Abingdon, Radcliffe Medical Press

Glasby, J. and Beresford, P. (2006) Who knows best? Evidence-based practice and the service user contribution, *Critical Social Policy*, 26(1), 268–84

Glasby, J., Lester, H., Briscoe, J., Clark, M. and England, E. (2003) *Cases for change in adult mental health (1997–2003)*. Leeds, NIMHE

Glasby, J. and Littlechild, R. (2002) *Social work and direct payments*. Bristol, Policy Press

Glasby, J. and Littlechild, R. (2004) *The health and social care divide: the experiences of older people* (2nd ed.). Bristol, Policy Press

Glasby, J., Littlechild, R. and Pryce, K. (2004) *Show me the way to go home: delayed hospital discharges and older people*. Birmingham, Health Services Management Centre/Institute of Applied Social Studies

Glasby, J. and Peck, E. (eds) (2003) *Care trusts: partnership working in action*. Abingdon, Radcliffe Medical Press

Glendinning, C., Hudson, B., Hardy, B. and Young, R. (2002a) *National evaluation of notifications for use of the section 31 partnership flexibilities of the Health Act 1999: final project report*. Manchester/Leeds, National Primary Care Research and Development Centre and Nuffield Institute for Health

Glendinning, C., Powell, M. and Rummery, K. (2002b) *Partnerships, New Labour and the governance of welfare*. Bristol, Policy Press

Goffman, E. (1961) *Asylums: essays on the social situation of mental patients and other inmates*. Harmondsworth, Penguin

Goldberg, D. and Huxley, P. (1992) *Common mental disorders*. London, Routledge

Golding, J. (1997) *Without prejudice: Mind lesbian, gay, bisexual mental health awareness research*. London, Mind

Goodwin, S. (1990) *Community care and the future of mental health service provision*. Aldershot, Avebury

Goodwin, S. (1997) *Comparative mental health policy: from institutional to community care*. London, Sage Publications

Goodwin, I., Holmes, G., Newnes, C. and Waltho, D. (1999) A qualitative analysis of the views of in-patient mental health service users, *Journal of Mental Health*, 8(1), 43–54

Gournay, K. and Brooking, J. (1994) The CPN in primary care: an outcome study, *British Journal of Psychiatry*, 165, 231–8

Gournay, K. and Brooking, J. (1995) The CPN in primary care: an economic analysis, *Journal of Advanced Nursing*, 22, 769–78

Grant-Pearce, C.M. and Deane, J. (1999) Joint working between the public and purchasing authorities to determine mental health information needs, in D. Bhugra and V. Bahl (eds) *Ethnicity: an agenda for mental health*. London, Gaskell

Gray, R., Parr, A.M., Plummer, S., Sandford, T., Ritter, S. and Mundt-Leach, R. (1999) A national survey of practice nurse involvement in mental health interventions, *Journal of Advanced Nursing*, 30, 901–6

Greenberg, J.S., Greenley, J.R., and Benedict, P. (1994) Contributions of persons with serious mental illness to their families, *Hospital and Community Psychiatry*, 45(5), 475–9

Greengross, R., Hollander, D. and Stanton, R. (2000) Pressure on adult acute psychiatric beds: results of a national questionnaire survey, *Psychiatric Bulletin*, 24(2), 54–6

Griffiths Report (1983) *NHS Management Inquiry Report*. London, DHSS

Griffiths Report (1988) *Community Care: an Agenda for Action*. London, HSMO

Grounds, A. (2001) Reforming the Mental Health Act, *British Journal of Psychiatry*, 178, 387–9

Grove, B. (1994) Reform of mental health care in Europe, *British Journal of Psychiatry*, 165, 431–3

Grove, B. and Drurie, S. (1999) *Social firms: an instrument for social and economic inclusion*. Redhill, Social Firms UK

Grove, B., Freudenberg, G.M. and Harding, A. (1997) *The social firm handbook*. Brighton, Pavilion

Gulliver, P. (1999) Two approaches to the joint commissioning of mental health services, *Mental Health Review*, 4(3), 21–3

Gulliver, P., Peck, E. and Towell, D. (2002) Balancing professional and team boundaries in mental health services: pursuing the holy grail in Somerset, *Journal of Interprofessional Care*, 16(4), 359–70

Gunn, J. (2000) Future directions for treatment in forensic psychiatry, *British Journal of Psychiatry*, 176, 332–8

Gunn, J. and Maden, A. (1998) Bed requirements in high security hospitals, *Health Trends*, 30(3), 86–8

Hall, S. (2001) Argument rages over Sarah's law, *The Guardian*, 13th December. Available online (accessed 09/02/04) via www.guardian.co.uk

Hall, S. (2002) Huntley fit to stand trial for murders, *The Guardian*, 9 October. Available online (accessed 09/02/2004) via www.guardian.co.uk

Ham, C. (1999) *Health policy in Britain: the politics and organisation of the National Health Service* (4th ed.). Basingstoke, Palgrave-Macmillan

Hancock, M. and Villeneau, L. (1997) *Effective partnerships: developing key indicators for joint working in mental health*. London, Sainsbury Centre for Mental Health

Hancock, M., Villeneau, L. and Hill, R. (1997) *Together we stand: effective partnerships: key indicators for joint working in mental health*. London, Sainsbury Centre for Mental Health

Hannay, D. (1979) *Health and lifestyles*. London, Routledge

Hannigan, B. (2003) The policy and legal context, in B. Hannigan and M. Coffey (eds) *The handbook of community mental health nursing*. London, Routledge

Hannigan, B. and Coffey, M. (eds) (2003) *The handbook of community mental health nursing*. London, Routledge

Harding, C.M. and Zahniser, J.H. (1994) Empirical correction of seven myths about schizophrenia with implications for treatment, *Acta Psychiatrica Scandinavica*, 3(1), 140–6

Harris, E.C. and Barraclough, B. (1998) Excess mortality of mental disorder, *British Journal of Psychiatry*, 173, 11–53

Harrison, G., Hopper, K., Craig, T., Laska, E., Siegel, C., Wanderling, J., Dube, K.C., Ganev, K., Giel, R., An der Heiden, W., Holmberg, S.K., Janca, A., Lee, P., León, C., Malhotra, S., Marsella, A., Nakane, V., Sartorius, N., Shen, V., Skoda, C., Thara, R., Tsirkin, J.S., Varma, V., Walsh, D., and Wiersma, D. (2001) Recovery from psychotic illness: a 15 and 25-year international follow-up study, *British Journal of Psychiatry,* 178, 506–17

Harrison, P. (1973) Careless community, *New Society*, 28 June

Hayward, R. (2000) Somerset's development of an integrated information system for mental health services: organisational foundations, *British Journal of Healthcare Computing and Information Management*, 17(1), 18–19

Healthcare Commission (2004) *State of healthcare report, 2004*. London, Healthcare Commission

Health Education Authority (1997) *Mental health promotion: quality framework*. London, Health Education Authority

Heater, D. (1990) *Citizenship: the civic ideal in world history, politics and education*. London, Longman

Heath, I. (1999) Uncertain clarity: contradiction, meaning and hope, *British Journal of General Practice*, 49, 651–7

Heath, I. (2004) The cawing of the crow...Cassandra-like, prognosticating woe, *British Journal of General Practice*, 54, 320–1

Henwood, M. (1998) *Ignored and invisible? Carers' experience of the NHS*. London, Carers National Association

Heron, C. (1998) *Working with carers*. London, Jessica Kingsley

Higgins, R., Hurst, K. and Wistow, G. (1999) Nursing acute psychiatric patients: a quantitative and qualitative study, *Journal of Advanced Nursing*, 29(1), 52–63

Higgitt, A, and Fonagy, P. (2002) Clinical effectiveness, *British Journal of Psychiatry*, 181, 170–4

Hill, M. and Hupe, P. (2002) *Implementing public policy*. London, Sage

Hill, R.G., Shepherd, G. and Hardy, P. (1998) In sickness and in health: the experiences of friends and relatives caring for people with manic depression, *Journal of Mental Health*, 7(6), 611–20

Hirschman, A. (1970) *Exit, voice or loyalty*. Cambridge (MA), Harvard University Press

Hoggett, P. (1992) The politics of empowerment, *Going Local*, 19, 18–9

Hogman, G. and Pearson, G. (1995) *The silent partners: the needs and experiences of people who provide informal care to people with a severe mental illness*. Kingston upon Thames, National Schizophrenia Fellowship (now Rethink)

Hogman, G. and Sandamas, G. (2001) Mental patients are at last asked about the drugs they are given, *The Health Summary*, January, 8–11

Home Office (1990) *Provision for mentally disordered offenders*. Circular 66/90

Hoult, J. (1986) Community care of the acutely mentally ill, *British Journal of Psychiatry*, 149, 137–44

House Deb, 6.6 (1845) c. 193

House of Commons (1948) Hansard, Volume 447, column 50, 9 February

House of Commons Health Committee (2002) *Delayed discharges.* London, TSO

Huang, M.C. and Slevin, E. (1999) The experiences of carers who live with someone who has schizophrenia: a review of the literature, *Mental Health and Learning Disabilities Care,* 3(3), 89–93

Hudson, B. (2002) Integrated care and structural change in England: the case of Care Trusts, *Policy Studies,* 23(2), 77–95

Hudson, B. (2003) Care trusts: a sceptical view, in J. Glasby and E. Peck (eds) *Care trusts: partnership working in action.* Abingdon, Radcliffe Medical Press

Hudson, B. and Henwood, M. (2002) The NHS and social care: the final countdown?, *Policy and Politics,* 30(2), 153–66

Hudson, B., Hardy, B., Henwood, M. and Wistow, G. (1997) *Inter-agency collaboration: final report.* Leeds, Nuffield Institute for Health

Hunkeler, E.M., Meresman, J.F., Hargreaves, W.A., Fireman, B., Berman, W.H., Kirsch, A.J. Groebe, J., Hurst, S.W., Braden, P., Getzell, M., Feigenbam, P.A., Peng, T. and Salzer, M. (2000) Efficacy of nurse in telehealth care and peer support in augmenting treatment of depression in primary care, *Archives of Family Medicine,* 9, 700–8

Hutchinson, M. (2000) Issues around empowerment, in T. Basset (ed.) *Looking to the future: key issues for contemporary mental health services.* Brighton, Pavillion

Huxley, P. and Thornicroft, G. (2003) Social inclusion, social quality and mental illness, *British Journal of Psychiatry,* 182, 289–90

Independent Police Complaints Commission (2004) *Policing and mental health: risks and realities.* One day conference, Birmingham, 20th January

Jenkins, R., Ustun, T. and Bedhiran, E. (1998) *Preventing mental illness: mental health promotion in primary care.* Chichester, Wiley

Jewesbury, I. (1998) *Risks and rights: mentally disordered offenders and public protection.* London, NACRO

Johnson, S. and Thornicroft, G. (1993) The sectorisation of psychiatric services in England and Wales, *Social Psychiatry and Psychiatric Epidemiology,* 28 (1), 45–7

Johnson, S., Nolan, F., Pilling, S., Sandor, A., Hoult, J., McKenzie, N., White, I,R., Thompson, M., Bebbington, P. (2005) Randomised Controlled Trial of Acute Mental Health Care by CRISIS Resolution Teams: The North Islington CRISIS Study. *British Medical Journal* 331, 599–602

Judge, J., Harty, M.A. and Fahy, T. (2004) Survey of community forensic psychiatry services in England and Wales, *Journal of Forensic Psychiatry and Psychology,* 15(2), 244–53

Kai, J. and Crosland, A. (2001) Perspectives of people with enduring mental ill health from a community-based qualitative study, *British Journal of General Practice,* 51, 730–73

Karp, D.A. (1996) Speaking of Sadness. *Depression, disconnection, and the meanings of illness.* Oxford, Oxford University Press

Katon, W., Robinson, P., von Korff, M., Bush, T.M., Ludman, E., Simon, G. and Walker, E. (1996) A multifaceted intervention to improve treatment of depression in primary care, *Archives of General Psychiatry,* 53, 924–32

Katon, W., Von Koerff, M., Lin, E., Simon, G., Walker, E., Umutzer, J., Bush, T., Russo, J. and Ludman, E. (1999) Stepped collaborate care for primary care patients with persistent symptoms of depression, *Archives of General Psychiatry,* 56, 1109–15

Kendrick, T., Millar, E., Burns, T. and Ross, F. (1998) Practice nurse involvement in giving depot neuroleptic injections: development of patient assessment and monitoring checklist, *Primary Care Psychiatry*, 4, 149–54

Kendrick, T., Bums, T., Garland, C., Greenwood, N. and Smith, P. (2000) Are specialist mental health services being targeted on the most needy patients? – the effects of setting up special services in general practice, *British Journal of General Practice*, 50, 121–6

Kenny, C. (2004) Spending reviews leaves social services counting up future cuts, *Community Care*, 12–18 August, 18–19

Kessler, D., Lloyd, K., Lewis, G. and Pereira Gray, D. (1999) Cross sectional survey of symptom attribution and recognition of depression and anxiety in primary care, *British Medical Journal*, 318, 436–9

Killaspy, H., Banerjee, S., King, M. and Lloyd, M. (1999) Non-attendance at psychiatric outpatient clinics: communication and implications for primary care, *British Journal of General Practice*, 49, 880–3

Killaspy, H., Banerjee, S., King, M. and Lloyd, M. (2000) Prospective controlled study of psychiatric outpatient non attendance, *British Journal of Psychiatry*, 176, 160–5

Killaspy, H., Dalton, J., McNicholas, S. and Johnson, S. (2000b) Drayton Park: an alternative to hospital admission for women in acute mental health crisis, *Psychiatric Bulletin*, 24(3), 101–4

King, M., McKeown, E., Warner, J., Ramsay, A., Johnson, K., Cort, C., Davidson, O. and Wright, L. (2003) *Mental health and social wellbeing of gay men, lesbians and bisexuals in England and Wales: a summary of findings*. London, Mind

Kingdon, D. (1989) Mental health services: results of a survey of English district plans, *Psychiatric Bulletin*, 13, 77–8

Kingdon, J.W. (1995) *Agenda, alternatives and public policies* (2nd ed.). New York, Harper Collins

Kingsland, J.P. and Williams, R. (1997) General practice should be central to community mental health services, *British Medical Journal*, 315, 13–77

King's Fund Institute (1988) *Health finance: assessing the options*. London, King's Fund Institute

Kmietowicz, Z. (2005) Rip up draft mental health bill and start again, says BMA. *British Medical Journal*, 330, 326

Koffman, J., Fulop, N., Pashley, D. and Coleman, K. (1996) No way out: the delayed discharge of elderly mentally ill acute and assessment patients in North and South Thames regions, *Age and Ageing*, 25(4), 268–72

Koffman, J., Fulop, N.J., Pashley, D. and Coleman, K. (1997) Ethnicity and use of acute psychiatric beds: one-day survey in North and South Thames regions, *British Journal of Psychiatry*, 171, 238–41

Kohen, D. (1999) Specialised in-patient psychiatric service for women, *Psychiatric Bulletin*, 23(1), 31–3

Kosa, J. and Zola, I.K. (1975) (eds) *Poverty and health: a sociological analysis*. Cambridge, MA/London, Harvard University of Press

Kupshik, G. and Fisher, C. (1999) Assisted bibliotherapy: effective, efficient treatment for moderate anxiety problems, *British Journal of General Practice*, 49, 47–8

La Grenade, J. (1999) The National Health Service and ethnicity: services for black patients, in D. Bhugra and V. Bahl (eds) *Ethnicity: an agenda for mental health*. London, Gaskell

Laing, R.D. (1960) *The Divided Self*. London, Tavistock Press

Laing, R.D. (1961) *The Self and Others*. London, Tavistock Press

Laming, H. (2003) *The Victoria Climbié inquiry: summary and recommendations*. London, HSMO

Lart, R. (1997) *Crossing boundaries: accessing community mental health services for prisoners on release*. Bristol, Policy Press

Laurance, J. (2003) *Pure madness: how fear drives the mental health system*. London, Routledge

Leason, K. (2003a) Mental health 'tsar' admits services suffer from institutional racism, *Community Care*, 17–23 July, 18–19

Leason, K. (2003b) Bennett case typical of way NHS treats black people, inquiry told, *Community Care*, 7–13 August, 12

Leason, K. (2003c) Author of mental health report says government diluted racism findings, *Community Care*, 17–23 July, 8

Leatherman, S. and Sutherland, K. (2003) *The quest for quality on the NHS: a mid term evaluation of the ten-year quality agenda*. London, TSO

Leavey, G., Healy, H. and Brennan, G. (1998) Providing information to carers of people admitted to psychiatric hospital, *Mental Health* Care, 1(86), 260–2

Lee, P. (2002) Shooting for the moon, in C. Barnes, M. Oliver and L. Barton (eds) *Disability Studies Today*. Cambridge, Quality Press

Lee, R. and Bradley, D. (2000) Wrong side of beds, *Health Service Journal*, 110(5726), 30–1

Leff, J. (1997) *Care in the community: illusion or reality?* Chichester, John Wiley and Sons

Leff, J., Trieman, N., Knapp, M. and Hallam, A. (2000) The TAPS Project: a report on 13 years of research 1985–1998, *Psychiatric Bulletin*, 24, 165–8

Lelliott, P. and Wing, J. (1994) A national audit of new long-stay psychiatric patients II: impact on services, *British Journal of Psychiatry*, 165, 170–8

Lelliott, P., Audini, B. and Duffett, R. (2001) Survey of patients from an inner-London health authority in medium secure psychiatric care, *British Journal of Psychiatry*, 179, 62–6

Lesperance, F., Frasure-Smith, N., Talajic, M. and Bourassa, M.G. (2002) Five year risk of cardiac mortality in relation to initial severity and one year changes in depression symptoms after myocardial infarction, *Circulation*, 105, 1049–53

Lester, H.E., Tritter, J. and England, E. (2003) Satisfaction with primary care: the perspectives of people with schizophrenia, *Family Practice*, 20, 508–13

Lester, H.E., Tritter, J.Q. and Sorohan, H. (2004) Managing crisis: the role of primary care for people with serious mental illness, *Family Medicine*, 36(1), 28–34

Lester, H.E., Tritter, J.Q. and Sorohan, H. (2005) Providing 'good enough' primary care: a focus group study. *British Medical Journal* 2005, 330, 222–8

Li, P.L., Logan, S., Yee, L. and Ng, S. (1999) Barriers to meeting the mental health needs of the Chinese community, *Journal of Public Health Medicine*, 21(1), 74–80

Lindow, V. (1999) Power, lies and injustice: the exclusion of service users' voices, in M. Parker (eds) *Ethics and community in the health care professions*. London, Routledge

Link, B.J. and Phelan, J.C. (2001) Conceptualising stigma, Annual Review of Sociology, 27, 363–85

MacInnes, D. (2000) Interventions in forensic psychiatry: the caregiver's perspective, *British Journal of Nursing*, 9(15), 992–7

Mac Gabhann, L. (2000) Are nurses responding to the needs of patients in acute adult mental health care?, *Mental Health and Learning Disabilities Care*, 4(3), 85–8

Maden, A., Rutter, S., McClintock, T., Friendship, C. and Gunn, J. (1999a) Outcome of admission to a medium secure psychiatric unit 1: short- and long term outcome, *British Journal of Psychiatry*, 175, 313–16

Maden, A., Friendship, C., McClintock, T. and Rutter, S. (1999b) Outcome of admission to a medium secure psychiatric unit: 2 – role of ethnic origin, *British Journal of Psychiatry*, 175, 317–21

Maguire, N. (1999) Models of imperfection, *Health Service Journal*, 109(5654), 20–2

Mallon, S. (2001) The therapeutic benefits of a women-only environment, *Nursing Times*, 97(37), 40–1

Mandelstam, M. (1998) *An A–Z of community care law*. London, Jessica Kingsley

Mannion, R., Davies, H.T.O. and Marshall, M.N. (2003) *Cultures for performance in health care: evidence on the relationships between organisational culture and organisational performance*. York, Centre for Health Economics

Markham, G. (2000) Policy and service development trends: forensic mental health and social care services, *Tizard Learning Disability Review*, 5(2), 26–31

Marmot, M. (2004) Evidence based policy or policy based evidence?, *British Medical Journal*, 328, 906–7

Marshall, R. (1990) The genetics of schizophrenia: axiom or hypothesis?, in R.P. Bentall (ed.) *Reconstructing schizophrenia*. London, Routledge

Marshall, T.H. (1950) *Citizenship and social class and other essays*. Cambridge, Cambridge University Press

Marshall, M. and Lockwood, A. (1998) Assertive community treatment for people with severe mental disorders (Cochrane Review), *The Cochrane Library*, 3, Oxford, Update Software

Marshall, M., Bond, G., Stein, L.I., Shepherd, G., McGrew, J., Hoult, J., Rosen, A., Huxley, P., Diamond, R.J., Warner, R., Olsen, M., Latimer, E., Goering, P., Craig, T.K., Meisler, N. and Test, M.A. (1999) PRiSM Psychosis study. Design limitation, questionable conclusions, *British Journal of Psychiatry*, 173, 501–3

Marshall, M., Lockwood, A. and Green, R. (1998) Case management for people with severe mental disorders. (Cochrane Review), *The Cochrane Library*, 1, Oxford, Update Software

Martin, J.P. (1984) *Hospitals in trouble*. Oxford, Basil Blackwell

Mauksch, L.B. and Leahy, D. (1993) Collaboration between primary care medicine and mental health in an HMO, *Family Systems Medicine*, 11, 121–35

Maunder, L., Cameron, L. and Liddon, A. (2001) Targeting services to meet need: a tiered approach to mental health care, *Mental Health and Learning Disabilities Care*, 4(11), 366–9

May, R. (2001) Crossing the 'them and us' barriers: an insider perspective on user involvement in clinical psychology, *Clinical Psychology Forum*, 150, 14–7

Maynard, A. and Tingle, R. (1975) The objectives and performance of the mental health services in England and Wales in the 1960s, *Journal of Social Policy*, 151–68

Mays, N., Goddwin, N., Killoran, A. and Malbon, G. (1998) *Total purchasing: a step towards primary care groups*. London, Kings Fund

McCabe, A. and Ford, C. (2001) *Redressing the balance: crime and mental health*. Manchester, UK Public Health Association

McCann, G. (1999) Care of mentally disordered offenders, *Mental Health Care*, 3(2), 65–7

McCormick, A., Fleming, D. and Charlton, J. (1995) *Morbidity statistics from general practice: fourth national morbidity study 1991–1992*. London, HMSO

McDermott, G. (1998) The care programme approach: a patient perspective. *Nursing Times*, Feb 25–Mar 3, 57–9

McDermott, G. and Reid, L. (1999) Model for integrated mental health care measures up, *Nursing Times*, 95(13), 46–7

McDonagh, M.S., Smith, D.H. and Goddard, M. (2000) Measuring appropriate use of acute beds: a systematic review of methods and results, *Health Policy*, 157–84

McFadyen, J.A. (1999) Safe, sound and supportive: forensic mental health services, *British Journal of Nursing*, 8(21), 1436–40

McFarlane, L. (1998) *Diagnosis: homophobic – the experiences of lesbians, gay men and bisexuals in mental health services*. London, PACE

McIntyre, B. (1999) Placement and community support needs of patients in a medium secure unit, *Mental Health Care*, 2(11), 379–82

McKenna, J., Shaw, J., Porceddu, K., Ganley, A., Skaife, K. and Davenport, S. (1999) 'Long stay medium secure' patients in special hospital, *Journal of Forensic Psychiatry*, 10(2), 333–42

McMillan, I. (1997a) Ancient and modern, *Nursing Standard*, 11(34), 28–9

McMillan, I. (1997b) Refuge reaching out, *Nursing Standard*, 11(39), 26–7

McMillan, I. (2000) One-stop service, *Nursing Standard*, 13(33), 16–17

Means, R. and Smith, R. (1998) *Community care: policy and practice* (2nd ed.). Basingstoke, Macmillan

Means, R., Richards, S. and Smith, R. (2003) *Community care: policy and practice* (3rd ed.). Basingstoke, Palgrave Macmillan

Medawar, C., Herxheiner, A., Bell, A. and Jofre, S. (2002) Paroxetine, Panorama and use of reporting ATDRs: consumer intelligence matters in clinical practice and post marketing drug surveillance, *International Journal of Risk and Safety in Medicine*, 15, 161–9

Meehan, E. (1993) Citizenship and the European Community, *Political Quarterly*, 64(2), 172–86

Mellor-Clark, J. (2000) *National survey of counsellors working in primary care: evidence for growing professionalisation?* (Occasional paper 79). London, Royal College of General Practitioners

Meltzer, H. Singleton, N., Lee, A. and Bebbington, P. (2002) *The social and economic circumstances of adults with mental disorders*. London, ONS

Melzer, D., Fryers, T., McWilliams, B. and Jenkins, R. (2002) *Quantifying associations between social position and the common mental disorders in Britain*. Unpublished paper commissioned by the Department of Health

Melzer, D., Tom, B.D.M., Brugha, T., Fryers, T., Gatward, R., Grounds, A., Johnson, T. and Meltzer, H. (2004) Access to medium secure psychiatric care in England and Wales 3: the clinical needs of assessed patients, *Journal of Forensic Psychiatry and Psychology*, 15(1), 50–65

Mental Health Aftercare Association (1999) *First national GP survey of mental health in primary care*. London, MACA

Mental Health Commission (1997) *Discrimination against people with experience of mental illness*. Discussion paper for the Mental Health Commission, Wellington, New Zealand

Mental Health Foundation (2003) *Surviving user-led research: reflections on supporting user-led research projects*. London, The Mental Health Foundation

Millar, B. (2000) All in a day's work, *Therapy Weekly*, 27(10), 48

Mind (1996) *Lesbians, gay men, bisexuals and mental health*. Mind factsheet (updated 2002), available online via www.mind.org.uk (accessed 04/02/2004)

Mind (2003a) *Developing a visual impairment and mental health*. Mind factsheet, available online www.mind.org.uk (accessed 04/02/2004)

Mind (2003b) *Deafness and mental health.* Mind factsheet, available online www.mind org.uk (accessed 04/02/2004)

Mind (n.d.) *Mind: the mental health charity.* Available online via www.mind.org.uk (accessed 04/07/2002)

Minghella, E. and Ford, R. (1997) Focal points?, *Health Service Journal*, 107(5583), 36–7

Minghella, E., Ford, R., Freeman, T., Hoult, J., McGlynn, P. and O'Halloran, P. (1998) *Open all hours: 24-hour response for people with mental health emergencies.* London, Sainsbury Centre for Mental Health

Ministry of Health (1962) *A hospital plan for England and Wales.* London, HMSO

Mohan, R., Slade, M. and Fahy, T.A. (2004) Clinical characteristics of community forensic mental health services, *Psychiatric Services*, 55(11), 1294–8

Monkley-Poole, S. (1995) The attitudes of British fund holding general practitioners to community psychiatric nursing services, *Journal of Advanced Nursing*, 21, 238–47

Mooney, H. (2004) Mental health changes slammed, *Health Service Journal*, 9th September, 5

Moore, C. and Wolf, J. (1999) Open and shut case, *Health Service Journal*, 109(5660), 20–2

Morgan, H. (1998) A potential for partnership? Consulting with users of mental health services, in A. Foster and V.Z. Roberts (eds) *Managing mental health in the community: chaos and containment.* London, Routledge

Morris, J. (2004a) *'One town for my body, another for my mind': services for people with physical impairments and mental health support needs.* York, Joseph Rowntree Foundation

Morris, J. (2004b) *Services for people with physical impairments and mental health support needs* (Joseph Rowntree Foundation Findings 574). York, Joseph Rowntree Foundation

Morrissey, M. (1998) Improving information for clients in mental health care, *Mental Health Nursing*, 18(2), 25–7

Mulvany, J. (2000) Disability, impairment or illness? The relevance of the social model of disability to the study of mental disorder, *Sociology of Health and Illness*, 22(5), 582–681

Murphy, E. (1991) *After the asylums: community care for people with mental illness.* London, Faber and Faber

Murray, S. (1998) Evaluation of shifted out-patient clinics, *Psychiatry Audit Trends*, 6, 64–7

Mynors-Wallis, L.M., Gath, D.H., Day, A., Baker, F. (2000) Randomised controlled trial of problem solving treatment, antidepressant medication, and combined treatment for depression in primary care, *British Medical Journal*, 320, 26–30

Nadkarni, R., Chipchase, B. and Fraser, K. (2000) Partnership with probation hostels: a step forward in community forensic psychiatry, *Psychiatric Bulletin*, 24(6), 222–4

National Institute for Clinical Excellence (2004) *Depression: management of depression in primary and secondary care.* London, NICE

National Institute of Health and Clinical Excellence (2003) *Schizophrenia: core interventions in the treatment and management of schizophrenia in primary and secondary care.* London, NICE

NIMHE (2003a) *Inside outside: improving mental health services for black and minority ethnic communities in England.* Leeds, NIMHE

NIMHE (2003b) *Engaging and changing: developing effective policy for the care and treatment of Black and minority ethnic detained patients.* Leeds, NIMHE

NIMHE (2004a) *Celebrating our cultures: guidelines for mental health promotion with black and minority ethnic communities.* Leeds, NIMHE

NIMHE (2004b) *From here to equality: a strategic plan to tackle stigma and discrimination on mental health grounds, 2004–2009.* Leeds, NIMHE

National Schizophrenia Fellowship (1997) *How to involve users and carers in planning, running and monitoring care services and curriculum development.* Kingston-upon-Thames, National Schizophrenia Fellowship (now Rethink)

National Schizophrenia Fellowship (2000) *No change?* London, National Schizophrenia Fellowship

National Schizophrenia Fellowship (n.d) *Carers facts and figures.* Available online at www.nsf.org.uk (accessed 26/06/01)

Neill, J. and Williams, J. (1992) *Leaving hospital: older people and their discharge to community care.* London, HMSO

Newnes, C., Long, N. and MacLachlan, A. (2001) Recruits you, sir, *OpenMind,* 108, 12

NHS Confederation (2003a) *The Draft Mental Health Bill: an assessment of the implications for mental health service organisations.* London, NHS Confederation

NHS Confederation (2003b) *The role of nurses under the new GMS Contract.* London, NHS Confederation

NHS Centre for Reviews and Dissemination (2001) *Counselling in primary care* (Effective Health Care, volume 5, number 2). York, NHS Centre for Reviews and Dissemination

NHS Executive (1994) *Introduction of supervision registers for mentally ill people from 1 April 1994.* HSG(84)5

NHS Executive (1996) *Workforce planning for general medical services* Leeds, NHS Executive

NHS Executive (1998) *Signposts for success in commissioning and providing health services for people with learning disabilities.* Leeds, NHS Executive

NHS Management Executive (1992) *Local voices: the views of local people in purchasing for health.* Leeds, NHS Management Executive

NHS Service and Delivery Organisation (2003) *SDO News,* 6 (December). London, National Co-ordinating Centre for NHS Service Delivery and Organisation Research and Development

National Institute for Clinical Excellence (2003) *Schizophrenia: full national clinic guidelines on core interventions in primary and secondary care.* London, Royal College of Psychiatrists and the British Psychological Society

Nocon, A. (1994) *Collaboration in community care in the 1990s.* Sunderland, Business Education Publishers

Nolan, P, and Badger, F. (2002) *Promoting collaboration in primary mental health care.* Cheltenham, Nelson Thornes

Nolan, P., Dunn, L. and Badger, F. (1998) Getting to know you, *Nursing Times,* 94(39), 34–6

Norfolk, Suffolk and Cambridgeshire Strategic Health Authority (2003) *Independent inquiry into the death of David Bennett.* Cambridge, Norfolk, Suffolk and Cambridgeshire Strategic Health Authority

Norman, A. (1985) *Triple jeopardy: growing old in a second homeland.* London, Centre for Policy on Ageing

Norman, I.J. and Peck, E. (1999) Working together in adult community mental health services: an inter-professional dialogue, *Journal of Mental Health,* 8(3), 217–30

Norman, R. and Malla, A. (2001) Duration of untreated psychosis: A critical examination of the concept and its importance, *Psychological Medicine*, 31, 381–400

Norman, R.M.G. and Townsend, L.A. (1999) Cognitive behavioural therapy for psychosis: a status report, *Canadian Journal of Psychiatry*, 44, 245–52

Office of the Deputy Prime Minister (2004) *Mental health and social exclusion* (*Social Exclusion Unit Report*). London, ODPM

Office of Health Economics (2000) *Compendium of health statistics* (12th ed.). London, OHE

Office for National Statistics (2002) *Labour Force Survey*, London, ONS

Office for National Statistics (2003) *Labour Force Survey, Autumn 2003*. London, ONS

Oliver, M. (1983) *Social work with disabled people*. Basingstoke, Macmillan

Oliver, M. (1990) *The politics of disablement*. Basingstoke, Macmillan

Oliver, M. (1996) Defining impairment and disability: issues at stake, in C. Barnes and G. Mercer (eds) *Exploring the divide: illness and disability*. Leeds, Disability Press

Oliver, M. and Sapey, B. (1999) *Social work with disabled people* (2nd ed.). Basingstoke, Macmillan

Onyett, S., Standee, R. and Peck, E. (1997) The challenge of managing community mental health teams, *Health and Social Care in the Community*, 5(1), 40–7

OPCS (2000) *Living in Britain: results from the 1998 General Household Survey*. London, HMSO

Organisation for Economic Co-operation and Development (OECD) (2001) *OECD health data*. Paris, OECD

Owen, A.J., Sashidharan, S.P. and Edwards, L.J. (2000) Availability and acceptability of home treatment for acute psychiatric disorders, *Psychiatric Bulletin*, 24(5), 169–71

Parker, G. (2002) Evidence based policy in practice: health services, *Managing Community Care*, 10(1), 22–6

Parkman, S., Davies, S., Leese, M., Phelan, M. and Thornicroft, G. (1997) Ethnic differences in satisfaction with mental health services among representative people with psychosis in south London: PRiSM Study 4, *British Journal of Psychiatry*, 171, 260–4

Parsons, T. (1964) *The social system*. London, RKP (first published 1951)

Payne, S. (1999) Outside the walls of the asylum? Psychiatric treatment in the 1980s and 1990s, in P. Bartlett and D. Wright (eds) *Outside the walls of the asylum: the history of care in the community, 1750–2000*. London, Athlone Press

Patmore, C. and Weaver, T. (1991) *Community mental health teams: lessons for planners and managers*. London, Good Practice in Mental Health

Paton, J.M., Fahy, M.A. and Livingston, G.A. (2004) Delayed discharge – a solvable problem? The place of intermediate care in mental health care of older people, *Aging and Mental Health*, 8(1), 34–9

Payne, G. (eds) (2000) *Social divisions*. Basingstoke, Macmillan

Payne, S. (1999) Outside the walls of the asylum? Psychiatric treatment in the 1980s and 1990s, in Bartlett, P. and Wright, D. (eds) *Outside the walls of the asylum: the history of care in the community*, 1750–2000. London, Athlone Press

Peat, L. (1979) Twenty five yeas of community psychiatric nursing, *Community Psychiatric Nurses Association Journal*, January.

Peck, E. (2002) Integrating health and social care, *Managing Community Care*, 10(3), 16–19

Peck, E. and Crawford, A. (2002) 'You say tomato': culture as a signifier of difference between health and social care, *Mental Health Review*, 7(3), 23–6

Peck, E. and Greatley, A. (1999) Developing the mental health agenda for primary care groups, *Managing Community Care*, 7, 3–6

Peck, E. and Norman, I.J. (1999) Working together in adult community mental health services: exploring inter-professional role relations, *Journal of Mental Health*, 8(3), 231–42

Peck, E., Gulliver, P. and Towell, D. (2002a) *Modernising partnerships: an evaluation of Somerset's innovations in the commissioning and organisation of mental health services – final report*. London, Institute of Applied Health and Social Policy, King's College

Peck, E., Gulliver, P., Towell, D. (2002b) Information, consultation or control: user involvement in mental health services in England at the turn of the century, *Journal of Mental Health,* 11, 4, 441–51

Peck, E., Gulliver, P. and Towell, D. (2003) The Somerset story: the implications for Care Trusts of the evaluation of the integration of health and social services in Somerset, in J. Glasby and E. Peck (eds) *Care trusts: partnership working in action*. Abingdon, Radcliffe Medical Press

Pelosi, A. and Birchwood, M. (2003) Is early intervention of psychosis a waste of valuable resources?, *British Journal of Psychiatry*, 182, 196–8

Percy Commission (1957) *The Report of the Royal Commission on Mental Illness and Mental Deficiency*. London, HMSO

Perring, C., Twigg, J. and Atkin, K. (1990) *Families caring for people diagnosed as mentally ill: the literature re-examined*. London, HMSO

Peterson, L., Jeppesen, P., Thorup, A., Abel, M., Ohlenschlager, J., Christenese, T.O., Krarup, G., Jorgensesn, P., Nordentoft, M. (2005) A Randomised Multi-centre Trial of Integrated Versus Standard Treatment for Patients with a First Episode of Psychotic Illness. *British Medical Journal*, 331, 602–9

Peveler, R., George, C., Kinmonth, A., Campbell, M. and Thompson, C. (1999) Effect of antidepressant drug counselling and information leaflets on adherence to drug treatment in primary care: randomised controlled trial, *British Medical Journal*, 319, 612–15

Pierre, S. (1999) The experiences of African and Afro-Caribbean people in acute psychiatric hospital: a qualitative study, *Mental Health Care*, 3(2), 52–6

Pilgrim, D. (2002) The biopsychosocial model in Anglo-American psychiatry: past, present and future?, *Journal of Mental Health*, 11(6), 585–94

Pilgrim, D. and Rogers, A. (1999) *A sociology of mental health and illness* (2nd ed.). Buckingham, Open University Press

Pinfold, V., Bindman, J., Thornicroft, G., Franklin, D. and Hatfield, B. (2001) Persuading the persuadable: evaluating compulsory treatment in England using Supervised Discharge Orders, *Social Psychiatry & Psychiatric Epidemiology*, 36(5), 260–6

Polczyk-Przybyla, M. and Gournay, K. (1999) Psychiatric nursing in prison: the state of the art?, *Journal of Advanced Nursing*, 30(4), 893–900

Porter, R. (1987) *Mind forged manacles*. Harmonsworth, Penguin

Porter, R. (1999) *A social history of madness: stories of the insane*. London, Orion Books

Porter, R. (2002) *Madness: a brief history*. Oxford, Oxford University Press

Powell, E. (1961) Speech to the Annual Conference of the National Association of Mental Health (now Mind)

Poxton, R. (1999) Primary and community mental health and social care: making a difference at the interface, *Mental Health Review*, 4(3), 24–7

Poxton, R. (2003) What makes effective partnerships between health and social care? in J. Glasby and E. Peck (eds) *Care trusts: partnership working in action*. Abingdon, Radcliffe Medical Press

Press Association (2003) Accusations, dates and appearances, *The Guardian*, 10 June. Available online (accessed 09/02/2004) via www.guardian.co.uk

Pressman, J. and Wildavsky, A. (1973) *Implementation*. Berkeley, University of California Press

Preston, C., Cheater, F., Baker, R. and Hearnshaw, H. (1999) Left in limbo: patients' views on care across the primary/secondary interface, *Quality in Health Care*, 8(1), 16–21

Price, J. (1997) *Queer in the head: an examination of the response of social work mental health services to the needs and experiences of lesbians and gay men*. Surbiton, Social Care Association

Priebe, S., Badesconyi, A., Fioritti, A., Hansson, L., Rienhold, K., Torres-Gonzales, F., Turner, T. and Wiersma, D. (2005) Reinstitutionalisation in mental health care: comparison of data in service provision from six European countries, *British Medical Journal*, 33, 123–6

Prior, D. (1993) *Social organisation of mental illness*. London, Sage

Quirk, A. and Lelliott, P. (2001) What do we know about life on acute psychiatric wards in the UK? A review of the research evidence, *Social Science and Medicine*, 53(12), 1565–74

Ramon, S. (1996) *Mental health in Europe*. Basingstoke, Macmillan

Rankin, J. (2005) *Mental health and social inclusion*. London, Institute for Public Policy Research

Rassool, G.H. (ed.) (2002) *Dual diagnosis: substance misuse and psychiatric disorders*. Oxford, Blackwell Science

Read, J. and Baker, S. (1996) *Not just sticks and stones: a survey of the discrimination experienced by people with mental health problems*. London, Mind

Read, J. and Reynolds, J. (eds) (2000) *Speaking our minds: an anthology*. Basingstoke, Palgrave

Reed, J.L. and Lyne, M. (2000) Inpatient care of mentally ill people in prison: results of a year's programme of semistructured inspections, *British Medical Journal*, 320, 1031–4

Regen, E., Smith, J. and Shapiro, J. (1999) *First off the starting blocks: lessons from GP commissioning pilots for PCGs*. Birmingham, HSMC, University of Birmingham

Rethink (2002) Missing millions: an unpublished report from Rethink cited in Rankin, J. (2004) *Developments and trends in mental health policy*. London, Institute for Public Policy Research

Rethink (2003a) *Reaching people early: a status report on the early support received by people with severe mental illness and their informal carers*. London, Rethink

Rethink (2003b) *Who cares? The experiences of mental health carers accessing services and information*. London, Rethink

Ridley, J. and Jones, L. (2002) *'Direct what?' A study of direct payments to mental health service users*. Edinburgh, Scottish Executive Central Research Unit

Rimington, L.D., Davies, D.H. and Pearson, M.G. (2001) Relationship between anxiety, depression and morbidity in adult asthma patients, *Thorax*, 56, 266–71

Ritchie Report (1994) *Report of the inquiry into the care and treatment of Christopher Clunis*. London, HMSO

Robert, G., Hardacre, J., Locock, L., Bate, P. and Glasby, J. (2003) Redesigning mental health services: lessons on user involvement from the Mental Health Collaborative, *Health Expectations*, 6, 60–71

Roberts, P. and Priest, H. (1997) Achieving interprofessional working in mental health, *Nursing Standard*, 12(2), 39–41

Robinson, R. (2002) Gold for the NHS: good news that raises questions on consistency and sustainability, *British Medical Journal*, 324, 987–8

Robinson, G., Beaton, S. and White, P. (1993) Attitudes towards practice nurses, *British Journal of General Practice*, 43, 25–9

Rogers, A. and Pilgrim, D. (2001) *Mental health policy in Britain* (2nd ed.) Basingstoke, Palgrave

Rogers, A. and Pilgrim, D. (2003) *Mental health and inequalities*. Basingstoke, Palgrave-Macmillan

Rogers, H. (2000) Breaking the ice: developing strategies for collaborative working with carers of older people with mental health problems, in H. Kemshall and R. Littlechild (eds) *User involvement and participation in social care: research informing practice*. London, Jessica Kingsley

Rogers, A., Campbell, S., Gask, L., Sheaff, R., Marshall, M., Halliwell, S. and Pickard, S. (2002) Some national service frameworks are more equal than others: implementing clinical governance for mental health in primary care groups and trusts, *Journal of Mental Health*, 11, 199–212

Romme, M. and Escher, A. (1989) Hearing voices, *Schizophrenia Bulletin*, 15, 209–16

Rooney, P. (2002) *Mental health policy implementation guide: adult acute inpatient care provision*. London, Department of Health

Rose, D. (2001) *Users' voices: the perspectives of mental health service users on community and hospital care*. London, Sainsbury Centre for Mental Health

Rosenhan, D.L. (1973) On being sane in insane places, *Science*, 179, 250–8

Royal College of General Practitioners (2001) *The primary care workforce*. London, RCGP

Royal College of General Practitioners (2002) *RCGP information sheet number 4: General Practice in the UK*. London, RCGP

Royal College of General Practitioners (2003a) *RCGP information sheet number 21: the primary health care team*. London, RCGP

Royal College of General Practitioners (2003b) *RCGP information sheet number 1: profile of UK general practitioners*. London, RCGP

Royal College of Psychiatrists (1997) *Community psychiatric nursing* (Occasional paper OP40). London, Royal College of Psychiatrists

Royal College of Psychiatrists (2002) *Acute hospitals should be at the forefront of psychiatric services* (press release, 1 March). London, Royal College of Psychiatrists

Ryan, T. and Bamber, C. (2002) A survey of policy and practice on expenses and other payments to mental health service users and carers participating in service development, *Journal of Mental Health*, 11(6), 635–44

Sainsbury Centre for Mental Health (1998a) *Keys to engagement: review of care for people with severe mental illness who are hard to engage with services*. London, Sainsbury Centre for Mental Health

Sainsbury Centre for Mental Health (1998b) *Acute problems: a survey of the quality of care in acute psychiatric wards*. London, Sainsbury Centre for Mental Health

Sainsbury Centre for Mental Health (1999) *The National Service Framework for Mental Health: an executive briefing*. London, Sainsbury Centre for Mental Health

Sainsbury Centre for Mental Health (2000) *Taking your partners: using opportunities for inter-agency partnership in mental health*. London, Sainsbury Centre for Mental Health

Sainsbury Centre for Mental Health (2001) *Setting the standard: the new agenda for primary care organisations commissioning mental health services*. London, Sainsbury Centre For Mental Health

Sainsbury Centre for Mental Health (2002a) *Being there in a crisis.* London, Sainsbury Centre for Mental Health

Sainsbury Centre for Mental Health (2002b) *An executive briefing on adult acute inpatient care for people with mental health problems* (briefing 16). London, Sainsbury Centre for Mental Health

Sainsbury Centre for Mental Health (2002c) *The search for acute solutions: a project to improve and evaluate acute mental health inpatient care.* London, Sainsbury Centre for Mental Health

Sainsbury Centre for Mental Health (2002d) *Acute inpatient care (mental health topics).* London, Sainsbury Centre for Mental Health

Sainsbury Centre for Mental Health (2002e) *Breaking the circles of fear.* London, Sainsbury Centre for Mental Health

Sainsbury Centre For Mental Health (2003a) *Policy paper 3: the economic and social costs of mental illness.* London, Sainsbury Centre For Mental Health

Sainsbury Centre for Mental Health (2003b) *Money for mental health: a review of public spending on mental health care.* London, Sainsbury Centre for Mental Health

Sainsbury Centre for Mental Health (2004) *Practice based commissioning in the NHS: the implications for mental health.* London, Sainsbury Centre for Mental Health

Sashidharan, S.P. (1999) Alternatives to institutional psychiatry, in D. Bhugra and V. Bahl (eds) *Ethnicity: an agenda for mental health.* London, Gaskell

Sashidharan, S., Smythe, M. and Owen, A. (1999) PRiSM Psychosis Study. Thro' a glass darkly: a distorted appraisal of community care, *British Journal of Psychiatry*, 175, 504–7

Saultz, J.W. (2003) Defining and measuring interpersonal care, *Annals of Family Medicine*, 3, 134–44

Sayce, L. (1997) Stigma and social exclusion: top priorities for mental health professionals, *Eurohealth*, 3(3), 5–7

Sayce, L. (1999) High time for justice, *Nursing Times*, 95(9), 64–6

Sayce, L. (2000) *From psychiatric patient to citizen: overcoming discrimination and social exclusion.* Basingstoke, Palgrave

Sayce, L. (2001) Social inclusion and mental health, *Psychiatric Bulletin*, 25, 121–3

Sayce, L. and Morris, D. (1999) *Outsiders coming in? Achieving social inclusion for people with mental health problems.* London, Mind Publications

Sayce, L., Craig, T.K.J. and Boardman, A.P. (1991) The development of community mental health centres in the UK, *Social Psychiatry and Psychiatric Epidemiology*, 26, 14–20

Schon, D. (1983) *The reflective practitioner: how professionals think in action.* London, Temple Smith

Scull, A. (1977) *De-carceration: community treatment and the deviant – a radical view.* Englewood-Cliffs, NJ, Prentice-Hall

Scull, A. (1979) *Museums of madness.* Harmondsworth, Penguin

Scull, A. (1993) *The most solitary of afflictions: madness in society in Britain, 1700–1900.* New Haven, Connecticut, Yale University Press

Secker, J., Pidd, F., Parham, A. and Peck, E. (2000) Mental health in the community: roles, responsibilities and organisation of primary care and specialist services, *Journal of Interprofessional Care*, 14 (1), 49–58

Sharpley, M., Hutchinson, G., McKenzie, K. and Murray, R.M. (2001) Understanding the excess of psychosis among the African-Caribbean population in England: review of current hypotheses, *British Journal of Psychiatry*, 178 (Supplement 40), 60–8

Shaw, J., Appleby, L. and Baker, D. (2003) *Safer prisons: a national study of prison suicides, 1999–2000 by the National Confidential Inquiry into Suicides and Homicides by People with Mental Illness*. London, Department of Health

Shelter (2003) *House keeping: preventing homelessness through tackling rent arrears in social housing*. London, Shelter

Shepherd, G. (1998) Models of community care, *Journal of Mental Health*, 7(2), 165–77

Shepherd, G., Beardsmoore, A., Moore, C., Hardy, P. and Muijen, M. (1997) Relation between bed use, social deprivation, and overall bed availability in acute adult psychiatric units, and alternative residential options: a cross sectional survey, one day census data, and staff interviews, *British Medical Journal*, 314, 262–6

Sign (n.d.) *Mental health services for deaf people: are they appropriate?* Beaconsfield, Sign

Sims, J. (2004) Sam's Bill, *Care and Health*, 4–18 February, 25

Singleton, N., Bumpstead, R., O'Brien, M., Lee, A. and Meltzer, H. (2001) *Psychiatric morbidity among adults living in private households, 2000*. London, TSO

Singleton, N., Maung, N.A., Cowie, A., Sparks, J., Bumpstead, R. and Meltzer, H. (2002) *Mental health of carers*. London, TSO

Smith, J., Mays, N., Dixon J., Goodwin, N., Lewis, R., McClelland, S., McLeod, H. and Wyke, S. (2004) *A review of the effectiveness of primary care-led commissioning and its place in the NHS*. London, The Health Foundation

Smyth, M. and Hoult, J. (2000) The home treatment enigma, *British Medical Journal*, 320, 305–9

Social Care Institute for Excellence (2003) *Users at the heart: user participation in the governance and operations of social care regulatory bodies*. London, SCIE

Sorohan, H., Lester, H.E., Hughes, E. and Archer, L. (2002) The role of the practice nurses in primary care mental health: challenges and opportunities, *Primary Care Psychiatry*, 8, 41–6

Spandler, H. and Vick, N. (2004) *Direct payments, independent living and mental health: an evaluation*. London, Health and Social Care Advisory Service

Stalker, K. (eds) (2003) *Reconceptualising work with 'carers': new directions for policy and practice*. London, Jessica Kingsley

Steadman, H.J., Mulvey, E.P., Monahan, J., Robbins, P.C., Appelbaum, P.S., Grisso, T., Roth, L.H. and Silver, E. (1998) Violence by people discharged from acute psychiatric inpatient facilities and by others in the same neighbourhoods, *Archives of General Psychiatry*, 55, 1–9

Stein, L.I. and Test, M.A. (1980) An alternative to mental hospital treatment, *Archives of General Psychiatry*, 37, 392–9

Stone, M. (1985) Shellshock and the psychologists, in W.F. Bynum, R. Porter and M. Shepherd (eds) *The anatomy of madness: volume 2*. London, Taverstock

Stott, N.C.H. and Davis, R.H. (1979) The exceptional potential in each primary care consultation, *Journal of the Royal College of General Practice*, 29, 201–5

Styron, W. (2001) *Darkness visible*. London, Vintage

Sullivan, H. and Skelcher, C. (2002) *Working across boundaries: collaboration in public services*. Basingstoke, Palgrave

Summers, A. (2003) Involving users in the development of mental health services: a study of psychiatrists' views, *Journal of Mental Health*, 12(2), 161–74

Swain, J., French, S., Barnes, C. and Thomas, C. (eds) (2004) *Disabling barriers – enabling environments* (2nd ed.). London, Sage

Swanson, J., Holzer, C., Gunju, V. and Jono, R. (1990) Violence and psyciatric disorder in the community: evidence from the epidemiological catchment area surveys, *Hospital and Community Psychiatry*, 41, 761–70

Symons, L., Tylee, A., and Mann, A. (2002) *Nurse facilitated open access depression clinic in primary care – London pilot.* London, Institute of Psychiatry (unpublished)

Szasz, T. (1960) The myth of mental illness, *American Psychologist,* 15, 564–80

Szasz, T. (1970) *Ideology and insanity: essays on the psychiatric dehumanisation of man.* Garden City, Double Day

Szasz, T. (2003) The psychiatric protection order for the 'battered mental patient,' *British Medical Journal,* 327, 1449–51

Tabassum, R., Macaskill, A. and Ahmad, I. (2000) Attitudes towards mental health in an urban Pakistani community in the United Kingdom, *International Journal of Social Psychiatry,* 46(3), 170–81

Taylor, P.J. and Gunn, J. (1999) Homicides by people with mental illness: myth and reality, *British Journal of Psychiatry,* 174, 9–14

Telfer, J. (2000) Balancing care and control: introducing the care programme approach in a prison setting, *Mental Health Care,* 4(3), 93–6

Telford, R. and Faulkner, A. (2004) Learning about service user involvement in mental health research, *Journal of Mental Health,* 13(6), 549–59

Thomas, R. and Corney, R. (1993) The role of the practice nurse in mental health: a survey, *Journal of Mental Health,* 2, 65–72

Thompson, N. (2001) *Anti-discriminatory practice* (3rd ed.). Basingstoke, Macmillan

Thomson, L., Galt, V. and Darjee, R. (2004) *An evaluation of appropriate adult schemes in Scotland* (Scottish Executive Research Findings 78/2004). Edinburgh, University of Edinburgh

Thorne, A. (2001) Blood-letting politics over Health Concern, *Birmingham Post,* 2 February

Thornicroft, G., Parkman, S. and Ruggeri, M. (1999) Satisfaction with mental health services: issues for ethnic minorities, in D. Bhugra and V. Bahl (eds) *Ethnicity: an agenda for mental health.* London, Gaskell

Thornicroft, G., Rose, D., Huxley, P., Dale, G. and Wykes, T. (2002) What are the research priorities of mental health service users?, *Journal of Mental Health,* 11(1), 1–5

Thornicroft, G., Strathdee, G., Phelan, M., Holloway, F., Wykes, T., Dunn, G., McCrone, P., Leese, M., Johnson, S. and Szmukler, G. (1998a) Rationale and design: PRiSM Psychosis Study 1, *British Journal of Psychiatry,* 173, 363–70

Thornicroft, G., Wykes, T., Holloway, F., Johnson, S. and Szmukler, G. (1998b) From efficacy to effectiveness in community mental health services. PRiSM Psychosis Study 10, *British Journal of Psychiatry,* 173, 423–7

Tien, A.Y. (1991) The distribution of hallucinations in the population, *Social Psychiatry and Psychiatric Epidemiology,* 26, 287–92

Tiemans, B., Ormel, J. and Simon, G. (1996) Occurrence, recognition and outcome of psychological disorders in primary care, *Psychological Medicine,* 153, 636–44

Tierney, A.J., Macmillan, M.S., Worth, A. and King, C. (1994) Discharge of patients from hospital – current practice and perceptions of hospital and community staff in Scotland, *Health Bulletin,* 52(6), 479–91

Timmins, N. (2001) Anger over local hospital gives real bite to underdog doctor's campaign, *Financial Times,* 28 May

Titmuss, R.M. (1968) *Commitment to welfare.* London, George Allen and Unwin

Todd, Lord A.R. (1968) *The Todd Report: Royal Commission on Medical Education.* London, HMSO

Took, M. (2002) Mental breakdown and recovery in the UK, *Journal of Psychiatric and Mental Health Nursing,* 9, 635–7

Tudor Hart, J. (1988) *A new kind of doctor*. London, Merlin Press

Tyrer, P. and Steinberg, D. (2003) *Models for mental disorders: conceptual models in psychiatry*. Chichester, John Wiley and Sons

Tyrer, P., Coid, J., Simmonds, S., Joseph, P. and Marriott, S. (2000) Community mental health teams (CMHTs) for people with severe mental illnesses and disordered personality (Cochrane Review), *The Cochrane Library*, 3, Oxford, Update Software

Ungerson, C. (1987) *Policy is personal: sex, gender and informal care*. London, Tavistock

Union of Physically Impaired Against Segregation (UPIAS) (1976) *Fundamental principles of disability*. London, UPIAS

Ustun, T.B., Rehm, J., Chatterji, S., Saxena, S., Trotter, R., Room, R. and Bickenbach, J. (1999) Multiple-informant ranking of the disabling effects of different health conditions in 14 countries: WHO/NIH Joint Project CAR Study Group, *Lancet*, 354, 111–15

Valios, N. (2000) Appeal court broadens definition of disability, *Community Care*, 22–28 June, p. 11

Valuing People Support Team (2004) *Green light for mental health* (parts A and B). London, Valuing People Support Team/Department of Health

Vanderwall, C. (1997) The role of the community forensic mental health nurse: initiatives for across agency working, *Psychiatric Care*, 4(6), 283–6

Vaughan, P.J. (1999) A consortium approach to commissioning services for mentally disordered offenders, *Journal of Forensic Psychiatry*, 10(3), 553–66

Vaughan, P.J. and Stevenson, S. (2003) An opinion survey of mentally disordered service users, *Prison Service Journal*, 147, 11–17

Vaughan, P., Kelly, M. and Pullen, N. (2000) Services for mentally disordered offenders in community psychiatry teams, *Journal of Forensic Psychiatry*, 11(3), 571–86

Victor, C. (1991) *Health and health care in later life*. Milton Keynes, Open University Press

Wade, D. and Halligan, P. (2004) Do biomedical models of illness make for good healthcare systems?, *British Medical Journal*, 329, 1398–401

Wahl, O.F. (1995) *Media madness: public images of mental illness*. New Jersey, Rutgers University Press

Wallcraft, J. and Bryant, M. (2003) *The mental health service users movement in England*. London, Sainsbury Centre for Mental Health

Walsh, E. and Fahy, T. (2002) Violence in society, *British Medical Journal*, 325, 507–8

Walsh, E., Buchanan, A. and Fahy, T. (2002) Violence and schizophrenia: examining the evidence, *British Journal of Psychiatry*, 188, 490–5

Walshe, K., Smith, J., Dixon, J., Edwards, N., Hunter, D.J., Mays, N., Normand, C. and Robinson, R. (2004) Primary care trusts: premature reorganisation with mergers, may be harmful, *British Medical Journal*, 329, 871–2

Walton, P. (2000) Psychiatric hospital care: a case of the more things change, the more they remain the same, *Journal of Mental Health*, 9(1), 77–88

Wanless, D. (2002) *Securing our future health: taking a long term view*. London, Department of Health

Warner, R. (1985) *Recovery from schizophrenia: psychiatry and political economy*. London, Routledge

Warner, L. and Ford, R. (1998) Conditions for women in in-patient psychiatric units: the Mental Health Act Commission 1996 national visit, *Mental Health Care*, 1(7), 225–8

Warner, R., Gater, R., Jackson, G. and Goldberg, D. (1993) The effects of a new mental health service based in primary care on the work of general practitioners, *British Journal of General Practice*, 43, 507–11

Warner, L., Rose, D., MacKintosh, G. and Ford, R. (2000a) Could this be you? Evaluating quality and standards of care in the inpatient psychiatric setting, *Mental Health and Learning Disabilities Care*, 4(3), 89–92

Warner, L., Nicholas, S., Patel, K., Harris, J. and Ford, R. (2000b) *National visit 2: a visit by the Mental Health Act Commission to 104 mental health and learning disability units in England and Wales – improving care for detained patients from black and minority ethnic communities (preliminary report)*. London, Sainsbury Centre for Mental Health

Watson, A. (1997) *Services for mentally disordered offenders in the community: an inspection report*. London, Department of Health

Watson, A. (2001) *Detained: inspection of compulsory mental health admissions*. London, Department of Health

Waxman, R., Tennant, A., Halliwell, P. (1999) Community survey of factors associated with consultation for low back pain, *British Medical Journal*, 317, 1564–7

Weaver, T., Taylor, F., Cunningham, B., Maden, A., Rees, S. and Renton, A. (1997a) The Bentham Unit: a pilot remand and assessment service for male mentally disordered remand prisoners, *British Journal of Psychiatry*, 170, 462–6

Weaver, T., Taylor, F., Cunningham, B., Kavanagh, S., Maden, A., Rees, S. and Renton, A. (1997b) Impact of a dedicated service for male mentally disordered remand prisoners in north west. London: retrospective study, *British Medical Journal*, 314, 1244–5

Webb, Y., Clifford, P., Fowler, V., Morgan, C. and Hanson, M. (2000) Comparing patients' experience of mental health services in England: a five-Trust survey, *International Journal of Health Care Quality Assurance*, 13, 6/7, 273–81

Webbe, A. (1998) Ethnicity and mental health, *Psychiatric Care*, 5(1), 12–16

Webster, C. (2002) *The National Health Service: a political history*. Oxford, Oxford University Press

Weinberg, A. and Huxley, P. (2000) An evaluation of the impact of voluntary sector family support workers on the quality of life of carers of schizophrenia sufferers, *Journal of Mental Health*, 9(5), 495–503

White, E. (1990) The work of the Community Psychiatric Nurses Association: a survey of the membership, *Community Psychiatric Nursing Journal*, 10, 30–5

White, E. (1993) Community psychiatric nursing, 1980–1990: a review of organisation, education and practice, in C. Brooker and E. White (eds) *Community psychiatric nursing: a research perspective* (volume II). London, Chappleman and Hall

White, J. (2000) Clinical psychology in primary care, *Primary Care Psychiatry*, 6(4), 127–36

White, E. and Brooker, C. (2001) The fourth quinquennial national community mental health nursing census of England and Wales, *International Journal of Nursing Studies*, 38(1), 61–70

Whittle, M.C. and Scally, M.D. (1998) Model of forensic psychiatric community care, *Psychiatric Bulletin*, 22(12), 748–50

Widgery, D. (1991) GP mourns the dying East End, *GP Magazine*, July, 32

Wilkinson, R.G. (1996) *Unhealthy societies: the afflictions of inequality*. London, Routledge

Williams, R. (1976) *Keywords*. London, Croomhelm

Willis, J. (1995) *The paradox of progress*. Abingdon, Radcliffe Medical Press Ltd

Wilson, M. and Francis, J. (1997) *Raised voices: African-Caribbean and African users' views and experiences of mental health services in England and Wales.* London, Mind Publications

Wilson, T. and Holt, T. (2001) Complexity science: complexity and clinical care, *British Medical Journal,* 323, 685–8

Winchester, R. (2001) Pushed to breaking point, *Community Care,* 7–13 June, pp. 18–20

Wistow, G. and Fuller, S. (1982) *Joint planning in perspective.* Birmingham, Centre for Research in Social Policy and National Association of Health Authorities

Witcher, S., Stalker, K., Roadburg, M. and Jones, C. (2000) *Direct payments: the impact on choice and control for disabled people.* Edinburgh, Scottish Executive Central Research Unit

World Health Organisation (1999) *The world health report: making a difference.* Geneva, World Health Organisation

World Health Organisation (2004) *WHO Guide to mental and neurological health in primary care.* London, Royal Society of Medicine Press

Wright, S., Bindman, J., Thornicroft, G. and Butcher, M. (2000) *Thematic review of NHS R&D funded mental health research in relation to the National Service Framework for Mental Health.* London, Institute of Psychiatry

Yates, M. and Deakes, C. (1998) Introducing multidisciplinary record keeping in a forensic setting, *Psychiatric Care,* 5(6), 204–7

Youth Justice Board (n.d.) *Speaking out: the views of young people, parents and victims about the youth justice system and interventions to reduce offending.* London, Youth Justice Board for England and Wales

Yuen, P. (2003) *Compendium of health statistics* (15th ed.). London, Office of Health Economics

Key legislation

Carers (Equal Opportunities) Act 2004
Carers (Recognition and Services Act) 1995
Carers and Disabled Children Act 2000
Community Care (Direct Payments) Act 1996
Community Health and Standards Act 2003
Disability Discrimination Act 1995
Equal Pay Act 1970
Health Act 1999
Health and Social Care Act 2001
Human Rights Act 1998
Mental Health Act 1983
National Assistance Act 1948
NHS Act 1946
NHS and Community Care Act 1990
NHS Reform and Health Care Professionals Act 2002
Primary Care Act 1997
Race Relations Act 1976
Race Relations (Amendment) Act 2000
Sex Discrimination Act 1975

Appendix A: Mental Health Policy Chronology, 1975–2004

1975	*Better Services for the Mentally Ill* published
1986	*Making a Reality of Community Care* published
1988	*Griffiths Report* published
1989	*Caring for People* published
1990	NHS and Community Care Act passed
1991	CPA introduced
1994	*Ritchie Report* published
1994	Supervision registers introduced
1995	Disability Discrimination Act passed
1995	Mental Health (Patients in the Community Act) passed
December 1997	*The New NHS: Modern, Dependable* published
December 1998	*Modernising Mental Health Services: Safe, Sound and Supportive* published
November 1998	*Modernising Social Services* published
April 1999	481 PCGs go live
April 1999	The Health Act passed
October 1999	*NSF for Mental Health* published
November 1999	*Richardson report* and *Green Paper on Reforming the MHA* published
April 2000	17 first wave PCTs go live
July 2000	*NHS Plan* published
October 2000	Human Rights Act 1998 came into effect
March 2001	First *Mental Health Policy Implementation Guide* published
July 2001	*Shifting the Balance of Power* published
August 2001	The Health and Social Care Act passed
January 2002	*Shifting the Balance of Power – the Next Steps* published
April 2002	*New Deal for Disabled People* goes national
April 2002	*Adult Acute In-patient Care Provision* published
April 2002	PCTs go live across England
June 2002	NHS Reform and Health Care Professionals Act passed
June 2002	Draft *Mental Health Bill* published
June 2002	Launch of NIMHE
October 2002	*Mainstreaming Gender and Women's Mental Health* published
September 2003	*Building on the Best: Choice, Responsiveness and Equity in the NHS* published
December 2003	*Mental Health and Social Exclusion* report published
June 2004	*The NHS Improvement Plan* published
June 2004	*Choosing Health: Making Healthier Choices Easier* published
November 2004	*The National Service Framework for Mental Health – Five years On* published
December 2004	*Delivering Race Equality in Mental Health Care* published

Index